WHERE LIFE, THERE'S LAWSUITS

WHERE THERE'S LIFE, THERE'S LAWSUITS

NOT ALTOGETHER SERIOUS RUMINATIONS ON LAW AND LIFE

JEFFREY MILLER

ECW PRESS

Copyright © Burden of Proof Research Inc., 2003

Published by ECW PRESS
2120 Queen Street East, Suite 200, Toronto, Ontario, Canada M4E 1E2

All rights reserved. No part of this publication may be reproduced, stored in a retrieval system, or transmitted in any form by any process — electronic, mechanical, photocopying, recording, or otherwise — without the prior written permission of the copyright owners and ECW PRESS.

NATIONAL LIBRARY OF CANADA CATALOGUING IN PUBLICATION DATA

Miller, Jeffrey, 1950 –
Where there's life, there's lawsuits: not altogether serious ruminations on law and life / Jeffrey Miller
ISBN 1-55022-501-4

1. Law — History. I. Title
K183.M548 2003   340'.09   C2002-905422-2

Cover and Text Design: Tania Craan
Copy Edit: Nadia Halim
Production and Typesetting: Mary Bowness
Printing: Marc Veilleux Imprimeur
Cover illustration for series (*Ardor in the Court!, Where There's Life*): The Art Archive / Bibliothèque des Arts Décoratifs Paris / Dagli Orti (A)

This book is set in Bembo and Trajan

The publication of *Where There's Life, There's Lawsuits* has been generously supported by the Canada Council, the Ontario Arts Council, and the Government of Canada through the Book Publishing Industry Development Program. Canada

DISTRIBUTION
CANADA: Jaguar Book Group, 100 Armstrong Avenue, Georgetown, ON, L7G 5S4

UNITED STATES: Independent Publishers Group, 814 North Franklin Street, Chicago, Illinois 60610

EUROPE: Turnaround Publisher Services, Unit 3, Olympia Trading Estate, Coburg Road, Wood Green, London N2Z 6T2

AUSTRALIA AND NEW ZEALAND: Wakefield Press, 1 The Parade West (Box 2066), Kent Town, South Australia 5071

PRINTED AND BOUND IN CANADA

ECW PRESS
ecwpress.com

TABLE OF CONTENTS

INTRODUCTION
WHO CARES WHODUNNIT? ix

CHAPTER ONE
YOU'RE NICKED, SUNSHINE
Crime and Punishment 1

CHAPTER TWO
FINDERS, KEEPERS
Property and Related Stuff 35

CHAPTER THREE
EVERYTHING MOM WARNED YOU ABOUT
The Private Wrongs Called Torts 65

CHAPTER FOUR
TAKING CARE OF BUSINESS
Contracts and Commerce 91

CHAPTER FIVE
THE MORON IN A HURRY
Intellectual Property Isn't Necessarily Smart   117

CHAPTER SIX
ALL IN THE FAMILY
Family Law   149

CHAPTER SEVEN
INLAWS AND OUTLAWS
Lawmakers, Lawbreakers   167

CHAPTER EIGHT
SOME OF MY BEST FRIENDS ARE BALD, DEAD WHITE GUYS
Human Rights   225

CHAPTER NINE
IF YOU CAN'T SAY SOMETHING NICE
Libel, Slander, Contempt, and Generally Minding One's Tongue   237

NOTES   275

INDEX   287

In memory of
Naomi Estelle Miller,
1929–2002,
who loved a good book.

INTRODUCTION

WHO CARES WHODUNNIT?

A few weeks into my law school education, my Property I professor admonished the class not to read the cases as though they were mysteries. "Some people like to go breathlessly through them like they're drugstore whodunnits," he said in disgust, "waiting to see how it all comes out in the end." I have spent the last 21 years ignoring such advice. And this book is Exhibit Number Three to that plea of guilty.

I come to law as a writer, more interested in the problem of justice in *The Merchant of Venice* than the rule in *Shelley's Case*. I have always read the case law as literature, a cultural artifact with its own mythic foundations — the legislature as the godhead; legal fictions such as "the reasonable person" one rung below, taking the role of Adam or Eve in a crimeless, lawsuit-free Eden; the plaintiffs and defendants — those ordinary Janes and Joes who, win or lose, relinquish a part of their souls in the law courts — heroically or antagonistically inhabiting the Fallen World; and final judgment representing Final Judgment. Judges are the priestly interpreters of this secular received wisdom: The Law translated into the law. In other words, I remain the English major I was before law school, one of those lucky enough to have taken Northrop Frye's "Literary Symbolism" course at the University of Toronto.

The actual writing of this book started 20 years ago, just after Butterworths Canada had launched the country's first newspaper for the legal profession. I worked in Butterworths' marketing department at the time, more or less gainfully combining my legal training with prior — if ambivalent — experiences as an English major and ad-agency copywriter while I waited for *The New Yorker* to anoint me the next James Thurber. It's been a long wait. Happily, however, a few weeks after *Ontario Lawyers Weekly* started publication in May, 1983, Geoffrey Burn, Butterworths' president of the day, came into my office and asked if I could "liven the thing up a bit with something allegedly humorous for the back page."

I haven't always been funny since then, even allegedly, but the paper soon went international and I still have the job. And I'm never short of material. The law is indeed a compelling, burgeoning literature, *pace* Professor Balfour of Property Law I, precisely because it depicts us *in extremis*. It shows us at our very worst, and sometimes at our very best. It distills the human condition in the way of good fiction, editing out all of the "one damn thing after another" of everyday life and shining its high beam on whether we have demonstrated grace under pressure. It provides a constant supply of allegedly humorous situations, or at least truly poignant and signal ones, such that I don't think anybody else in the world has a newspaper job quite like mine. Which is to say that, although there are several collections of purported "legal humor" or "legal oddities and curiosities," I hope that this particular offering goes beyond that, and recounts some real truth, at least here and there, about the human condition.

As for the organization of the book, the more I worked on it, the more it seemed that I could have put the essays in any order. To abate my publisher's fears about chaos reigning, I have grouped them by the category of law that seemed most suitable (any one subject can fit in various legal categories, of course), and within the categories I have grouped them again more or less chronologically, older to more recent subjects. That is the only reason why the essay on the disembowelment of criminals, for example, appears before the essay about vasectomies not being mayhem. They both concern criminal law, but happily, probably, the state stopped disemboweling convicts a long time ago. In some instances, such as the mayhem essay, the topic took me through several centuries of history. In such cases, to determine where the essay would appear in the chapter I asked myself, "Overall, does this feel more historical or modern?" which usually proved to be a pedantic way of flipping a coin. The point is, you do not need to read the book in any particular order. In fact, I would encourage you just to leap in wherever the spirit takes you. Life is more bemusing that way, which is the point of the thing.

In addition to Geoffrey Burn, who gave me the push down the road that deposited all of us here, I want to acknowledge my editors at *The Lawyers Weekly* over the years, every one of them indulgent and supportive: Michael Fitz-James, Donald Brillinger, Beverley Spencer, Jordan Furlong, and Thomas Claridge — as well as interim editors Norman MacInnes, Jim Middlemiss, and Richard Furness. I should mention Ann Macaulay, too, for the days she used to proofread me at TLW — those days when computer typesetting was young, and corporate downsizing an unknown disease.

Sir Robert Megarry's *Miscellany-at-Law* and *Second Miscellany-at-Law* helped show me how it was done, those two decades ago, and gave me some brilliant leads. All of the staff at the magnificent Great Library of Osgoode Hall (the historic site of the law society of which I am a proud member) have been similarly indispensable. By these presents I hereby beg pardon of Riitta Nummela-Recouso and Margaret Revell for sending them to rummage around in the rare book room on more occasions than they care to think about. Special thanks, as well, to Jeanette Bosschart, Theresa Roth, Karen Teasdale, Florence Hacker, and Charles Mackie.

Some of the material in this book had an airing in a different form on "Basic Black," the Saturday variety show on CBC Radio. Producer David Malahoff brought me in as the show's legal correspondent after host Arthur Black and I met on the air to talk about one of my earlier books — one that had nothing whatever to do with law. In the early years of my legal journalism career, Joe Coté and Mareka Mayer at CBC Toronto's "Metro Morning" were similarly supportive, as were Phil Jackman and the op-ed staff at the *Globe and Mail* in Toronto.

Tracey Millen, Joy Gugeler, and Jen Hale at ECW PRESS have worked hard, thoughtfully, and cheerfully as literary midwives, and we should all thank our lucky stars that their boss, Jack David, remains both the Ben and Jerry of publishing, a more or less caring not-exactly-capitalist and reflexive adopter of waif-and-stray writers — never mind his fondness for the worst Greek restaurants in the Beach. And with her intelligence, forbearance, and professional regard for the book-making process, Nadia Halim remains my all-time favorite copy editor in the known universe.

In reviewing my French translations of some portions of the book, Anne-Marie Brinsmead bolstered my confidence in the English originals while reassuring me that after 37 years of studying a second language, I actually had moved beyond advanced beginner. I think.

As to help with specific material covered in these pages, Brian Burns, Chief Deputy Clerk of the Rhode Island Supreme Court, assisted me with real aplomb on the Goldshine naughty novelties case (Chapter One). Maître J. Daniel Phelan of Montreal valiantly tried to explain to me the civil law of *viager* (Chapter Two), although I remain unconvinced that anyone will ever really figure it out. Vancouver lawyer Gale Raphanel kindly pointed me to the Maupassant stories that I mention in the same essay.

Ishmael Reed gave me some awesome leads, and quotable remarks, on reckless eyeballing, Chapter Three. Robert Spoo of Debevoise & Plimpton, NYC, was generous with his views and work on the copyright problems of James Joyce's *Ulysses*, as were Toronto lawyers Sheldon Burshtein and Paul Sanderson on the Napster litigation (Chapter Five). Martin Rudland, a barrister in Leeds, England, generously provided details of *The Queen v. Anonymous* and other information about standing mute (Chapter Seven), while Rex Bell and James Tufteland, respectively District and Chief Deputy District Attorney for Clark County, Nevada, were extremely helpful on *Nevada v. Anderson*, Chapter Eight. Andrew Blumen, Mr. Anderson's attorney, provided supplementary information on the case.

Tax law expert David Sherman and Rubin Cohen, accountant-psychotherapist, advised me on windfalls and related taxation bemusements such as "reasonable expectation of profit," not something many writers have. Leo Rosten (*al'av hasholem*) provided cantankerous and entertaining remarks (true to form) on the possible etymology of *gazump* (Chapter Nine). And on its website the Rutgers Animal Rights Law Center conveniently assembled statutory material on agricultural defamation, a.k.a. veggie libel, Chapter Nine.

Then, of course, there was my grandmother, Gertie Smookler, to whom I read *Les Misérables* while she did her housework and I thereby learned that law and justice are not the same thing; and then there is my wife, Phyllis, who patiently listens to me still going on, and on, about the difference.

CHAPTER ONE

YOU'RE NICKED, SUNSHINE

Crime and Punishment

1 In beer, truth — and then there's the morning after

Traitors to God and State have always suffered the *ultimum supplicium*, the ultimate sanction. Of course time has refined the ultimate so that some jurisdictions view the psychological pain of long imprisonment as a fate equal to, if not worse than, death. But there have been setbacks along this supposedly enlightened path. At the beginning of the British "Enlightenment" the House of Lords held that it was not only possible but theoretically mandatory that after a traitor had been drawn (dragged through the streets, sometimes without the benefit of a hurdle), hanged, and disembowelled, his entrails were to be burned while he watched.

The issue arose in the curious — and curiously gruesome — case of *R. v. Walcott*. The Old Bailey judges had convicted Thomas Walcott of treason. Thomas' son John appealed, chiefly on the ground that the sentence passed against his father was not in the conventional form. The trial judgment properly said that after Thomas had been drawn and hanged his innards were to be wrenched from his body. But the judges had omitted the prescription that the entrails should be "burned while he was yet alive." Because the judgment did not insist that Thomas watch the final indignity, the judgment, said John, was void.

As both the ultimate crime and ultimate punishment were at issue, the appeal court studied the case very closely. First it called an adjournment so that the London Clerk of Indictments, Mr. Tanner, could be summoned to testify. When Tanner appeared, the prosecution proved that the proper words — *"ipsoque vivente comburentur"* — had been entered on the attainder (the formal judgment depriving Walcott of his rights as a Crown subject) and indictment. The judgment could therefore be amended, the prosecutor urged, to conform with these records.

The prosecutor also said that the "drawing, hanging and quartering are the substantial parts of the judgment, and the other words are *in terrorem* and may be therefore omitted." It was "inconsistent in the nature of man," he proposed, to continue living after disembowelment. But Walcott's lawyer insisted that, given the gravity of the offense, the judgment "ought to be certain and very exact." As to the possibility of carrying out the full sentence, he waxed schoolmasterly: "Tradition saith that Harrison, one of the Regicides [of Charles I], did mount himself, and give the Executioner a Box on the Ear after his Body was opened."

Legend might have been a better word than *tradition*. In any case, the court agreed that death was *ultimum supplicium* (*supplicium*, which otherwise means prayer or supplication, reputedly acquired the connotation of "execution" in homage to prisoners beheaded while kneeling). But death was the punishment for any felony, and therefore treason, the ultimate felony, carried an even "harsher" penalty.

In support of this seeming illogic, the court proffered a string of earlier bloody-minded prosecutions, culminating in *Lord Stafford's Case*, where ten judges determined that the convict could not be beheaded because he would need his eyes after execution: "His bowels should be ripped up before his face and thrown in the fire." The *Walcott* court was loathe to wink at procedural laxity, it said, because of a danger of what judges like to call "opening the floodgates" — in these cases, to "new punishments as they should think more suitable to the crimes," such as a "Jewish judgment," perhaps, "that the offender should be stoned to death; or a Turkish judgment, that he should be strangled...." (Even today, in some countries where Islam predominates, judges routinely order amputation of a finger, hand, or limb. In 1990 in Sudan, robbers were crucified. In Iran, a man was thrown from a cliff for sexual abuse of a child, while, in the U.S., a man jailed for similar offenses pled unsuccessfully that he should be castrated.) Moreover, the court declared, judgments which incorporated the words missing in this instance could be overturned where they called for a "heavier punishment" than the common law demanded.

Finally, taking notice that "Colonel" Harrison had indeed been cut down alive and disembowelled only to rise up and strike his executioner, the court found for the prisoner Walcott: because the sentence had omitted the words "burned while he was living," the court set aside the treason conviction.*

---

*It was not only the criminal courts that preferred gory metaphysics to biology. At the turn of the 17th century, a man named Astrigg had put about a rumor that Sir Thomas Holt had "struck his cook on the head with a cleaver, and cleaved his head; the one part lay on the shoulder, and another part on the other." When Sir Thomas successfully sued Astrigg for slander, Astrigg appealed on a point of evidence: Sir Thomas's case was defective, he said, because he did not prove Astrigg had said he had cleaved the cook's head so that the cook "was thereby killed." The appeal judges agreed, remarking that "notwithstanding" the cleaving, "the party may yet be living," in which case the alleged crime would be not murder but mere "trespass," not something that would leave a serious stain on Sir Thomas' reputation.

The court did not mention that Queen Elizabeth had earlier ruled the punishment unacceptable to the Crown. This was especially thoughtful of her considering that the practice came to her attention through a particularly nasty plot on her life, a plot that was only one of several that gave the sovereign good reason to be her father's daughter in the paranoid and ruthless despot department.

The Babington Conspiracy was a plot by a small group of English Catholics to murder Queen Elizabeth and install Mary Queen of Scots on the throne. It failed miserably because of an intelligence coup worthy of James Bond. Every week or so, Mary was permitted a shipment of beer to the house where she was imprisoned. Elizabeth's double-agents had convinced Mary that it was safe to send and receive messages in a secret drawer built into a beer barrel. Thus was born the not very famous maxim, "In lager, truth."

The most famous member of the conspiracy was probably Chidiock Tichbourne, who managed to immortalize himself the night before his execution by writing a poem in the Tower. It has become known, appropriately enough, as *Elegy for Himself*, and has the understandable tone of a young man prematurely enduring a mid-life crisis:

> *My prime of youth is but a frost of cares,*
> *My feast of joy is but a dish of pain,*
> *My crop of corn is but a field of tares [weeds],*
> *And all my good is but vain hope of gain;*
> *The day is past, and yet I saw no sun,*
> *And now I live, and now my life is done.*

According to *Howell's State Trials*, which reports the proceedings against the conspirators as well as those against Mary, Tichbourne tried to plead both guilty and not guilty — he knew of the plot, he confessed, but otherwise had no hand in it. You would think that under the law of the day this amounted to standing mute (and that

Tichbourne was placing himself at risk of the *peine forte et dure**) but the court entered a plea of not guilty. Then, after all of his confederates had pled guilty, Tichbourne bowed to the inevitable and followed suit.

Speaking after the court passed sentence, Tichbourne hoped that he might be an example to rash adolescents and bemoaned that "I am descended from an house, from 200 years before the Conquest, never stained till this my misfortune." He apologized to the queen and "hoped steadfastly, now at this his last hour, his faith would not fail."

In addition to being immortalized by his own poem, and thereby contradicting what the poem says, Tichbourne was one of the few of the Babington gang to be cut down from the gallows while still alive to watch himself be mutilated and incinerated. When Elizabeth heard about these barbarities, she ordered them stopped, at least to the point that disembowelment should *follow* death, beginning a convention that should have rendered *Walcott* moot.

2   New wine in old bottles, or: tracking down one indecent young lord

When you write about legal history for a living, sooner or later you are going to consider indecency. At first you will wonder if it is a fit topic for a person of your talents and standards. Then you will notice that it is two hours to your deadline.

---

*See page 182.

In fact, seemliness has nothing to do with it. It's a matter of detachment and scholarship. As Masters might have said to Johnson, the basic urges are, well, basic. They have featured prominently, and basically, in legal history.

If you read even a little in the legal history of indecency, you are bound to come across *Le Roy versus Sr. Charles Sidley*, as it is styled in Siderfin's *King's Bench Reports*. I first encountered it, I think, in *Redd v. State*, a 1910 prosecution in Georgia of two men charged with open lewdness when they "in a public place, adjacent to a highway and in the presence of a lady and several children, caused a bull and a cow to copulate."

The trial judge, Judge Powell, declined to follow a Tennessee case which said that the public exhibition of a stud horse constituted a public nuisance. But Judge Powell ruled that if someone dressed monkeys to look like people and encouraged them to have sex on a stage, this would debauch public morals. He admitted that the patriarch Jacob publicly marked Laban's male cattle by making them jump over a stick dipped in fresh paint. But then, noting that "King Solomon with his thousand wives would not be tolerated in Georgia," he found Redd guilty: "The act of the animals was not the thing indecent. The indecent thing was the conduct of the defendants."

In canvassing the relevant authorities, Judge Powell cited Siderfin on Sidley, remarking that the accused had thrown bottles containing an "offensive liquor" from a balcony. When I checked Siderfin, I found him coy, and in Law French, no less. He wrote that Sir Charles *"monstre son nude corps in un balcony in Covent Garden al grand multitude de people & la fist tiel choses & parle tiel parolls &c."* (showed his nude body . . . and did certain things and said certain words, etc.). Siderfin added in parentheses that the indictment set out *"particulars de son misbehavior,"* but he refused to do the same.

He did reveal that Sir Charles pled guilty and that insofar as he was a *"gent'home de trope aunc family"* (a gentleman of a very old family) the justices fined him 2000 marks, imprisoned him for a week, and ordered him to be of good behavior for three years. Lucky for him his family was not young and poor.

In the ensuing ten years I wrote nothing about the case because I knew nothing more of it. Then one day, in the middle of some unrelated research, I discovered that the law reporter Keble had documented a matter he called *Sydlyes' Case*, where he described the offense as "shewing himself naked in a balcony, and throwing down bottles (pist in) *vi et armis* among the people in Convent Garden, *contra pacem*, and to the scandal of the government." I went straight to the *Dictionary of National Biography*, where I eventually tracked "Sydlye" down under the moniker of Sir Charles Sedley (1639?–1701), "wit and dramatic actor," baron, member of Parliament and, of course, roisterer.

The DNB said nothing about bodily fluids in projectiles, but did refer to a "shameful drunken frolic" mentioned in Samuel Pepys' diaries. The library's Everyman Pepys had the relevant entry for July 1, 1663, but carried a note warning that the details Pepys had reported were "too gross" for publication. The note advised that Samuel Johnson's *Lives of the Poets* contained particulars suitable for family reading.

Now Samuel Johnson could speak his mind when the occasion presented itself, but in matters of offensive liquors in bottles I preferred to put my trust in candid Pepys. It wasn't for nothing that he wrote his diaries in code. Fortunately, Volume IV of the comprehensive Pepys contained the July 1 entry, including the gross details of "Sir Charles Sydly's" conduct on the balcony.

Sidley (the "correct" spelling) had stood accused, I at last learned, of "coming in open day into a Balcone and showed his nakedness — acting all postures of lust and buggery that could be imagined, and abusing of scripture and, as it were, from thence preaching a Mountebanke sermon from that pulpitt." In the middle of his discourse, he seems to have remarked that he

> *hath to sell such a pouder as should make all the cunts in town run after him, a thousand people standing underneath to see and hear him. And that being done, he took a glass of wine and washed (his genitals) in it and then drank it off; and then took another and drank the King's health.*

Pepys reports that the Chief Justice (Lord Foster) scolded Sir Charles that "it was for him and such wicked wretches as he ... that God's anger and judgments hung over us, calling him 'Sirrah' many times."

So there it is — Intensive Legal Research — Historical. Of course, if Sir Charles were alive, I would have had to phone his office and put him on trial all over again. But that's another essay — Intensive Modern Journalism.

3 Vasectomies do not constitute mayhem

> *"Vasectomies do not constitute mayhem."*
> HEADNOTE, JESSIN V. THE COUNTY OF SHASTA, 1969

Sado-masochists, or the merely curious, can legally consent to be spanked, whipped, or even "tortured," at least to the extent that they are not really hurt. Nowhere in the Anglo-American world, however, can you legally consent to mayhem.

According to Lord Coke, Attorney General to Elizabeth I,

> *"Mayhem," mahemium, membri mutilatio, or obtruncatio, commeth of the French word mehaigne, and signifieth a corporall hurt, whereby hee loseth a member, by reason whereof hee is less able to fight; as by putting out his eye, beating out his fore-teeth, breaking his skull, striking off his arme hand or finger, cutting off his legge or foot, or whereby he loseth the use of any of his said members.*

From this, legal scholar William Blackstone concluded in his 1769 *Commentaries on the Laws of England* that mayhem is "the violently depriving another of the use of such of his members as may render him the less able in fighting, either to defend himself, or to annoy his enemy." It is, in other words, a battery, and close etymological relative of *maim*. Originally it signified "an atrocious breach of the king's peace, an offence tending to deprive him of the aid and assistance of his subjects" — especially in military endeavors.

At common law, ears and noses didn't count as members capable of mayhem because severance did "not weaken but only disfigure him." Arms, legs, and fingers always counted: every first-year law student reads the 1705 battery case where Cockroft sued Smith for mayhem after "a scuffle" in which Cockroft "ran her fingers towards Smith's eyes," and Smith "bit a joint from the plaintiff's finger." So did, in Blackstone's words, "those parts, the loss of which in all animals abates the courage." More recently, this has been jurisprudently termed "disabling the testicles."

Coke's list has never been definitive. Perhaps he and his brethren kept it short because the punishment on conviction of mayhem was an eye for an eye. Of course, as Blackstone reasonably remarks, "the law of retaliation . . . is at best an inadequate punishment." Then again, as Blackstone more than reasonably adds, "upon repetition of the offence the punishment could not be repeated." The punishment for castration by mayhem, by the way, was not a testicle for a testicle, but death.

By the time of Charles II (1660–85), it had become a felony to "on purpose, with malice aforethought, unlawfully cut out or disable the tung or put out the eye" — these being favorite deterrents that criminals used to intimidate their victims or eyewitnesses who might otherwise testify against them — "slit the nose or lip, or cut off or disable any limb or member, or disfigure him in any of the manners with intent to maim or disfigure him." Slitting the nose slipped in under the *Coventry Act* (1682), named after John Coventry, who suffered that battery in the street "in revenge (as was supposed) for some obnoxious words uttered by him in Parliament."

Statutorily, other types of injuries were added to the offense over time, and in California, at least, the category may still be expanding. In 1980, the California Court of Appeal declared involuntary tattooing mayhem after two hoodlums beat a woman and tattooed "MFFM" ("Misfits Forever, Forever Misfits") on her breast, "Property of G.P." on her abdomen, and "Mine Too," with an arrow, on her left thigh — pointing, one presumes from the sensitivity and wit here displayed, north.

One hoodlum contended that although California courts had said knife wounds could constitute mayhem, tattooing was different because its purpose was not injury and many people even paid money to have it performed on them. The court was not impressed. "That argument," the judges pointed out, "is the equivalent to saying that a defendant who cuts off a person's leg against his will is not guilty of mayhem because some people voluntarily have their legs amputated for medical reasons." Although the other hoodlum likely had never heard of Lord Coke, he argued that the breast and abdomen are not "members" of the body. Without blinking an eye, the court threw back at him a contrary ruling from an especially gruesome California case, in which a woman's heart had been cut out and her mutilated external genitalia were found to be a "member."

While probably any permanent disfigurement can now amount to mayhem, the courts have reassured us that voluntary vasectomies are an exception. In 1969, the California county of Shasta tried to rely on the old "disabling the testicles" argument to avoid paying for a vasectomy on a "qualified medical indigent"— a man who could not afford medical care, partly because he already had several children to support.

Lawyers for the county evidently thought themselves clever in having dug up an old opinion of the state's attorney general that, except in cases of extremity such as grave illness, sterilization of prison inmates could amount to mayhem. Apparently they concluded from the opinion that if sterilization was mayhem, it was a criminal medical procedure, just as abortion can be criminal in certain circumstances. But the California District Court called the opinion "archaic and illogical." This is perhaps extreme: it is not difficult to imagine situations where a prisoner might find it easier to submit to sterilization than risk offending authorities by refusing. (There persists a view that crime is in some senses genetic, and more than one would-be reformer has proposed the sterilization of the "lower orders of society.") In any event, consent by coercion is no consent.

In the Shasta County case, the district court found that county-funded vasectomies were an "acceptable method of family planning" that would hardly "render the patient impotent or unable to fight for the king." A perhaps stronger answer would have been that if the court declared vasectomies to be mayhem in welfare cases, they would be mayhem for all other purposes. That is, no one, no matter how rich or poor or overawed with children, could obtain one (nor could any doctor perform one), because you cannot consent to mayhem.

The Supreme Court of North Carolina had made that clear eight years before, in *State v. Bass*. George Bryson had gone to Bass, who was evidently Bryson's family doctor, and asked Bass to deaden the fingers of his brother, Walter Rogers. The men told Dr. Bass that they were going to cut off Walter's fingers to collect insurance money.

At first, Bass refused their request. He called the idea "foolish." But when Bryson paid him the $65.60 he owed on account, and another $29.00 for the anesthetic, business prevailed over professionalism. Bass deadened Walter's fingers with Procaine. He also gave the brothers a tourniquet and showed them how to use it, so that Walter wouldn't bleed to death. The brothers departed for Walter's house, where George took a skill-saw and cut the four fingers off of Walter's left hand.

When Bass was charged with being an accessory before the fact to mayhem, he pled that, because Walter consented to everything that happened, there was no "malice aforethought" — no intent — and therefore no crime. Noting that North Carolina was originally within the common law jurisdiction of Britain, Justice Moore of the Supreme Court canvassed the entire history of the law of mayhem. He directed particular attention to a 1603 prosecution described by Lord Coke which was "remarkably similar" to Bass's case (and which seems to signal an early case of indigence as both a performing art and idleness *in extremis*):

> *In my circuit in anno 1 Jacobi regis, in the County of Leicester, one Wright, a young strong and lustie . . . rogue, to make himselfe impotent, thereby to have the more colour to begge or to be relieved without putting himselfe to any labour, caused his companion to strike off his left hand; and both of them were indited, fined and ransomed therefore, and that by the opinion of the rest of the justices for the cause aforesaid.*

(In his 1877 digest of criminal law, which served as a model for later Anglo-American criminal codes, Sir James Fitzjames Stephens writes of another case where a dentist removed a soldier's front teeth so that he could avoid an exercise in which he was obliged to bite down on cartridges. Stephens thought that both the dentist and patient would be guilty of mayhem.)

Judge Moore's opinion is not exactly a hallmark of judicial clarity, but he appears to accept a very wide definition of malice — one that would give philologists a headache: "To me," he says "it seems that if [an act] is done on purpose, it is done with malice." Logically and semantically, this simply does not follow. In any event, where the Shasta County case was glib about public policy, Judge Moore was earnest:

> *Our government is deeply concerned, financially and otherwise, for the health of its citizens and that they not become a public charge. Likewise our commonwealth needs the services of its citizens quite as much as the kings of England needed the services of theirs.*

Whether there was malice in Dr. Bass' actions was immaterial. The common law rule on mayhem clearly said that Walter could not consent to have his fingers deadened for cutting off with a skill-saw.

The same, of course, usually applies to affrays or so-called "consensual fights." The more civilized view, anyway, seems to be that, outside regulated sport, you cannot legally consent to a fight such as the typical brawl in the tavern parking lot. Even in violent contact sports, there is a boundary where a "hit" becomes assault and battery. But in some jurisdictions, at least until guns and knives came into daily play, fisticuffs have been legal as long as the combatants respect the *unspoken* rules — fists only, and never to the point of grave injury.

This view recognizes that the "choose ya" fight of the schoolyard or parking lot is in many ways as formal as its forebear, the gentlemanly duel. But our common law has always held private duelling with lethal weapons to be criminal. A man who killed another in a private duel was considered a murderer. According to William Hawkins' *Treatise of the Pleas of the Crown*, the victor's seconds were also held guilty, as accessories, "whether they fought or not; and some have gone so far as to hold, that the Seconds of the Person killed are also equally guilty."

The Canadian *Criminal Code* forbids anyone even to attempt to throw down the gauntlet, fixing a maximum penalty for arranging a duel at two years. But, as Blackstone remarked two and a half centuries ago, no law has stopped men who think "it their duty as gentlemen" to make "wanton with their own lives and those of their fellow creatures." Those twin devils, pride (or *machismo*) and fashion, make us do it:

> *It requires such a degree of passive valour, . . . arising from the false notions of honour too generally received in Europe, that the strongest prohibitions and penalties of the law will never be entirely effectual to eradicate this unhappy custom; till a method be found out of compelling the original aggressor to make some other satisfaction to the affronted party, which the world shall esteem equally reputable, as that which is now given at the hazard of the life and fortune, as well as of the person insulted.*

Most authorities say that private duelling arose from trial by combat, a public mode of settling disputes developed in the Middle Ages, when proving legal wranglings by other means had become an exercise in cynicism. Trial by compurgation (bringing in witnesses to swear that you were a truthful sort) and by ordeal had been too easily finagled. On the one hand, your friends might be too willing to stretch the truth for you. On the other, soft-hearted clerics, responsible for officiating at ordeals, might let the iron bar cool a bit before you carried it (if the resulting wounds healed in a specified time you were deemed innocent by act of God), or might declare your riding low in a pond or well with your hands and legs bound the sort of "sinking" that proved your divinely-assisted innocence.

Barrister and legal historian Charles Rembar records that in one parish at the turn of the 12th century, all 50 accused tried by ordeal were miraculously found not guilty.

Judicial combat — formal, state-sanctioned duelling in which, again, God supposedly smiled upon the most deserving litigant or his champion (this sort of duelling, in other words, was not only lawful, it was The Law) — was abolished in England in 1819, but duelling in private disputes had yet to reach its popular zenith. It had been imported from Italy in the late 1400s and was "considerably facilitated," says the *Encyclopedia Britannica*, "by the fashion of wearing a sword as part of everyday dress."

In North America, duelling clothed itself in the looser-fitting habit of democracy. Here, even the common man found that if he couldn't prevail by free speech, there was always free gunplay as an alternative. So, on July 11, 1804, Aaron Burr killed Alexander Hamilton on a New Jersey bluff where Hamilton's son had died the same way three years earlier. Burr still failed to become president, though he had imagined that Hamilton was the only obstacle in his path. And then, of course, there were all those westerly meetings on Main Street at high noon.

The *Canadian Encyclopedia* records that at least 12 people have died in formal duels in this country. In the early 1800s, a physician and a member of the Quebec legislature took up pistols over whether Montreal General Hospital should hire lay nurses to assist medically-trained nuns. The only serious casualty was public policy: "The result was that untrained lay nurses were hired." Formal duelling in Canada ended in 1873, in St. John's, Newfoundland. Although the dispute was deadly serious, the seconds had loaded the pistols with blanks. The last Canadian killed in a duel was Major Henry Warde. Robert Sweeny shot Warde in Verdun, Quebec, on May 22, 1838, for having sent a love-letter to Sweeny's wife.

The experience in the U.S. and Canada seems to have proved

Blackstone prophetic. In days when few could resort to civil remedies, laws against duelling "were irregularly enforced." Despite what judges said about duelling being illegal, juries sometimes preferred codes of gentlemanly behavior. As late as 1990, the government of Uruguay approved a duel between a police inspector and a newspaperman.

La Republica, a Montevideo newspaper, had accused police inspector Saul Claveria of being an accessory in a smuggling incident. Claveria, described in news reports as "strapping," challenged the paper's editor, Federico Fassano, to a duel.

News reports describe Fassano as "pudgy." Unhindered by such characterizations, he accepted the duel, and the Uruguayan government formally gave its blessing. A 1920 law there permitted the settling of private disputes by formal combat.

About a week after the Uruguayan government had approved the Claveria-Fassano shootout, seconds for Claveria declared that Fassano had violated the duellist's code by making public statements. The seconds probably did not appreciate the historical irony in their complaint: in the old European days, duelling was strictly kept secret. When this led to cheating — such as when one duellist ambushed the other — convention declared that to maintain fairness the combatants should formally go public. That was how seconds came into the picture. And sure enough, editor Fassano, who had called Inspector Claveria's challenge a farce, appreciated the publicity value of seconds. As his seconds, he chose a 90-year-old ecologist and a congresswoman.

Convention, of course, has always denied women, and men over 60, the right to participate in duels. "Consenting adults" meant men of a certain age. Because of the publicity resulting from Fassano's "breaches of honor," prominent Uruguayans were heard to wonder if maybe the old duelling law wasn't barbaric. A local senator remarked that government authorization of the duel might be an abridgement of the editor's freedom of speech. If so, it is no wonder that Claveria's seconds didn't like Fassano yelling loudly enough for the world to hear. Sometimes it takes a little incivility to remind us what civilization means.*

4   "The Naked Truth" and the shop that time (not to mention sensitivity) forgot

Amid the amputated genitalia, the shopkeeper is glaring at me. Finally, inevitably, he asks, "Can I help you?" But he doesn't mean it. He doesn't need my kind of bother. He gets so much aggravation here at Yonge and Bloor, the crossroads of Canada. Giggling nervously (this is my first time), I tell him I'm just doing research for an office party, "looking for things that might be appropriate." What else can I say? That I just got hold of the record for a 1918 Rhode Island sex-toy prosecution and I'm trying to get a newspaper column out of it?

What's really bugging him is that I'm writing things down. Fortunately, even I can barely read what my notebook says:

> *Plastic casts of male/female organs.*
> *Business card: "Sex Instructor. First Lesson Free." Space for your telephone number.*

---

*If the duel ever came off, there is no public record of it. Fassano, in any event, survived. At this writing, he's still niggling away at rightists and authority figures from the helm of *La Republica*. In 1997, he was acquitted of "attacking the honor of a foreign president," Paraguayan leader Juan Carlos Wasmosy.

> *Golf ball with woman's breasts.* "GUARANTEED *to keep your* EYE *on the ball.*"
>
> *White porcelain whale for spare change labelled* "*Sperm Bank.*"

That's the tamer stuff. I guess it's standard novelty-store merchandise, rarely better than puerile, never surpassing the sophomoric. There's also the "dirty diaper" (disgustingly true-to-life), the fake vomit and dog-do, the "Pet Cock" (boxed just like, you guessed it, a pet rock), a tiny bikini with striptease tassels labelled "Congratulations: A Gift for Your New Baby Girl." And if you think that's in bad taste, you should see the "Instant Abortion" kit. It's the shop that time, and sensitivity, forgot.

There is a merkin labelled "For the golfer having trouble with his putts"; candies shaped like sex parts and naked female torsos; condoms big enough for an elephant marked "Capable Male Wanted to Fill This Opening"; licenses to have sex and fart; knitted "socks" styled as "Golfer's Ball Warmer, Guaranteed to Improve Your Drive" (scientifically untrue, I believe). . . . So yes, we have come a long way, which way I don't know, but a long way, since 1918, when Rhode Island Justice Walter Vincent was so outraged by a contract to sell these sorts of "joke gifts" that he refused to tell anyone exactly what they were.

"We do not feel warranted," his honor wrote in his reasons for judgment, "in particularly describing the effects which may be produced by the manipulation of these so-called 'novelties.' To do so would only serve to extend the knowledge of and give permanency to obscene and indecent devices." But Justice Vincent added that the exhibits were "part of the record in the case, and will be subject to the examination of those who may need to inspect them." It was the sort of invitation I couldn't resist.

At issue in the case was the fact that Harry Goldshine had sold Henry Glass $151.61 worth of this stuff, wholesale. Glass in turn offered the novelties for sale in his retail store, but refused to pay

Goldshine. Goldshine instituted a lawsuit to get his money, but was nonsuited in the Superior Court.

Without quoting a single authority, Justice Vincent, sitting on appeal, denied wholesaler Goldshine his remedy:

> *Samples of the articles introduced in evidence at the trial bear unmistakable proof of their obscene and indecent character which fully justified the court in its refusal to submit that question to the consideration of the jury. We do not need to cite authorities to the effect that a contract based upon a violation of the [obscenity] statute referred to cannot be enforced in a court of law.*

"I of course don't want to embarrass you," I told the Rhode Island Supreme Court Clerk's Office when I called them about Goldshine's case, "but I would be grateful if you could check the record. All the case report says is that the toys looked innocent until set in motion and had names such as 'Bear Charms,' 'Bull Charms,' 'Modern Dancers,' and 'Naked Truth.' I assume their context was sexual."

If Brian Burns, the Chief Deputy Clerk, was embarrassed, he didn't say so. He provided me the old record, which explains that "Bear Charms" was a disc, suspended in a metal frame, with a bear depicted on either side. When someone spun the disc, the bears seemed to copulate. In a similar way, "Bull Charms" showed the named animal solidly answering a call of nature. "Modern Dancers" was a metal token covered with a filmy scrim which depicted a naked woman doing the "hootchy-cootchy" when a lighted match was played behind it. And "The Naked Truth" featured a cardboard envelope with a cardboard picture of a woman's legs protruding from its opening. When the legs were pulled from the envelope, a spring-loaded metal snare snapped the puller's thumb, and the woman's "chemise" was revealed, printed with the word "Stung."

The store at Yonge and Bloor does not carry many mechanical

novelties — some wind-up false teeth, electric dildos, a funnel-and-bottle rig to "stop messy leaks in your car" ("fits all male connections"), a plastic statue of a friar, called "The Merry Monk," who gets so excited when you pat his tonsured head that his robe parts below the belt. Closing my notebook, I feel as though I should buy something, but can't think what. As I am about to creep out (empty-handed), I hear a couple conversing at the open door.

She: "Oh, they have funny mugs in there. Let's go look." He, very reluctant: "It's just garbage." She: "But I want to look." He: "Okay, but it's just garbage." She hesitates in the doorway and turns to him: "Come with me."

I'm caught, ogling, nervous, the counter-man scowling. They come in and carefully slide past me, the type she thinks she needs protection from — the kind that hangs around stores that sell rubber sex dolls, fake dog crap, and golf balls with pink plastic ta-tas.

5   That's *hung*, officer, not *hanged*

"Mr. Kelly had been a police officer of fourteen years' experience. He felt that the respondent's ability to operate his vehicle was clearly impaired by alcohol, rating him a seven on a scale of one to ten. He wouldn't qualify as a ten because he 'wasn't laying down.'"

That is how Justice Robert Zelinski, of the Ontario Court's General Division, characterized eyewitness testimony in the trial of Thomas Laframboise. In 1993, Justice Zelinski heard the Crown's appeal of a trial decision that, despite such graphic evidence, Laframboise was not guilty of impaired driving.

The more or less hapless Laframboise had made the mistake of drinking two beers while he was taking the tranquilizer Halcion by prescription. He "breathalyzed" at 70 and 80, surprising the police, who had assumed from his behavior that he was intoxicated to the point of just about laying down. (Under Canadian law, a reading of 80 — 80 milligrams of alcohol per 100 milliliters of blood — constitutes impairment.) Kelly, the former police officer and now quasi-expert witness, had seen Laframboise driving on two flat tires. When he shouted this information at Laframboise, the latter continued blithely on into a shopping mall lot, hit a car parked there, and then lurched off on foot, seemingly oblivious, into the mall.

Kelly called the police, who arrested Laframboise after he said that he had drunk a beer and that his physical handicaps were obesity, low self-esteem, and being "hung like a horse." "Persons who do not suffer the disabilities of the respondent," Justice Zelinski found, "may be of the view that the second and third of the respondent's complaints are contradictory." But contradictions or none, his lordship upheld Laframboise's acquittal, ruling that there was a reasonable doubt whether Laframboise had been aware that taking Halcion could affect his driving ability. Justice Zelinski expressed no further opinions on Laframboise's other endowments.

Drunk drivers can take evasive action more deliberately, of course, despite their impairment, and with a sort of perverse ingenuity. Especially memorable in this vein is the 1985 case of Donald Zurfluh, at the time an 18-year-old from Stettler, Alberta. When a police constable stopped him on suspicion of drunk driving, Zurfluh agreed to take a breathalyzer test. As the constable was driving Zurfluh to the police detachment for the test, Zurfluh tore off a piece of his underwear and began chewing it. He later explained that he thought the cotton in the material would absorb the alcohol on his breath. It turned out that while this tactic was of dubious effect, Zurfluh blew at exactly the legal limit — which, as the trial court said, made him not guilty of driving while impaired.

In *Baxter v. The Queen*, an April, 1993 case from Ontario's General Division, neither the impaired nor the "blowing over" charge stuck.* John Baxter was on business in Sault Ste. Marie, Ontario, having driven there from his hometown of Kitchener. A police officer stopped him upon seeing his car suddenly swerve on the roadway.

At the station, the officer attempted to help Baxter reach his Kitchener lawyer, but the phones had been wired so as to make long distance calling impossible. The officer hit on the idea that the local duty counsel might be able to use their phones to call Kitchener for Baxter. But when the officer phoned the Sault 1-800 number and asked for help, the lawyer on duty replied, "I'm not a God-damn answering machine."

It can be hard to keep your dignity at duty counsel rates. In any event, Baxter spoke briefly to the duty counsel who was not a God-damn answering machine and then, not knowing what else to do, he chose a lawyer from the Kitchener phone book. So as not to take a total shot in the dark, Baxter selected a lawyer named Baxter. After speaking to Baxter the lawyer, Baxter the accused took the breathalyzer tests.

Justice Gladys Pardu excluded the breathalyzer certificates from evidence and ordered a new trial, finding that the lack of that long distance feeling at the Sault cop shop deprived Baxter (the accused) of a reasonable opportunity to retain and instruct counsel of his choice.

---

*In criminal law, your ability to drive can be impaired even if you do not "breathalyze at" or "blow over" the legal limit. While charges of "driving with a blood-alcohol ratio exceeding the lawful limit" presume that anyone is impaired at the limit, some people get drunk at levels well below the breathalyzer limits; others drive while impaired by drugs (prescription or not), or because of hunger, lack of sleep, etc.

Bruce Reynolds of Canmore, Alberta, wasn't so lucky in his bid to beat a "blowing over" rap. Apparently Reynolds did not challenge the accuracy of the breathalyzer readings. However, he claimed that he did not have care or control of the car he was sitting in on arrest.

It was not a bad argument, considering that the car was broken down and under tow when police came upon Reynolds at the wheel. But it was not an argument that impressed Judge Davie of the Alberta Provincial Court. His honor found that because Reynolds' car was being towed by a single chain (and not on a bed or by a rigid bar), he had to work the steering and brakes. This amounted to "operating" the motor vehicle, Mr. Justice Davie held, and in that respect Reynolds' case paralleled *Rex v. Miller*, a 1944 conviction of a man steering a military tank that was under tow. In *Miller*, a five-ton truck had been pulling the tank along the street when the tank swerved and hit an oncoming car. The trial judge found that it was "obvious that the unit could not proceed unless there was someone at the wheel of the tank to steer or drive it in the proper direction."

6   Pleading guilty in Latin was all Greek to me

When I was 17 I was involved in a traffic accident. I was driving the Corvair I'd bought out of my after-school earnings. "The Mixmaster," my friends called that car, in a day when the term described a machine for making cakes, not rap music. It was the closest that I could get to a European sports car. It had only "three on the floor," but I'd put a knob on the shifter that gave the impression it was four. Although this made operating the car a bit of a puzzle for other drivers, it was cheaper than buying an actual European sports car, and my father tended to favor automotive products made in America. My father, after all, paid the license fees and insurance.

My Corvair was American, all right, even if it was unsafe at any speed, and even if its heating and defrosting system might as well have been Sumatran. I don't have anything against Sumatra, of course, but as far as I know Sumatra doesn't make cars. And the heating-defrosting system in my Corvair was non-existent.

It was cold and rainy the day of the accident, the radio was blaring, and my friend Paul and I were yammering about whatever teenagers yammered about in 1968. The windshield was badly fogged by all that hot air and I didn't see that a traffic light had turned red. A car coming off the highway broadsided my Corvair, knocking Paul out cold, briefly, and gashing the forehead of the passenger in the other car. I was left dazed, with two bloodied elbows and a totally destroyed automobile. Paul stopped talking for a total of maybe two minutes.

Everybody told me anxiously, "You'll have to plead 'guilty with an explanation.'" In the continuing fog, this sounded sensible: I'd run the light, and I had an explanation. It never occurred to me until I entered the courtroom months later that there might have been other alternatives.

My Uncle Oscar knew a bail bondsman, my relatives said. Maybe Uncle Oscar would talk to the bail bondsman, who would accidentally-on-purpose get to talking with the judge in the steam-baths or courthouse canteen about how this certain decent kid was coming up on a certain careless charge and this kid was not the sort of decent kid who would normally run a red light, and definitely not the sort of decent kid who would thrive in the county clink.

This sounded fine, too, until it occurred to me that the judge would think that I personally was trying to pervert the course of justice, which would make him madder than ever, so that he'd bang me up for years in the state pen, like the drug smuggler in *Midnight*

Express. By the time I got to court, I was in a terrible state. I wasn't sure what my explanation was, but I was ready to plead guilty with an explanation to anything, including killing Jimmy Hoffa, even though he wasn't dead yet.

Most of that day is a fog, itself, but I remember that several people whose cases were called before mine pled guilty with an explanation. This seemed to provoke nothing more serious than boredom in the judge, although at each plea he'd grumble something I couldn't make out. Even if his honor didn't appear to think much of pleading g.w.e., the defendants all seemed to get off with fairly light fines. When my turn came, I pled "Guilty with an explanation," too. I don't think my knees even shook that much.

By then I'd convinced myself that I should take whatever happened like a man because: (1) despite his manifest boredom, the judge might be impressed; (2) if the other cases were any indication, it would be over in a minute; (3) maybe it would expiate the terrible guilt I felt about the whole thing; (4) I didn't have a heck of a lot of choice.

"No low contendree," the judge seemed to say, and, though my memory may be melodramatic about this, I think he actually banged his gavel on his desk, the way they do in the movies. Then he asked me for my explanation, and I mumbled something about the inadequacies of manifold exhaust heating systems in not-very-recent compact automobiles manufactured by General Motors.

The judge fined me $75, which was a lot of money to a 17-year-old making $1.50 an hour in 1968. But compared to the agony of guilt and fear I'd experienced until judgment, it was a cake-walk. In fact, I was disappointed that the judge virtually took no notice of me before he went on to the next malefactor, who of course pled "Guilty with an explanation." I don't think he even looked at me. I almost wished he'd bawled me out or something, so that I could have felt purged or maybe angry at him, so that he could have shared the guilt.

Only now do I understand the great favor his honor did me by entering a plea of *nolo contendere*. Although there are no traces of the plea *per se* in the Canadian legal system, supposedly it was in use in Britain as early as the reign of Henry IV (1367–1413). When William Hawkins explains "implied confession" in his *Treatise of the Pleas of the Crown* (1716), he is generally thought to be describing the *nolo contendere* plea:

> *An implied confession is where a defendant, in a case not capital, doth not directly own himself guilty, but in a manner admits to be yielding to the King's mercy, and desiring to submit to a small fine.... The defendant should not be estopped to plead not guilty to the action for the same fact.*

We defendants in Colorado in 1968 were doing just that — hoping the state would look kindly on us for admitting we'd blown it, but blown it without deliberation or bad faith. We were not pleading guilty *guilty* (in which case we would have been able to "speak to sentence" anyway — explain to the judge why he should consider imposing a light sentence or discharge), but guilty *kind of*. The guilty mind, as lawyers put it, wasn't really, truly, deeply so.

I knew that this did not oblige the judge to go any lighter on me (and in fact, I was never very impressed by Uncle Oscar's connections after that), but by changing my plea to "I do not contend the charges," he most certainly did me a mercy. He reserved my right to deny liability if the people in the other car sued me.

This is the principal virtue of the *nolo contendere* plea today in the United States. You can plead it only at the court's discretion, and it is not allowed for capital offenses. (It has been accepted, however, for serious crimes such as rape and burglary.) Unless you expressly reserve your right of appeal, the plea usually compromises that right. It won't necessarily mitigate punishment. But like a guilty plea it saves court time and expense; not only do you waive your right to a trial, your explanation does double duty as your submissions concerning the proper sentence. And although a plea of *nolo contendere* can be put forward in other actions as proof of the fact that you pled it, it cannot be used in subsequent proceedings as proof of your guilt or liability.

In my case, fortunately, *nolo contendere* was not much more than "a plea of guilty in Latin," as one wag has defined it. The people in the other car did not sue. But historically, the plea has been popular in prohibition and anti-trust prosecutions — prosecutions for crimes that are not *malum in se*, but *malum prohibitum* (not conduct wrong in itself, but conduct prohibited by mortal law). Thus the other rationale its defenders give for it: it allows time-saving quasi-confessions for minor breaches of the state's peace — "Yeah, I did it, but the harm was really incidental."

Obviously, this argument has little weight when the plea is proffered for more serious offenses. But it proved more than serviceable to a young man who made a mistake that could have been very serious, indeed.

7   You are my sunshine, and have the right to remain silent

"You're nicked, sunshine!" Pronounced correctly, "Yowar nickt, sowanshoyn" — drawled with that careful blend of righteousness and easy menace just before you read the tosser his rights and tell him that anything he says will be taken down in evidence — these are words that can make you the coolest dude in the English-speaking world.

Yowar nickt, sowanshoyn! It's a gourmet's version of *Gotcha!* Feel how the first two syllables play up and down your tongue, the way you get to draw out the "Gotcha!" sentiment for maximum sadistic enjoyment, until the comma hits your teeth for a heartbeat, then slides smoothly into the sibilant spitting-out of "sunshine" in a *frisson* of haughty disgust. Talk about your rule of law!

And that's only the beginning. There is still the villain's response, itself delicious to hear and contemplate. For a strict, even courtly, protocol governs this intercourse, and the adversaries must display a grudging mutual respect. To the Declaration Sadistically Victorious, "You're nicked, sunshine," the Reply Graciously Masochistic invariably must be, "Ya got me bang to rights, guv'nor."

Real villains never say this, of course. And in order to announce "You're nicked, sunshine" without having passersby grin nervously at the sidewalk as you approach, you have to be an English copper, preferably on a British television show. The rest of us are left with rather impoverished substitutes, as evidenced by a recent article in the *Independent* by the medical correspondent, Theodore Dalrymple (not, apparently, his real name), headed "Get Stuffed, Sunshine."

Dalrymple discusses there the social implications of swearing, and specifically the occasion on which a distraught mother brought her eight-year-old boy into his examining rooms. "He won't do what he's told," the mother complained, "he never sits down, he smashes things, and you should hear his fucking language!" When Dalrymple gently suggested that maybe the kid was picking up certain habits from his familiars, the woman marched out, but not before advising, "Now listen here, sunshine, I've had just about enough of your lip."

Dalrymple seems to imply that he believes parents make a difference, a view at odds with *The Nurture Assumption*, a recent book in which an American researcher contends that parenting has little effect on how a child turns out. The book became a bestseller, thanks to baby-boomers whose children have been brought up by videos and half-educated housemaids. Of course, the book's conclusions do not accord with the experience of most parole officers and social workers.

Probably everyone would agree, however, that we are being ironic when we use "sunshine" to describe someone we consider villainous. Jonathon Green's *The Slang Thesaurus* lists "sunshine" under "terms of friendship," along with *ace, amigo, babycakes, buggerlugs, diddums,* and *lovey.* Somehow, though, "You're nicked, buggerlugs" doesn't have quite the same *je ne sais quoi.*

Dalrymple refers to the book *The Future of Swearing and Improper Language* by the British writer Robert Graves, a book I stumbled upon in my earliest days as a law student. To relieve the bipolar tedium and high anxiety of first-year law, I checked Graves' little book out of the university's main library. But it wasn't all playing hooky, babycakes. Soon enough I was cast back into the law reports and statute books, where I discovered that, in Britain, swearing — not just blasphemy, but everyday profanity — used to be a specific statutory crime. The penalties escalated according to one's rank in society, a shilling for working people, in one era, on up to five shillings for gentlemen and more exalted toffs.

Evidently the Normans brought in the penalty scale which, under Henry I, ranged from a 40-shilling fine for foul-mouthed dukes to a whipping for the penniless page. Not surprisingly, under Cromwell the fines more than tripled, and culprits risked having their tongues bored with hot iron.

Ah, the price of civilization. Perhaps this supports Dalrymple's point that all the middle-class cussing one hears these days is democratic slumming. "Among the middle class, especially among its more intellectually-inclined members," Dalrymple writes, "impurity of language is taken as a symbol of purity of political and social sentiment. It is democratic to swear, and the more one does it, the more democratic one is. . . . The use of bad language is thus — by implication — an act of compassion and solidarity."

And here you'd put it down to high taxes and road rage. Maybe this democracy business explains the guy on the expressway. He cut in front of me at 120 kilometres per hour (75 mph), and I blew my horn — the automotive equivalent of "Watchit, sunshine." Perhaps it was an act of compassion and solidarity when he stuck his head out the window for the Reply Courteous, a cell-phone attached to one ear, a styrofoam coffee-cup supporting his extended middle finger, as he steered with his pelvis and screamed into the ozone-weary wind, "Why don't you stick it where the sun don't shine?"

8   Knock, hold your nose, and ask for Tim Horton

French fries and eel pies are meat, our courts say: *Bullen v. Ward* (see page 189). Bicycles are carriages: *Corkery v. Carpenter*, [1951] 1 King's Bench Reports, 102. Parking lots are bawdy houses: *R. v. Pierce* (1982), 37 Ontario Reports (2d) 721 (Court of Appeal). And now, sniffing the foyer constitutes an illegal search.

Call it, in fact, the "scratch 'n' sniff test." If a legal proposition makes the ordinarily reasonable person scratch his head and sniff, "Huh?" it has to be coming soon to a law report near you.

The Canadian Supreme Court's 4:3 sniffing decision in *R. v. Evans* seems right in law. Nonetheless it has the unmistakeable savor of the barnyard. I choose that locale advisedly. In his minority decision in *Evans*, Justice John Major quotes the leading "knock-and-look" case, *Robson v. Hallett* from 1967, and the famous Dickens truism therein:

> *For my part, it is no doubt true that the law is sometimes said to be an ass, but I am happy to think that it is not an ass in this respect,*

> *because I am quite satisfied that these three police officers, like any other members of the public, had implied leave and licence to walk through that gate up those steps and to knock on the door of the house. We are not considering for this purpose the entering of private premises in the form of a dwelling-house, but of the position between the gate and the front door. There, as it seems to me, the occupier of any dwelling-house gives implied licence to any member of the public coming on his lawful business to come through the gate, up the steps, and knock on the door of the house.*

Thus we have the common law rule that, absent evidence to the contrary, John and Jane Occupier extend an implied invitation to the world at large to knock at their door, including snoopy coppers.

Of course, the police in *Evans* knocked on the door *with the intention of sniffing*, and that little extra, really, is what makes all the difference. A neighbor of the Evanses had called Crimestoppers about marijuana cultivation in the Evans household. The police checked to see if the Evanses had criminal records, and scoured the Evanses' electricity bills for industrial-level power consumption. They stood around whistling nonchalantly on the public sidewalk while taking the occasional unassuming glance at the Evans house. It was all for nought. In fact, the police had begun to doubt the Crimestoppers tip.

As a last resort, plainclothes officers went up to the Evanses' door, apparently resolved to ask straight out if they were growing blow in the basement. One of the officers told the trial court:

> *Instead of just concluding the file at this point, I felt obliged to go and ask the occupant if in fact he was growing marijuana in his house and after doing so, I would conclude the file. There were many possibilities of things that may have happened, and we discussed them. Perhaps no one would be home at that particular time, perhaps he would deny such a thing, or another thing that we did talk about was*

> while we were speaking to the occupant, if somebody did answer the door and if in fact he was cultivating marijuana in the residence, we could get a whiff or a smell might come out at us. So we talked about that as well, and we talked about what we would do if this occurred.

So really, no one had the intention of sniffing so much as the anxious hope of getting an inculpatory whiff.

Still, legally the cops ended up no different than robbers at the lintel. Writing for the majority, Justice John Sopinka observes that "it would be ludicrous to argue that the invitation to knock invites a burglar to approach the door in order to 'case' the house. The waiver of privacy interests that is entailed by the invitation to knock cannot be taken to go that far." At the same time, Justice Sopinka holds that the reasonable expectation of privacy protected by section 8 of the *Canadian Charter of Rights and Freedoms* (the section that forbids unreasonable searches or seizures) extends to the aromas in our dwellings. And sure enough, most of us would just as soon that the neighbors did in fact keep the Jenny's Garlic 'n' Goat Cheese Surprise to themselves. But Justice Sopinka goes farther than that: knocking with the idea of sniffing is an unreasonable search, at least where sniffy police have no warrant or reasonable and probable grounds to make an "olfactory search."

How far, then, is the "that far" that the waiver of privacy interests goes? Cops and robbers can't knock to case the joint without probable cause, but is it unreasonable to deliberately breathe, prick up our ears, and stand wide-eyed when selling Policeman's Ball tickets at the local bawdy house? Does *Evans* extend to the other two senses, touching and tasting? "Is that a doughnut, ma'am, or is your hash brownie just happy to see me?"

Evidence is admissible, Justice Sopinka holds, if the police spot it upon knocking to make an innocent request to use your phone or to ask for directions. So perhaps we can expect an unusual surge of urgent police communication requirements in undesirable neighborhoods — "P.C. phone home!" And sure enough, that's three times tonight Cruiser 5307 has pulled up at Bugsy Malone's place to ask for the shortest route to the Mister Donut.

In a bizarre twist on the already exotic circumstances, the Supreme Court seems to leave open the question of what conduct would amount to withdrawing the implied invitation to knock. The majority does not treat the question at all. Justice Major observes that one is not obliged to answer the door, or put out the welcome mat:

> *Obviously, the residents of the home may refuse permission. They retain a full measure of choice and control over who may enter and who may not, whom they will speak to and whom they will ignore. They may also choose to revoke this implied licence explicitly, for example by installing a locked gate at the entrance to the property, or posting signs to that effect.*

Yet in concurring with Justice Major in all other respects, Justice Claire L'Heureux-Dubé states: "Since these issues do not arise in this appeal and were not argued before us, they are strictly *obiter* [off-point] and I prefer to leave them for another day."

What there is to consider on that other day is unclear. It remains mysterious what else one would use beyond gates, locks, and signs to revoke the implied invitation to knock, short of land mines on the front lawn. Meanwhile, it looks like we're safe from midnight raids by the S.W.A.T. team to catch us causing a nuisance by frying onions in a particularly odoriferous fashion. Would it be outside Parliament's jurisdiction to pass the *Occupier's Fryability Act*?

CHAPTER TWO

FINDERS, KEEPERS

Property and Related Stuff

9   The bedtime story they call Will's will

When the subject is Shakespeare, one of the few things scholars are fairly confident about is that he left a will. In general, it is not an unusual testamentary document for 1616, when it was made. In fact, the man who found it, Joseph Greene, vicar of Stratford-Upon-Avon, was worried that it would give the wrong impression. It was "so dull and irregular," he wrote in 1747, just after he'd come upon it, "so absolutely void of ye least particle of that spirit which animated our great Poet, that it must lessen his Character as a Writer, to imagine ye least sentence of it his production."

The vicar's unworldly opinion was echoed over 100 years later by the anonymous author of the magazine piece, "Who Wrote Shakespeare?" You will notice right away, however, that the title is not "Who Wrote Shakespeare's Will?" — the assumption being that the bloke who wrote the plays and poetry could not be the Shakespeare who drafted a will "as plain and prosaic as if it had been the production of a pig-headed prerogative lawyer." But not everybody since has been so bored by the will. In fact, several hogsheads of ink, and probably a few drams of blood, have been spilt over the provision near the end of the document, "Item. I give unto my wife my second best bed with the furniture."

This is the only mention of poor Anne Shakespeare in the entire 11-page document. Worse, given that it's an "interlineation" — meaning that it's scrunched between two of the otherwise more or less evenly-spaced lines of the will — it seems to be an afterthought. And to add yet more insult to the injury, "with the furniture" does not mean "and all the rest of the stuff in the house, including, of course, my *best* bed." It means the accessories, as they would say at Bloomingdales — the valance, bed linen, etc. that go with the second-best bed.

Yet was insult and injury the testamentary intent? Could it be, a great number of Bard enthusiasts have been asking for about two and a half centuries, that the poet bequeathed only "second best" to the woman who kept the kids quiet during the final draft of *Romeo and Juliet*?

The most blood-stirring theory is that the Shakespeare marriage was an unhappy, or even a blunderbuss affair. There is evidence, as they say, that Anne was with bairn before the banns, and that the marriage was all hugger-mugger hurry-up. And the consensus is that while the bridegroom was only 18, by Elizabethan standards, bride Anne, at 26, was just short of cronehood.

Proponents of the marriage-breakdown theory will refer you to two passages in the Works: first, the Duke's advice in *Twelfth Night* to Viola, who is disguised as a boy, "Let still the woman take an elder than herself"; and again, Prospero's advice in *The Tempest*, one of Shakespeare's last plays, that you should marry a virgin lest "barren hate, sour-eyed disdain and discord bestrew the union of your bed." But the legally knowledgable have pointed out that under the common law of dower Anne probably would have been automatically entitled to a third share of all of her husband's property. Some say it follows that Shakespeare thought it unnecessary to spell out her entitlement, but mentioned the second-best bed because the very best bed would have been part of the furnishings of the house, which under the will went to daughter Susanna.

Others counter that the poet's lawyer had once set up a real estate transaction for him so as deliberately to avoid dower, and that dower may not have been customary in Stratford at the time anyway. Still others say that the best bed was where William slept when he didn't sleep with Anne — making it seem even more likely that he was cocking a snook at her from the grave.

Mind you, when I was young my family called the dog's biscuits "crumpets," I suppose because the biscuits were crumbly and crunchy, and possibly because price-wise they were pretty upper crust. Apparently many families engage in such *jeux-de-mots*, so perhaps the Shakespeares had a family joke about best beds. Considering all the word-play that could have enlivened the day's dull care around New Place, Stratford, 1611–1616 (imagine old Bill padding around the kitchen in his slippers and robe trying out lines on the extended family like, "If nothing hath my something grief, then something hath the nothing that I grieve"), it seems at least possible that there were *two* best beds, the second being best for sleeping in, say, and the first being livelier and therefore best for, well, *not* sleeping in. In 1616, what would a 60-year-old widow have wanted with a bed that wasn't good for sleeping in?

There is, perhaps, a final, appropriately poetic, possibility. Shakespeare had thought a lot, and deeply, about time and tide during his career, and at the last had perhaps opted for the Christian gamble, had made the best of death by accepting the grave as his very best bed, as the cradle of eternal heavenly peace. Tradition, anyway, says that at her death Anne wanted to share her husband's last, best resting-place, but had to settle for second best (again) when the sexton was scared off by the words on William's gravestone:

> *Good friend, for Jesus' sake forbeare*
> *To dig the dust enclosed here;*
> *Blest be the man that spares these stones,*
> *And curst be he that moves my bones.*

10   That's no bitch; that's my pet otter!

We tend to think that legal casuistry, "getting him off on a technicality," is a modern development, when it is at least as old as Adam. Even under Anglo-American law, there are many aged examples. In 1844, Thomas Cox was acquitted of stealing "three eggs ... of the goods and chattels of Samuel Harris" because the indictment had not specified that they were eggs of a guinea-fowl and not "adder's eggs, or some other species of eggs which cannot be the subject of larceny." The next day, Cox's prosecutor crossed the courtroom before the same judge to defend a man accused of committing bestiality "in and upon a certain animal called a bitch." Apparently full of confidence and sure of the court's point of view, he relied on *Cox* to make the very point that had killed his case the day before: as in *Cox*, the lawyer asserted, the bestiality indictment did "not describe the animal with sufficient certainty," *bitch* by itself signifying perhaps a fox or otter bitch, or whatever animal. While repeating what he had said in *Cox* about the necessity of precise identification of the animal, the judge anyway pronounced the bestiality indictment good, and the lawyer lost once more.

In 1823, Thomas Halloway was acquitted of "stealing a brass furnace" on the argument that, by the time he had brought the object within the jurisdiction of the court, he had broken it into pieces so that it was no longer a furnace. It was a memorably lucky day for Halloway: on the same date, the same court acquitted him of pinching "two turkies" because the indictment should have specified that the turkies were dead. In a practice note to their report of Halloway's good fortune, Carrington and Payne, barristers of Lincoln's Inn, explain that live animals such as turkies are in law *ferae naturae* (free-roaming beasts) and cannot be owned, let alone stolen. Ancillary to this, stealing the skin of a dog, they say, is a felony, but stealing the living dog is not, "dogs being considered in law of base [wild] nature." They say nothing of bestiality with bitches, mind you, but add that, regarding indictments for theft, counsel should remember that a man charged with stealing a "pair" of stockings was acquitted because the stockings did not match, and that another accused escaped punishment for stealing a duck because the converted bird was a *drake*.

People who sneer at acquittals on legal technicalities forget, of course, that many have been *convicted* on technicalities — found guilty of theft, not to mention other sorts of behavior with ill-defined animals. Rather poignant in theft law is the more recent example of Lorne Pace, a petty officer who had served as a cook in the Canadian navy and air force for 11 years. On the day in question, in 1965, he had baked some orange-raisin loaves for dessert and knew the leftovers were going to be thrown out. Rather than see the loaves consigned to the garbage or sold off as animal food, he took one home to his children. When his superiors found out, they called the police and had Pace charged with stealing the cake.

The prosecution admitted that the loaf's cash value was maybe 50 cents. But it was also true that Queen Elizabeth II, the nominal head of the air force for whom Pace cooked, sold these leftovers as pig swill. The evidence showed that Pace knew that Her Majesty made a practice of selling leftovers to farmers. The court, therefore, "would not hear him" say he thought that the loaf was ownerless or abandoned. Even if he thought the loaf was of no use or value to the air force, it was still Crown property. On this reasoning, it could be said that Petty Officer Pace intended to deprive Her Majesty of her swill. To Pace's defense that he wouldn't have taken the loaf had he thought anyone would object, the court said the fact that those in charge would not object did not mean they would consent. It upheld his conviction for theft, as well as the nominal fine of "one dollar or one day in the city prison."

In a sense, Pace was arguing impossibility: you cannot steal something that does not belong to someone. (On similar reasoning, it used to be that a wife could not sue her husband: at common law, they were one flesh, the man's, and a person could not sue himself.) For a short time, this even applied to criminal attempts: if you tried to pick a pocket but couldn't because it was empty, you could not be convicted of criminal attempt. This was so illogical, it did not stand up very long: whether the pocket was full or empty, the would-be thief had still intended to pick it and had attempted that illegal act.

The Queen v. Brown, a case of a man indicted for attempting to commit unnatural acts with ducks, is the high-water mark of judicial retraction from the old law of impossible attempts. The case is notable for a lot of nervous behind-the-scenes shuffling.

Brown was formally charged with attempting to commit unnatural offenses with an animal, "to wit, a domestic fowl." When he admitted the offense at the Essex assizes in 1889, the Chief Justice of England, Lord Coleridge, dispassionately sentenced him to 12 months at hard labor. Later, someone, probably another judge, advised Lord Coleridge that a man in an earlier case had been acquitted of the same offense on the grounds that a duck was not an animal and therefore the offense as charged could not be proved. His lordship decided to submit the case to a judicial panel.

The supposed precedent was not recorded in the law reports, but Lord Coleridge was able to contact several of the judges who had heard it. Evidently, it turned out that the man in that earlier case had been acquitted on the basis of impossibility, but not because a duck was not legally an animal. The court had found him not guilty because it decided it was physically impossible for a human to "have connection" with a duck. On the basis of the old law, it would therefore also be impossible to attempt to have connection with a duck.

The evidence in Brown's case was that penetration of some sort was possible. The Crown proved that Brown had made a habit of attempted bestiality and that his yard was littered with "torn and bleeding" birds and duck corpses. In the end, although *Brown* is rather obscure, it seems to stand for the propositions:

(1) in law, a duck is an animal;
(2) in law, even if a duck is not an animal, it is possible to attempt the impossible;
(3) in fact as well as in law, it is possible to fuck a duck;
(4) even if in fact it is impossible to fuck a duck, it is possible to attempt to fuck a duck;
(5) the accused was guilty as charged.

11 Feets, and deceased pheasants, do their stuff

Feet come up a lot in law. It all started with the lord chancellor, or, rather, with John Selden taking the measure of his lordship's dogs in the late 1600s. At the time, the common law courts were battling the increasing popularity of the courts of equity. The former had begun losing favor for their rigidity and unfortunate tendency to fashion the law according to the sovereign's whim. Although under the direction of the lord chancellor the courts of equity put a higher premium on fairness, no matter what the "black letter law" said, Selden was skeptical:

> *Equity is A Roguish thing, for Law wee have a measure [and] know what to trust too. Equity is according to ye conscience of him yt is Chancellor, and as yt is larger or narrower soe is equity. Tis all one as if they should make ye Standard for ye measure wee call A foot, to be ye Chancellors foot; what an uncertain measure would this be; One Chancellor has a long foot[,] another A short foot[,] a third an indifferent foot; tis ye same thing in ye Chancellors Conscience.*

No doubt someone has done a doctor of laws on what an "indifferent foot" is in equity.

Around Selden's era, Justice Twisden "remembered" out loud, during argument in court, an earlier defamation matter in which "a shoemaker brought an action against a man for saying that he was a cobbler, and though a cobbler be a trade of itself, yet it was held that the action lay." Translation: a shoemaker sued a man for saying that he was a cobbler. And he won damages for slander. At common law, we mind our tongues.

There is that practice note in Carrington and Payne's Reports for 1823 which tells of a man acquitted of stealing a "pair" of stockings because they did not match. Then there is the modern British solicitor, very much living but perhaps thinking "I could have just *died*," whose socks made legal news during our own era. Martin Morrow was sitting in Falkirk Magistrates Court when his musical stockings "went off." Apparently he was able to hide his embarrassment under the counsel table during the ten minutes it took him to stop the music.

But shoes were the real foot-law newsmaker around the same time, when 52-year-old Charles Jones admitted to New York Justice Richard Andrias that he had more than a passing interest in women's shoes. Jones was acting as publicity agent at the time to Marla Maples, the pulchritudinous love-interest of Donald Trump, the American real estate magnate. Indeed, Jones was before Judge Andrias on charges of stealing dozens of pairs of Maples' footwear. Just how many pairs varies with the source, the accounting running from 200 to 78, 65, "more than 40," and 30.

Jones admitted to taking only one pair of boots, but prosecutors say that he had also stolen some of Maples' soiled bras and underpants — which police found in his desk drawers and behind radiator covers in his office — as well as Maples' diary and nude photos of the pneumatic former showgirl. (Police found a duffel bag of other women's underthings in Jones' office. He told them that he couldn't remember where it all came from. I used to have a stamp collection in similar disarray.)

Maples had been reporting missing footwear to the police for three years. In 1992, she hid a video camera in her closet, just like the ones at the bank and the Seven-Eleven. It caught Jones stuffing her clothing in his pockets. (Again, accounts differ: one says "black stiletto heels"; another says something from the dirty laundry pile.) When testifying for the prosecution, Maples refused to touch her own Jourdans, Fayvas, et. al., seized from Jones' custody, unless equipped with court-order latex gloves. It seems that for a collector such as Jones, the shoe is the actual sex object, with the True Owner being pretty well of secondary interest, supplementary nude photos or not.

Jones admitted to having "a physical sexual relationship" with the shoes, and to slashing the boots so that he could experience more intimate knowledge of the footprints therein. When the prosecutor asked him the love-object question, he agreed, "It's mostly the shoe." Some reports say that his infatuation was so profound, Jones rejected a plea-bargain which required him to return Maples' footwear. But the depth of his feeling did not discourage hilarity among courtroom spectators. Jurors burst out laughing when Jones testified that the matter was "deeper" than a fetish. It was an "irresistible impulse," he explained, but "not the overriding force in my life." He claimed, as well, that, though he is an ex-Marine, the complainant and her mother beat him up on discovering he was the shoenapper: "I've seen Marla Maples in action. She could take Donald Trump down."

Apparently Jones had got past security guards at Maples' apartment building by showing them a forged note: "Hi, Chuck. Here's some especially great clothes and shoes, sexy and casual." In the end, though, it was no joke. While recognizing that Jones was suffering from mental problems, Justice Andrias sentenced him to a maximum of four-and-a-half years in prison for burglary, criminal possession of stolen property, and criminal possession of a weapon. (Police found three handguns among the women's wear in his office.)

Meanwhile, Maples wasn't the only Trump wife screaming robbery and using covert surveillance. A detective agency sued ex-spouse Ivana Trump for $233,000 U.S., for services rendered in spying for Ivana ... on Marla Maples. The total bill was $308,000. Ivana said that she told the agency not to perform more than $100,000 worth of work on her divorce case against "The Donald" (with Maples as what the law used to call the "co-respondent"). The detectives claimed that Ivana's lawyer advised them they could spend more.

As an instance of the agency's extravagance, the lawyer, Ira Garr, pointed to $38,000 they charged Ivana to serve a subpoena on Maples. Who says the rich don't pay?

12 Stop in the name of the law — or Rollo!

This is the scene as the news services made it out:

The complainant, Paul Armorgie, marches up to a bulldozer. The machine's operator is digging a house foundation next to Armorgie's hotel on the Channel Island of Sark, near the hotel's pool. Armorgie throws his hat to the ground and raises his hands to the sky. He shouts: "*Je fais haro sur vous.*" Armorgie has just performed the medieval equivalent of applying for an injunction. He has just invoked — or at least he believes he has just invoked — the venerable *clameur de haro*.

Tourists sometimes make the mistake of thinking that the *clameur de haro*, the "clamor of haro," is a bit of play-acting for their benefit, the sort of "historical re-enactment" you see at those little farms where you pay $15.00 for a woman dressed like Laura Secord or Dolly Madison to satisfy your every desire, so long as that desire happens to be watching her make cookies that taste like sawdust while she fills you in on more than you wanted to know about farm wives in the 19th century. But hoary and quaint though the clamor of haro might be, it is still good law in the Channel Islands. Historians there believe that the Vikings introduced it, when they invaded the area during the early 900s. Some say the phrase derives from an appeal in the name of an especially fierce Viking leader, Rollo, his name having been shortened to "haro" from "Ha, Rollo!" Rollo's ravages prefigured the invasion of England by William of Normandy: Rollo became the first duke of Normandy when Channel Island leaders tried to make peace by ceding that territory to him.

Understandably, the lexicographers at the *Oxford English Dictionary* remain unconvinced by the *Ha, Rollo!* etymology. They prefer to derive *haro* from the Norman *haro*, which was used in roughly the same way as the Anglo-Norman *hu et cri*, which by law obliged citizens to raise the "hue and cry" of "Stop thief!" and to give hot pursuit to criminals. (Even if the criminal made it across village boundaries, custom dictated that the denizens of the second village take up the chase, and so on through each region, until the villain was in hand. Then, usually, the captors executed him summarily. The thief had become an outlaw in the literal sense — completely outside the law's protection.)

In a rare case of English-French rapprochement, the French language authority *Robert* seems to agree with the OED. *Robert* defines *haro* as, "Cry of help by a victim of a flagrant wrong, by which cry all hearers were obliged to intervene." For *clameur de haro*, *Robert* gives, "Form of words that gave others the right to arrest a malefactor." And for "to cry haro against" (*crier haro sur*) *Robert* says, "Denounce for public repudiation." This latter definition comes closest to the way the clamor of haro is used in the Channel Islands. There, it works as a sort of anytime, do-it-yourself cease-and-desist order. And it's regarded with the utmost gravity. As one guidebook warns: "Practical jokers should be warned that invoking the *clameur* needlessly also carries a heavy penalty."

Mind you, if you invoke it needlessly while following Paul Armorgie's method, you can probably plead that there was no criminal act. For if the news reports are right, Armorgie's version fits none of the proper *clameur* forms described by commentators. The accepted precedent observes the following protocol:

> *(1) The claimant drops to his knees in front of the person committing trespass against his property. (In Armorgie's case, this was the bulldozer operator, who was attempting to begin house construction next to Armorgie's swimming pool. If the claimant wants to throw his hands up in the air, custom permits it, apparently. And yes, if the claimant is prudent, he will remove his hat: as will become clear, supplication is the idea, to sovereign and Sovereign.)*

(2) The claimant shouts: "Haro, Haro, Haro! A l'aide, mon Prince. On me fait tort!" ("Help me, my Prince. This person has done me harm!" Some sources insist that you say "Haro" exactly three times.)

(3) The claimant recites the Lord's prayer in French (evidently in the hope that if one sovereign does not intervene on his behalf, perhaps another One will).

And *voilà*! If the alleged malefactor doesn't stop what he's doing pending trial of the dispute, he could face sanctions for contempt. According to the *Daily Telegraph*, a properly pleaded *clameur* will stop construction for a year and a day "unless challenged before the sovereign." Warburton's 1822 *History of Guernsey* warns that if the crier fails to litigate the merits of the dispute, "then the person against whom the haro was cried may bring his action against him who cried haro." It seems, in other words, that you might be able to seek damages against a person who cried haro at you but who later could not convince authorities that his case had merit.

Apparently the clamor of haro has been used successfully on the Islands to enjoin logging, the building of roads by the military, and the installation of a crane in the air-space of a newsstand on Jersey.

13   Exactly 1,711 angels, actually, on your standard pinhead

Lord Greene says that there is probably always room for another angel to dance on the head of a pin. The National Research Council disagrees: there's room for only a sedate 1,711, the council insists, and not a cherub more.

It is commonly thought that medieval philosophers whiled away the hours over this question. Science and law have shied away from it on the assumption that it is a problem of metaphysics beyond empirical analysis. In his 1982 book *The Angels and Us*, U.S. philosopher Mortimer Adler professed to have solved the problem logically once and for all. But first he was determined to set the record straight on medieval philosophers.

The idea that they debated the angel-cotillion issue vexed him as "simply one of the many modern inventions contrived to make a mockery of medieval thought." Seraphic pin-hoofing "never occupied the attention of a single thinker in the Middle Ages. . . . Nor was it among the disputed questions that scholastic theologians and philosophers have been traditionally supposed to wrestle with in endless — and fruitless — debate."

As Prof. Adler wrestled Jacobeanly with the question, he decided that the number of angels that could dance on the head of a pin, or anywhere else, was one. Angels, he explained, are by definition bodiless minds. When

> *an angel acts spiritually on a particular body, its presence at the place occupied by that body is also an occupation of that place. Just as the physical presence of one body at a place excludes all others from occupying the place, so the spiritual presence of an angel at a place excludes all others from occupying that place. One angel intensively occupying the head of a pin excludes all others from being spiritually present there.*

While in many ways Prof. Adler's angels were comparable (he contended) to corporations — angels can exercise influence on earth without leaving Heaven, "just as a corporation that has its legal residence in Delaware can act in Honolulu without leaving" the east coast — corporations are more like God than like angels: like God (and unlike angels), they can be in many places at once.

Then again, only God can be everywhere at once.

Despite his sober legal mind, Lord Greene seems to have held a more miraculous view, to which he gave vent in *In re Grosvenor*, a case arising out of the Battle of Britain. During an air raid on September 14, 1940, the Grosvenor brothers, Randolph, 73, and Edward, 66, had taken refuge in the basement of their Chelsea neighbor, Mrs. Price-Jones. Also present were the brothers' housekeeper and Mrs. Price-Jones's daughter. The house took a direct hit and all five people were killed.

In his will, Randolph had left money for Edward and the housekeeper. Edward had left property in his will to Randolph and to, among others, Mrs. Price-Jones. But now, everyone had died at about the same time, in the same accident. The problem, obviously, was whose heirs got what. Who had survived whom?

The *Law of Property Act* said that where it was not clear who survived whom, death was "presumed to have occurred in order of seniority." In other words, Randolph, being oldest, would be deemed to have died before Edward, who would have predeceased the 60-year-old Mrs. Price-Jones, who inherited the lot. That is, her surviving heirs would take accordingly. That is what a trial court told the other Grosvenor boy, Robert, to his financial disappointment. Robert pressed on to the Court of Appeal, which obliged him, two judges to one: the seniority rule did not apply, the court said. The bomb had not exploded until it penetrated the basement; so powerful was its force that the five victims had been mutilated beyond recognition. They had, the Court of Appeal found, died simultaneously; there was no "order of death."

Lord Greene scoffed at the idea that simultaneous death was impossible under the laws of succession. Insofar as "time is infinitely divisible," as the impossibility view had it, "it must always be certain that one of two persons in fact died before the other. . . . The statement that time is infinitely divisible," his lordship retorted,

> *was said to be a scientific fact. I should prefer to call it a metaphysical conception. No doubt, when a bevy of angels is performing saltatory exercises on the point of a needle it is always possible to find room for one more, but propositions of this character appear to me to be ill suited for adoption by the law of this country which proceeds on principles of practical common sense.*

At the House of Lords, however, another majority of two found the infinite divisibility of time eminently practical, sensible, and legal. Robert couldn't claim a penny. The oldest-die-first scheme of the *Law of Property Act* ruled out simultaneous death, the law lords found. Even if, as Lord Simonds put it, simultaneous death were scientifically possible, where survivorship is not proved, "the only alternative is uncertainty."

So be it, as well, you would think, with angels and pinheads. But at the National Research Council, Canadian government scientists managed to get a very definite 1,711 angels on the *point* of a pin. (Following Adler's reasoning, whether seraphic bugalooing is on the head of a pin or the point of a needle is irrelevant.) Her Majesty's physicists performed this seemingly impossible act of multiplication *and* divisibility using — no surprise here — technology of Japan (where angels are sometimes called bodhisatvas), an ion-beam etcher that scratched the conventional western idea of an angel (choir-robed, bewinged, be-haloed) 1,711 times on an area the size of a pin prick.

The machine took all of 40 seconds to do this. A more practical application is evidently (but not as believably) the etching of circuits on *individual atoms*, thereby making micro-micro chips for computers. And this is what our philosophy has come to: how many computer chips can do the binary two-step on the dust of a molecule?

14 Losing your head over real estate

Vincennes, *stone, one head, 85 yrs., in occupation, 73 sq. metres, 6th flr., elevator, condo., $130,000 down, $270/mo.*
One head, *75 yrs., in occup., 50 sq. m., 6th flr., elevat., condo., $79,000 down, $200/mo. Call 48.88.93.07.*
Rue de la Paix, *prestige home, 85 sq. m., in occup., 98 yrs., no down-payment. $900,000. Phone 43.28.83.46.*
Vacant in '98, *Sceaux (downtown), townhouse, six rooms, garden, $11,000 down + $8,300/mo. Call Cruz Viagers, 42.66.19.00.*

(FREELY TRANSLATED FROM LE FIGARO CLASSIFIEDS, DEC. 9, 1993.)

"Someone's invented a device that kills people in the most horrible, gruesome way possible, while leaving buildings standing untouched. It's called a mortgage."

BRITISH COMEDIAN ALEXEI SAYLE

Eighty-five-year-old heads. A 98-year-old who's just now setting up a life annuity for herself. It was Pascale, my French teacher at the continuing education division of the Toronto Public School system, who first attempted to explain to me this curiosity of the Napoleonic legal code called *viager*.

On earlier evenings, Pascale had admitted that her understanding of law in general was idiosyncratic. For example, in the days before she decided that she was too dangerous to drive, she found herself informing a dumbfounded Toronto police constable that she always parked her Austin Mini on the sidewalk near the St. Lawrence Market. The way she understood the law, boulevard parking was a driver's customary right, as long as she was doing business somewhere in the surrounding five miles.

Pascale, who was about 40 when I met her, grew up in Paris, in a professional family. (To protect the innocent — or the *soi-disant naive* — I am calling her by a pseudonym.) She had traveled and worked all over Europe. She had taught French in Africa. She did her Ph.D. at the University of Toronto in analytical philosophy and she had lived in Toronto for 20 years or more, trying to help anglophones like me become officially bilingual. But her soul remained in Gaul.

If I wanted to exchange ideas with Pascale, I was obliged to speak French even outside of class — which might explain some of my confusion about *viagers* and many other things in Pascale's solar system. The no-English rule was not for my betterment as her protégé, but because Pascale claimed that her English scared people.

Soon after she arrived in Canada she attempted to teach philosophy at the University of Toronto, but her students kept asking her, "Are you sure you mean that?" In a philosophical context this had the makings of a nervous breakdown — or, as Pascale put it, shuddering characteristically and using her favorite expression: *"C'était l'horreur!"* She didn't know if they were challenging her thinking or her English.

After she quit teaching philosophy, she looked in the newspaper for jobs. She saw an ad by an outfit seeking topless women to work for high wages. Fortunately, before she went for an interview someone explained that the advertiser was not looking for women who were insuperable in their field.

She attempted to improve her English by watching television, but the commercials upset her so much, she sold her TV within weeks of buying it. Years later, she claimed she still couldn't hear the word "Kraft" without getting nauseated.

Pascale soon came to avoid English as much as possible. Sometimes she had no choice in the matter, such as the lunchtime she ordered a peanut butter sandwich and became enraged when the waiter brought two anorexic sheets of wholewheat bread ("food for cattle") smeared with a tan, odoriferous substance that reminded her of animal droppings. She thought "peanut butter" meant "pineapple." Why she had wanted a pineapple sandwich I can't tell you.

Not long after that, she asked an astonished florist if he had "any penis." She wanted a posy of peonies for a friend. Her mercantile malapropisms seem to run along this line. More recently she dumbfounded another male victim in a drug store by pointing at his nether regions and demanding loudly, "'Ow do you call zose?" She wanted to know how to ask for shoelaces, but the man thought what a man thinks. As I imagine it, he was as shocked as the friends of Nabokov's Pnin when the emigré professor announced that he had been shot, when he meant he had been fired.

As for *viager*, our French class concluded that it had to describe some sort of reverse mortgage. But to Pascale, it seemed to denote the Amityville Horror Reverse Mortgage. Informing all of her other eccentricities, you see, was her thing about death. She wouldn't make a will because she thought that this would open the door to terminal cancer or tempt fate the next time she cleaned the outsides of her third-storey apartment windows. Instead, she daily sneered in the reaper's face, living on *tira misu* from Grano, the trendy *ristorante* down the street from her North Toronto digs, 12 cups of espresso, and three packs of Gauloises a day.

Her chief pedagogical technique was a constantly evolving "Song of Myself" in which she described, sometimes in epic detail worthy of Proust, her pathological mistrust of doctors, dentists, old people, and chrysanthemums. When a student gave her a potful of mums one end of term, she was sure that it was an omen she was about to die, because the French send mums to funerals. Her worst fears were confirmed when she unloaded the flowers on a friend, who immediately took sick.

In any event, Pascale refused to die in Canada. "When I know the time will be close," she proclaimed, "I will return to France. I once heard that the ground here was frozen so hard, they had to put a dead man in the refrigerator until spring. I couldn't take that. Even if they could dig, I don't like the cold."

Probably this sensitivity explains why she made the *viager* system sound like an undertaking only a coroner could stomach. And granted, there is something morbid about the *viager* ads in French newspapers, although I'm not sure that I'd have picked it up if Pascale hadn't wailed over them, cringing and eye-rolling and oh-la-la-ing. She told us to look for the ads in *Le Figaro*, a daily she assured us she never read, her demonstrative preference having been for the Communist *Liberation*.

Morbidly fascinated by her Cronenbergian build-up ("Be afraid, be very afraid!"), I rushed over to *Maison de la Presse* in Yorkville and bought the two most recent issues of *Le Figaro*. And, yes, some of the *"Viagers"* classifieds displayed a certain clinical *je ne sais quoi* — for example, "One head, woman, 98 years, nothing down," meaning, apparently, that the vendor was a 98-year-old woman who would sell her home for monthly advances, without demanding a lump sum "annuity" settlement.

Generally, *viagers* seem to be what we might call a self-directed pension plan for retired homeowners. To fund their old age, the owners sell their interest in their homes, but, as with reverse mortgages, they keep title, and sometimes possession, until they die. As purchaser, you can get immediate possession if the owner is in a nursing home, say, or living with family. In any event, your interest vests immediately if you're willing to buy now, get title who knows when. But as far as I can tell, if the vendor dies tomorrow, you hit the jackpot: you owe nothing more. You get full title, forever, even if you've paid only one or two monthly instalments.

Then again, there is at least some gamble that you will never get anything for your money at all. This happened recently, in fact, when Jeanne Calment of Arles, in the south of France, lived to be 121 years old. At the time, she was the oldest person in the world with the documents to prove it, a distinction that brought her the nickname Jeanne D'Arles — a sobriquet recalling the French martyr who died much younger, Jeanne d'Arc, a.k.a. Joan of Arc.

Calment's age, or rather, the fact that she outlived her solicitor, gave her a second claim to fame. When notary André-François Rattray died in Arles on Christmas, 1995, Jeanne d'Arles became an icon in the civil law of *viager*.

In 1965 Rattray entered a *viager* contract under which he agreed to pay Jeanne Calment rent of what today would be about $675 U.S. per month. He was 47, she 90. No doubt he figured that faster than he could say "Bob *est ton oncle*" he would have been owner in fee simple of Calment's spacious town-center apartment. But *pauvre* Rattray died 30 years later without equitable title, having paid Calment more than twice the market value of her apartment. On the day of his death, Calment enjoyed a Christmas dinner of roast duck, foie gras, cheese, and chocolate cake. What we would call legal title (the right to possession when Calment died) passed to Rattray's estate, making his heirs responsible for continuing rent to Calment, while they waited, and waited, for full equity ownership.

Calment predated the Eiffel Tower and, in about 1889, she sold pencils to Van Gogh, the genius she described as an ugly misery-guts who smelled of booze. She lived in a nursing home during the last 11 years of her life, after all her possible heirs pre-deceased her. Although she was blind, deaf, and virtually immobile near the end, she rode a bicycle until she was 100, smoked to the age of 117, and consumed port and chocolates daily. She attributed her longevity to a sense of humor, taking every day as it came, and avoiding stress and too much work. As well, she once remarked that maybe part of the reason she had made it into the *Guinness Book of World Records* was that God had forgotten about her — a new twist on Nietszche's concept of *Deus absconditus*. The remark the world will remember Jeanne Calment for, however, is what she said to poor old André-François Rattray at her

120th birthday party, shortly before he died: "We all make bad deals in life." A more accurate translation might be, *C'est la vie*.

From my teacher Pascale's perspective, the most interesting thing about the *viager* concept was its morbidity. She insisted that *viager* ads in *Le Figaro* typically read, "One head, 81 years, sickly widow, heart condition, dicky liver, one lung half gone, blind, sclerotic, bedridden. . . ." I'm not saying that I disbelieve this. But I have never been able to find any ads with such compelling salestalk in them. *Dommage!*

And as I say, as usual, and melodramatics aside, Pascale was on to something. Buying a house by *viager* looks a lot like a bloody-minded variation on selling short in the stock market. You pay your money and you hope the vendor buys the farm, sooner than later. You gamble on someone's death.

Pascale told us that there was a Maupassant story about a man who stacked the deck. He did a *viager* deal with some old-timer and then scared the codger to death, in order to get vacant possession for a song — or, more precisely, a eulogy. But again, I searched out the story in vain, although I later learned that Maupassant did write about a *viager* type of deal, in his short story "The Little Keg."* Pascale had confused this Maupassant story with another, "The Devil," that has to do with a sort of wager on when an old woman will die, but has nothing to do with *viagers*. An avaricious son pays an old woman a lump sum to sit with his mother as she dies. The woman usually works for a daily fee, and when she sees that the old woman might live for longer than expected, she begins to feel cheated. So she scares the woman to death.

---

*There, an innkeeper persuades an old woman to let him pay her 50 écrus a month until she dies, at which point her farm will become his. The innkeeper gets impatient when, like Jeanne Calment, the feisty old vendor lives on and on. The innkeeper gets her addicted to fine brandy (in "little kegs"), which surely enough kills her within the year.

I didn't doubt Pascale's word that Maupassant had written the *viager* story she described, but it had seemed just as possible that she made the story up and attributed it to Maupassant. I say that as a compliment. It's an example of what I like about Pascale. Other people would steal a Maupassant story and claim that they made it up. Pascale would make it up and not take the credit. After all, according to Pascale, the *Highway Traffic Act* says the sign reading "Fine for parking" means just that, and on the sidewalk, too.

15   Your body is absolutely priceless, and beyond redemption, too

When I was in junior high school, I learned that the human body was worth exactly one dollar and six cents. At the time, this was the equivalent of about four or five hamburgers, with the works. Having got our attention with this stark insult, our teachers would explain that the human animal was 98 percent water. The remaining two percent of calcium, phosphorous, magnesium, xanthan bean gum, and Yellow Dye Number Three was worth a mere four packs of baseball cards — cheaper by far than the battered and adulterated contents of my Gilbert Chemistry set.

I'm not sure why this melancholy statistic was on the curriculum. Perhaps it simply confirmed our teachers' general impression that we were just about worthless. Assuming a less sinister pedagogical intent, maybe they wanted us to understand that a person is greater than the sum of his parts. Although church was clearly separated from state-run public schools at the time, brimming with good intention they perhaps meant to imply that it is the inner person that counts.

Forty years have passed since grade nine science, in which time I would guess that the same $1.06, if preserved in the form of legal tender, would amount to approximately four bucks. In other words, I would expect something in the range of 300 percent inflation. But according to a recently-reported case of the Ontario Court (General Division), this too, too solid flesh has melted. In *Mason v. Westside Cemeteries*, Justice Ann Molloy holds that cremated human remains "have no value whatsoever."

Given that the cremated human remains in this case were those of the plaintiff's mother and father, stored in urns "about the size of a coffee can," and given that Westside Cemeteries seemed to have lost those coffee-can-sized urns, Justice Molloy awarded the plaintiff one dollar special damages for Mother, and one dollar special damages for Father. Doing her best in the circumstances, her honor had put her mind to what human ashes might fetch at market, and she seems to have taken judicial notice that "even if cremated human remains were a commodity capable of being bought and sold, there would be no arms-length purchaser who would want to buy them. There is no ascertainable 'market price' for human ashes." Maybe a safer way of putting it is that we would not want to meet the arms-length purchaser who would want to buy them.

Mason had argued that his parents' remains possessed considerable sentimental value for him. But a review of the cases persuaded Justice Molloy that courts granted damages for sentimental value only where the underlying property had intrinsic value — where you were talking about a telescope, say, that had been awarded to its owner for heroism and which somebody then stole, or where you were considering a very special farm dog shot dead by an unkind neighbor. Justice Molloy acknowledged "that the difficulty of assessing damages based on the value of the goods involved does not absolve a trial judge from his or her duty to nevertheless arrive at an assessment." However, her honor held that in the circumstances "the quantification of value goes beyond 'difficult.' It is impossible. In my opinion the cremated remains of the plaintiff's parents have no monetary value whatsoever."

Although *Mason* does not say so, there is venerable precedent for its low valuation of human remains. It turns out, indeed, that our teachers really were quite generous in valuing us at pocket-change (and half a pocket at that) on the open market.

Very old, and presumably settled, law follows The Law, biblically speaking, in asserting that a dead body is "but a lump of earth." This, anyway, is what the justices of Serjeants' Inn held in 1614 when William Haynes came before them on charges that he "had digged up several graves of three men and one woman, in the night, and had taken their winding sheets." Apparently Haynes argued that the providers of the burial sheets had given them to the deceased as gifts. Thus, there was no theft because the property was, well, nobody's.

The justices were unimpressed with this quasi-metaphysical approach. They reasoned quite physically that the sheet's living owners might have harbored a settled intention to "gift" the sheets to the corpses in the hope that the departed donees would accept the gifts upon the great Resurrection. But, as mere dust, a dead body could not own property in the first place. Property remained in "him who had property therein when the dead body was wrapped therewith" — the donors of the sheets.

Indeed, the court went further than Justice Molloy was prepared to venture in *Mason*, holding that not only could a corpse not own property, it could not *be* property.*

---

*An interesting sidelight to the winding-sheets case is that four sheets in all were stolen, but only three of the thefts were declared felonies. The violated corpses were those of three men and a woman. My guess is that the petty larceny charge was for the theft of the woman's sheet, she being by her sex not a legal person and therefore incapable of possessing property even in life.

16 Semper ubi sub ubi*

A friend from Leeds in the north of England, a friend who likes to think he's a bit of a rake, once told me of a motoring adventure in Buffalo, New York. For some minor, rakish infraction, he was stopped, he claimed, by a female police officer. "She told me," my friend explained, 'Anything you say may be taken down and used against you.' So I said, 'Knickers.'"

Although I've since been cautioned, by a Glaswegian who likes to think he's a bit of a rake that this joke is as old as my "grandmother's socks," I thought the joke was funny. Mind you, that was in less "politically correct" times, before Shakespeare was found wanting because he didn't write from the point of view, as one critic has noted, of oppressed Guatemalan women. The *first* wave of Puritans merely burned down his theater.

Now of course if someone *wants* you to hold her panties against yourself, this is correct enough even for the new millennium, but a whole new set of legal problems arises. One question for the serious legal reporter becomes: are the panties an *inter vivos* gift (a gift between living people), abandoned by the donee (and thereby the True Owner) and therefore capable of passing, as chattels, to a subsequent *bona fide* finder with or without notice of the new possessor's suspect interest? In other words, if someone throws her underwear at you, do you own it?

Alison Rose brought this question to mind in, of all places, the pre-Tina Brown *New Yorker* some years ago, a fastidious *New Yorker* in which undergarments rarely made an appearance, not even in lubricious short stories by Philip Roth or John Updike. Having attended

---

*A young Latin scholar's idea of a joke maxim, literally, "Always where under where."

a Tom Jones concert in Manhattan, Rose reported that many of the women in the audience threw underpants on stage, mostly "little white panties," sometimes black panties, and, in one case, "leopard bikini panties."

A woman standing near Rose "with the panties in her pocketbook wouldn't have been able to hit the stage with them from where she stood." Which was just as well, seeing how Jones ignored the panties when he wasn't "trampling" on them, kicking them out of his way, or perspiring obliviously on them as he sang "It's Not Unusual."

Rose tracked down Tom Jones after the concert and asked him "what generally happened to all those panties." Jones smiled at her with "gentlemanly bemusement" and replied, "I have no idea."

On these facts, presumably, Jones is the donee (his lack of gratitude notwithstanding). The gifts are apparently *inter vivos* (which are subject to different laws than gifts in wills), unless, of course, some donor shouted, "I'd die for him" or "He kills me" as she launched her bloomers stageward, which I suppose would make that particular pair *donatio mortis causa*.

Jones finishes his act. Stagehand finds the underwear, decides to keep it, or some select garments. Discuss the legal issues.

As far as I know, this case is unique. However, my files contain a 1984 precedent where the true owners were deprived of 143 bikini *bathing suits* — *without* their consent.

It seems that a fellow in Ste. Marie De Beauce, Quebec, had been stealing the swimwear from clotheslines. Police said his motive was "to get back at women who didn't pay enough attention to him." When arrested, he had been steadfastly assembling his collection for eight years.

He could have taken heart from a 1986 U.S. case, in which authorities *returned* 300 pieces of women's underwear to a thief. These were among his ill-gotten gains acquired while he was on parole for some other misadventure. For the parole violation and thefts, a court sentenced him to three years in the nick, but the 300 "panties, bras, and body suits" remained unclaimed by the thief's 12 victims. A deputy district attorney explained the disposition: "There was no evidence they were stolen, so the court gave them back."

Women's underwear was in the news a lot in 1984, even as outerwear. That was the year that women's groups produced cardboard panties to fit *over* their clothing as bum armor, after Canadian Prime Minister John Turner shocked the nation by patting the behind of the female president of the Liberal Party.

That was also the year of the Loblaw's supermarket promotion which suggested that thieves *buy* "Can Can Panty Hose," because there was "nothing more aggravating when you're pulling a bank job than having your pantyhose run, thereby revealing your face to the world." Loblaw's contended that this offer was "tongue in cheek," oblivious of a contemporary robbery at a Toronto gas bar, performed by a man with a pair of underpants over his head. Despite the disguise, witnesses easily identified the robber in court: he had put his head through the underpants' leg-hole.

Also that year, a butcher from Bowmanville, Ontario, attempted to market "stainless steel, chain-link underwear" to "help prevent rape." The Bouwhuis Protective Undergarment weighed about 14 ounces, with padlock, and was to sell for $179.50, mail-order. Evidently Bouwhuis got the idea from chain-mesh butchers' gloves and aprons, which are impenetrable even by sharp objects.

According to newspaper accounts, he believed that the mere sight of the garment could scare assailants away. Lawyer Jane Pepino, chair at the time of a Toronto task force on violence against women and children, was not impressed. She told the (Toronto) *Globe and Mail* that the idea "reinforced the belief that only a woman herself is responsible for her own protection."

Then, in 1985, there was the man who attempted to walk out of a Vancouver liquor store with a mickey of vodka stuck down his pants. The trouble was, he hadn't managed to zip up the trousers or, at least, store the bottle firmly in his underwear. He legitimately purchased a bottle of beer but answered "no" when the cashier asked if he wanted to pay for anything else. The Smirnoff's sticking obtrusively out of his fly eventually gave him a charge, all right, of theft under $200. Now you know why your doctor recommends boxer shorts instead of bikinis.

CHAPTER THREE

EVERYTHING MOM WARNED YOU ABOUT

The Private Wrongs Called Torts*

17   The probative weight of a swan-song

They taught us in school that real swans don't actually sing just before they die. Only *proverbial* swans sing swan-songs. Real swans, and the politicians who cast them crusts of bread, squeak when they're threatened with extinction, like the proverbial squeaky wheel. For reasons that will soon become clear, you could call the swan-song canard a poetic misstatement — a euphemism for what is not so much a song as a sob-story peddled by poetic license.

---

*Some law school joker once called torts, from the French for *wrongs* — as opposed to *tortes*, from the French for *pastries* — "everything Mom warned you about." This is because, in legalese, *torts* describes private wrongs, trespasses to property and to our fellow humans. If you rear-end the car in front of you or break your leg on the ice in a parking lot, if you think the coffee at Macdonald's caused third-degree burns to your lap — or, come to think of it, if you break your teeth on a walnut shell in French pastry — you have entered the Purgatory of torts.

For Canada's 100th birthday in 1967, Queen Elizabeth gave the Dominion a dozen white or "mute" swans. The royal swans were fruitful and multiplied on the Rideau. One even lived to be at least 22.

According to news reports, the Rideau royal known officially as Swan 113, and unofficially as Art, was so decrepit and hard of hearing that one day he went crashing over a waterfall, sleeping with his head tucked under his wing all the while. In 1974, Canada traded some of the white royals for Australian black swans. You could call it penal transportation in reverse.* Or call it convicts' revenge: the Aussie swans proved even more fruitful and multiplicative than the royals. By the 1990s it got so that it was costing Ottawa about $50,000 for the winter room and board of the Rideau swans. And this being the era of the bottom line, in 1992 Ottawa city council started talking about privatizing the swans. More ominous suggestions included birth control, extradition to other jurisdictions (transportation in double reverse?), and the death penalty — the sort of economizing politicians apply to other helpless groups these days.

A public outcry ensued and the politicians grew mute on the Rideau swan issue, until December 19, 1995. On that day, the Ottawa councillors voted six to five to cut the Rideau swans' funding, even though the cost of keeping them was now thought to be about $27,000, around half of original estimates. The Ottawa council majority felt that, royal gift or no royal gift, the swans could go to a zoo somewhere else or otherwise get off the public payroll. One councillor called them "a frill," and there is no truth to the rumor that he was really talking about the Senate.

---

*During the 18th and 19th centuries, Britain "transported" (deported) criminals — often, people whose "crime" was poverty — to penal settlements in Australia and Van Diemen's Land (Tasmania).

Which is where Cognos Inc. comes in. Many know the company as an Ottawa computer software firm. Lawyers remember it as the defendant in Canada's principal case on negligent misstatement, *Queen v. Cognos Inc.* A Cognos manager had lured Douglas Queen and his family from Calgary to Ottawa on the understanding that, for at least two years, Queen was to enjoy an integral role in the development of Cognos' new accounting software. However, within five months of the Queen family's move to Ontario, the project began to founder, and Queen was back out on the street 13 months later. The Supreme Court of Canada ruled that Cognos had negligently misled Queen regarding the security and importance of the job. Following in the majestic wake of *Hedley, Byrne v. Heller*, the leading case in the area, the court set up a five-part test for determining whether someone had made such a negligent misstatement, or perhaps a misstatement like "These swans and all their heirs and assigns will have government-funded housing on the Rideau as long as there is an Ottawa":

(1) There must be a duty of care based on a "special relationship" between the representor and the representee.
(2) The representation in question must be untrue, inaccurate, or misleading.
(3) The representor must have acted negligently in making the misrepresentation.
(4) The representee must have relied, in a reasonable manner, on the negligent misrepresentation.
(5) The reliance must have been detrimental to the representee in the sense that damages resulted.

By the time Ottawa city council was proposing to downsize the Rideau swans, it seemed that Cognos Inc. was taking the Supreme Court ruling to heart. At least the company had found a way to salvage the duty of care, if not always a duty of caring, that the council had assumed during the 28 years since the royal swan endowment. The politicians seemed to be turning their backs on those years, on what part one of the *Cognos* test called a special relationship. As to parts two, four, and five, the swans and Ottawa ratepayers — who relied on the city's tender mercies — could honestly say that council's past behavior implied that the birds had security of tenure. And conventional wisdom seems to hold that acting negligently in making representations (number three) constitutes a dictionary definition of "politician." (In fact, in his *Devil's Dictionary*, Ambrose Bierce begins his entry on "politician" with, "An eel in the fundamental mud upon which the superstructure of organized society is reared" — including the mud of the Rideau Canal, no doubt. Bierce bitterly concludes: "As compared with the statesman, he suffers the disadvantage of being alive.")

In any event, Cognos Inc. sailed to the rescue. To that point, there had been two heroic legends about swans. There's the one you learn when you study poetry in grade school, about the hero singing his swan-song, and then dying majestically. The subtler poets took this as a symbol of their immortality through their art. "Ageynist his dethe" Chaucer wrote in the late 1300s, the poet "shall sing his penanse."

Then there's the story about Wagner's opera *Lohengrin*. The libretto calls for the protagonist to enter on a boat towed by a swan. At one legendary performance, the stagehand sent the swan off without Lohengrin, who calmly turned to the stagehand and asked, "What time does the next swan leave?"

Now Canada contributes a third swan romance: the defendant in Canada's leading statement on *Hedley Byrne* has become Canada's leading defender of the Rideau swans. As Cognos Inc. has agreed to look after the swans' bed and board, the Rideau fauna have been successfully privatized. Now if we could only say the same about the Senate.

Like the city of Ottawa, the philosopher Karl Popper was once concerned with large flocks of swans and what they say about the way we think. In a fascinating section of their 1990 book, *Follies and Fallacies In Medicine*, Petr Skrabanek and James McCormick quote Popper on swans to show that basing one's case on the "weight" of evidence can be dangerous — or, as the common law puts it, prejudicial:

> *Karl Popper used the example of the black swan: the statement 'all swans are white' is little strengthened by the sight of the thousand and first white swan, but destroyed by the sight of one black swan.*

For lawyers, the lesson might be that when we speak of deciding cases by the weight or balance of the evidence, we must be clear that we're talking about more than mere quantity. As the authors put it, "Judging validity by the weight of confirmatory evidence is reminiscent of the tailor whose catch cry was: 'Never mind the quality, feel the width.'" Mere accretion of facts on one side of an argument can weigh logic down as easily as a thumb on the butcher's scale. A particularly interesting "fallacy" which Skrabanek and McCormick report has an obstetrician seeking a second opinion from a colleague.

The patient — that is, the expectant mother — is tubercular. The father has syphilis. Of the four previous children, the first is blind, the second died, the third is unable to hear or speak, and the fourth is tubercular. The colleague advises that this is a clear case for abortion. The obstetrician replies (smugly), "Then you would have murdered Beethoven."

Apparently the story is a favorite among anti-abortionists, who don't look at what the evidence actually shows. The "weight of the evidence" proves nothing more than that a tubercular mother and syphilitic father are apt to produce children with serious problems. This is a long way from showing that parents in dire circumstances are apt to produce offspring with unusual gifts and abilities, or that the best course for anyone in this situation is allowing the pregnancy to come to term.

18   No escape from the law's long limb

> ***Fruit of the poisoned tree doctrine:*** *This doctrine is to the effect that an unlawful search taints not only evidence obtained at the search, but facts discovered by process initiated by the unlawful search.*
>
> BLACK'S LAW DICTIONARY

A few summers ago, I was out on the deck when my neighbor to the north called out over the fence, "Hi! Do you mind if I prune some of these branches?" He meant the overhangs on the hawthorn, in the northeast corner of my yard, branches which drooped toward his own deck. I shrugged and answered, "Well, they're in your yard, so you can just go ahead. I mean, thanks for asking, but you didn't have to."

"I knew that," he said, rather sharply, I thought. "I'm a lawyer."

Quite clearly he had known nothing of the sort. But that didn't bother me. What bothered me was my own *esprit de l'escalier*, or, rather, my *esprit du jardin*. After he'd gone back into his house, I kicked myself because I had failed to retort, "You're a tree lawyer, are you?" Maybe he hadn't known that I was a lawyer, too, and painfully aware that membership in the law society didn't mean that you could draft a will, give independent legal advice on a marriage contract, superintend a commercial lease deal, argue a murder appeal, design a prospectus for an IPO, and practice tree law all off the top of your head.

Anyway, you would think that the perfect escape from life at the bar is the garden, never mind my former neighbor, the tree lawyer. That's what I was thinking when I checked *The English Gardening School*, by Rosemary Alexander and Anthony du Gard Pasley, out of my local library. I am not much of a flower gardener, but I had this idea that I wanted to design a sort of "peace garden" by the stucco wall of the garage, looking toward the aforementioned hawthorn. Unfortunately, the first thing I fell upon when I opened the book on my deck was a dense, photograph-bereft section entitled "LEGAL CONSIDERATIONS."

Planning permissions. Nuisance by noise (leaf-blowers, lawn-mowers . . .). Nuisance by smells. (Come to think of it, the tree lawyer was not too happy that hot August day we found the furry baked beans in the northeast corner of our fridge and consigned them to our compost bin, hard by his deck). Statutory restraint on tree-cutting, weeds, and the cultivation of certain plants. (In England, apparently they have the *Weeds Act 1959*, which enjoins the abetting or toleration of dock, ragwort, and thistles). Serious penalties for allowing herbicides and pesticides and pig manure to flow off your land or contaminate the ground water. A few minutes of this and, even if you're not a lawyer, you begin to multiply reasons not to go out in the garden. Your neighbor's child might get hurt fiddling with your weed-whacker. You might dig too deep and hit a common gas line. The roots of your hawthorn might interfere with your neighbor the tree lawyer's drainage pipes, for which you are liable, apparently, although the fruit of any overhanging branches belong to you. Then again, as every budding tree lawyer learned in law school, if the tree is poisoned, the fruit might not be admitted into evidence.

I was rather taken, though, with the authors' discussion of ancient lights: "If the landowner and those who preceded him have received daylight through their window for twenty years or more, they will have acquired a right to continue to have a reasonable amount of light while the house stands." This was really quaint, in an English garden way, especially the "reasonable" part, although, speaking as a man of a certain age, I'm not sure I find it reasonable that something that is 20 years old is "ancient."

But at least you can't violate a right to ancient lights with a tree or a rosebush. Only buildings are impeachable, including garden sheds, greenhouses, and the like. Also, apparently, motor vehicles. When Virginia Ironside, the "Living" columnist for the *Independent*, published a column about city parking problems some years ago, "readers wrote in making legal points about highways and byways, they wrote about the laws of obstruction and about boundary disputes, they wrote in about the 'law of ancient lights' when a large parked van shades one's windows."

The English Gardening School was due the following week, but I returned it before then. To get a break from law, I had begun considering croquet instead of this peace garden business. Mind you, there was that case, come to think of it, the one you read in first-year Torts. I believe it was about cricket, actually, but didn't a woman who was standing at a bus stop or something sue after she got whacked by a ball from the adjoining pitch?*

---

*The case was *Bolton v. Stone*, [1951] 1 All England Reports, page 1078, and the cricket club escaped liability. Bolton claimed that the club acted negligently in allowing balls to fly off the pitch onto the public roadway, but the court disagreed. Although balls had gone onto the road before, the chance of injury was sufficiently remote to defeat Bolton's claim.

19 Can a kiss be battery?

> Beauty and White et. al. v. Charming:
> Action by plaintiffs against defendant prince for battery, indecent assault, and nervous shock. Plaintiffs allege unconsented-to osculation and subsequent rude awakening in the middle of enchanted forest crawling with bugs and other slimy, noxious fauna. In answer, defendant claims that galloping cavalierly past comatose plaintiffs would have constituted negligence by nonfeasance. He pleads that his kiss was necessary to plaintiffs' survival (the "kiss of life") and that plaintiffs' consent to same was implied.
>
> FROM THE LAW REPORTS OF GRIMMLAND, 1823

"Can a kiss be a battery?" That's what my law school Torts text wanted to know. "What if you are kissed while you are asleep," it continued, "and only find out about it later?"

The obvious, and lawyerly, reply is that it depends, your honor, on who's doing the kissing. Romance can be downright disenchanting. Unfortunately for Prince Charming, it is probably no longer true that all the world loves a lover. Several feminists quite vocally do not: the dance of courtship as the courtiers knew it is, like Sleeping Beauty in her REM phase, pretty much moribund. Politically correct revisionists do not accept the old fairy-tale wisdom that only the kiss of virtue can awaken Virtue herself. Love does not conquer much, if politics is involved. The prince's traditional defense that the press of his lips has bestowed a public service would be drummed out of court with the pot-beating clamor of one of those old charivaris purportedly reserved for wife-abusers. (See page 160.)

But does our princely defendant have a defense of consent — the excuse that in fact or by implication Princesses Sleeping and Snow gave him permission? The "Snow White" most of us know from childhood, diluted and bleached by 400 years of nervous paternalism, suggests as much. In that familiar version, the handsome prince on his white steed has acted very mildly and properly. Yet, in "Snow White" according to the brothers Grimm in 1823, the prince doesn't kiss Snow's comatose virgin flesh, but purchases it from her enterprising dwarves — bringing up all sorts of nice new legal questions.

But never mind whether Snow White's body was property that the dwarves could blithely dispose of how they would.* When in the Grimm original the prince takes possession of Snow's coffin, his jostling dislodges the poisoned apple from her probably blue lips and she revives, quickened and blushy. Whether or not she immediately files a writ against the prince, the sexual overtones signal loudly towards the tale's roots in fertility legends. In an old version of the related "Sleeping Beauty," the sleeper is awakened only after a king has sex with her inanimate self.

Can a kiss be battery? In a South African case in 1947, one judge wrote:

> *If a man wooing a girl should tentatively and with due decorum test his prospects by a ventured kiss or embrace, such an action on his part might actually be against the woman's will in the sense that she has given no previous consent to it, express or implied . . . but I can scarcely conceive of a charge being brought in such a case, or, if brought, that any punishment would be meted out in respect of it.*

This was over 56 years ago, mind you, in days less sensitive about the sexual prerogatives of women. Now or then, what about jostling an

---

*In 1614, the justices at Serjeants' Inn in Fleet Street held that a corpse does not have a property interest in its own winding-sheet, let alone in itself. (*Haynes's Case*, 12 Coke's Reports, page 113). See page 59.

apple out of someone's mouth?* Is the king who revives Sleeping Beauty with more than a kiss guilty of an assault under modern law? Astonishingly, there is a modern case almost directly on point.

One day in the early 1960s, a Yukon Territories man named Ladue got drunk and began feeling amorous. He was perhaps not exactly a Prince Charming. He had sex with his girlfriend, even though she was inanimate, apparently asleep. The girlfriend did not awaken or respond. This was because she was dead. Ladue was charged with "indecently interfering with a dead human body," also known under the Canadian *Criminal Code* as "offering an indignity to a corpse."

Ladue pled that he was too drunk to know the woman was dead. In other words, he had made what lawyers call a mistake of fact (versus a mistake of law, which is usually no excuse). Because he didn't *intend* to have sex with a corpse, he claimed he wasn't guilty of that crime: how could he interfere with a dead body if he didn't know the person was dead?

It seems a good question, but it gave no pause to the justices of the Yukon Territories Court of Appeal. Ladue knew that the woman was not conscious. He knew, in other words, that she was not consenting to sex. If the woman had been functional, the chief justice remarked, Ladue would have been "raping her." As commentators have pointed out, this conclusion is not strictly logical: insofar as a corpse is not a person, you cannot rape a corpse. (An "alive corpse" is obviously a contradiction in terms.) While Ladue could not commit the impossible, he could certainly try to, making his crime *attempted* rape. Still,

---

*Sex aside, in tort law a battery can be "the merest touching," and even not exactly a touching at all. In 1897, North Carolina prosecuted a pharmacist as an accessory to a battery after he sold a laxative to a customer, knowing that the customer probably intended to sneak it into another man's drink.

relying on the argument that Ladue would have been forcing sex on his girlfriend had she been alive, the court held that "it is impossible for him to argue that, not knowing her to be dead, he was acting innocently. An intention to commit a crime, although not the precise crime charged, will provide the necessary *mens rea*" — illegal intent — under the law.

The court's disgust is manifest in its apparent determination to convict, despite legal illogic. The charge was interfering with a dead body. Yet the chief justice concludes, "I do not consider knowledge that the body is dead to be a specific ingredient" of interfering with a dead body. And he does not tell us how the intent to (attempt) rape can be the same as the intent to offer an indignity to a corpse.

What if you're *just looking* without consent? A law professor once wrote of sexual politics that "there's no harm in asking." But is there harm in reckless eyeballing?

Reckless Eyeballing is the title of an angry, preachy, not always coherent novel by Ishmael Reed. It was published in 1986, and based, Reed explains,

> upon a remark that Susan Brownmiller made in her book, Against Our Will. *She said that, for wolf whistling at a white woman, [a teenaged boy] was just as guilty as the men who murdered him. It's the kind of logic that keeps me in business.*

Reed is referring to Brownmiller's account of the murder of Emmett Till. Till was a 14-year-old black boy from Chicago visiting Money, Mississippi. He had, Brownmiller writes, been "regaling the black youth of Money with tales of his exploits with white girls up North," and had flashed around a photo of one such conquest. The Money youth dared him to ask the wife of a local white store-owner for a date. Young Till took the dare and the woman chased him out of the store with a pistol. As she chased him, he 'wolf-whistled' at her. The woman's husband and his half-brother abducted Till at two o'clock the next morning, sadistically beat him, shot him in the head, tied a weight to his neck, and threw him in the Tallahatchie River. An all-white, all-male jury acquitted the killers, ostensibly because the body pulled from the Tallahatchie was so mutilated, authorities couldn't identify it.

Brownmiller concluded:

> *We are rightly aghast that a whistle could be cause for murder but we must also accept that Emmett Till and [the husband] shared something in common. They both understood that the whistle was no small tweet or hubba-hubba or melodious approval for a well-turned ankle. Given the deteriorated situation . . ., it was a deliberate insult just short of physical assault.*

Mr. Reed tells me that "black folklore is full of tall tales about black men walking up the side of buildings in order to avoid colliding with white women on the street." An article in *Ebony* in the 1950s recounted a case in Mississippi, he says, of a man arrested for "reckless eyeballing" — looking at a white woman.

All of this was the raw material for the novel. *Reckless Eyeballing* is about a black playwright on the outs with feminists. In an attempt to win their favor and restore his grants, he writes a play about a man who is lynched for recklessly eyeballing a white woman. The woman demands that the corpse be exhumed and put on trial. The play's producer, a black woman, remarks that "because he leered at [the woman] the black [man] was just as guilty as the white men who murdered him."

In a letter about his book, Reed told me that, during the 1990s, charges of reckless eyeballing seemed to be making a comeback among feminist students where he taught in California — or at least that "white feminists are giving black men the evil eye" there. In 1989, a student at the University of Toronto made headlines for months by lodging a complaint of the type Reed might have had in mind.

During her regular swim at the pool in Hart House — until fairly recently, an athletic and social club restricted to male students and professors — a professor harassed her, the student told the university's sexual harassment board, by swimming near her in a snorkel mask and flippers, and ogling her. The board upheld the complaint and banned the professor from the pool for five years. As well, it ordered the professor to take counselling. The professor admitted looking at the student, but denied harassment. He said that he was a keen student of human nature and the human form, especially in athletic pursuits.

Many observers, this writer among them, at first thought such disputes should be settled quietly and "reasonably." Privately. Some of us were reminded of the bad old 1950s, when little schoolgirls could not wear shiny shoes because of prurient vice-principals and their fantasies about reflections of the little girls' panties. It seemed insane, or at least nerve-wracking and uncivilized in itself, that we might have to obtain consent before looking at someone. While it was clear that leering was rude and stupid, to make it illegal seemed wildly reactionary. But then, after both the student and the professor made their cases on television, faces were put to the complaint and it became clear that the freedoms involved were heartfelt and interlocking as well as contentious. This was not the same case as using sexual insecurities as an excuse for racial persecution.

Suppose a silent, oddly-dressed stranger followed closely behind you when you walked down Main Street. He didn't say or do anything in particular, but he stared at you. It happened twice, three times, four times. Should you confront him? Should you call out to other pedestrians? How? For what? What if he were deranged and reacted violently to your desire to be left alone?

It turned out that the Hart House disputants had attempted to settle their problem between themselves, without success. But whatever happened there, you have to wonder why a woman should be obliged to resort to self-help in these cases. In other situations, the law specifically *forbids* self-help where alternatives are available. The swimmer must have known she risked humiliation by going public. In fact, it would have been easier to persist in self-help.

Ishmael Reed is a provocative and valuable writer who has sound, historical reasons for his anger, and for his worry that people will equate looking at someone with illegal harassment. But as the University of Toronto board seems to have decided, there is a definable border where reckless eyeballing crosses into intrusion or menacing. (Whether a board of this sort should have the highfalutin' power to order someone to take counselling is another matter.) By going public, the swimmer has provided all of us a chance to think about that line.

We live in an age when physically normal people stuff their chests with plastic, suck fat from their thighs, prance around in their underwear in public, and then complain when other people take notice. They may not be asking for trouble, but they seem to invite appreciation. They seem to be consenting to at least a smoky gaze. But the Hart House swimmer did not clamor for attention and then scream when it was not the kind she wanted. She did not ride the subway or flounce down Main Street in one or two wisps of cotton or velvet, as we all have seen men and women do. She was just going for a swim.

20 You've heard about the Midnight Rambler

There is an old ballad about a mesmerizing musician, a Scots-English Orpheus called Glasgerion. Like Orpheus, Glasgerion can harp fish out of the water, water out of stone, and milk from a maiden's breast "though bairn she never had nane." After one such performance at court, Glasgerion makes a date with a fine lady sometimes said to be a princess of Normandy. The lady extends an irresistible proposal: if Glasgerion comes to her bower before the cock has crowed, he "shall be a welcome guest."

Glasgerion asks his servant Jack to wake him before cock-crow. Instead, Jack dons his master's clothes and rides off to the lady's bower on Glasgerion's steed. Worse comes to worst. Jack "sore mistrusted that lady gay" — who, evidently gritting her teeth, remains politely cheerful despite her mistake of taking Jack for his employer:

> He did not take the lady gay
> To bolster nor to bed;
> But down upon her chamber floor,
> Full soon he hath her laid.

When the truth is revealed, the lady kills herself with one of those little pen-knives women in ballads always seem to have on their persons: "Says, There never shall be no churl's blood,/Spring within my body." Glasgerion arrives to discover his lover's corpse, whereupon he kills Jack and, propping his sword's pummel against a stone, takes his own life.

Outside music and movies, people usually react less violently in such situations. But variations on the Glasgerion story are shockingly common in everyday life and in our law reports. The reasons for judgment of Lord Justice Edmund Davies of the English Court of Appeal relate an instance from 1972. An 18-year-old woman was sleeping naked very near an open window. At about 3:30 or four o'clock on a Sunday morning, she was awakened by a figure crouched there in the moonlight. In court, she could not recall whether the figure was already in the room, or on the part of the sill outside it. "The young lady," Justice Edmund Davies found, "then realized several things: first of all that the form in the window was that of a male; secondly that he was a naked male; and thirdly that he was a naked male with an erect penis." Thinking it was her boyfriend "paying her an ardent nocturnal visit," the young woman invited the man into her bed.

She did not discover until after she had sex with the man that he was not her boyfriend but 19-year-old Stephen Collins. Collins testified that he was acquainted with the young woman because he had done odd jobs around her mother's house. He had a drinking problem, he told the court, and on the night in question, he was inebriated. He had seen a light in the woman's window and moved a ladder to it. When he climbed up, he saw her sleeping naked in the room, descended, and removed all of his clothes except his socks. Then, he climbed back up to the window. Apparently "he took the view," Justice Edmund Davies said,

> *that if the girl's mother entered the bedroom it would be easier to effect a rapid escape if he had his socks on.... That is a matter about which we are not called upon to express any view, and would in any event find ourselves unable to express one.*

Justice Edmund Davies must have been ignorant of the dialogue in "Glasgerion" when Jack, disguised as his master, gains entrance to the lady's bower. The lady remarks,

> *O ragged is your hose, Glasgerion,*
> *And riven is your sheen [shoes]*

> *And ravelled is your yellow hair,*
> *That I saw yestere'en.*

To which Jack replies,

> *The stockings they are Jack, my man's*
> *They came first to my hand;*
> *And this is Jack, my man's, shoon,*
> *At my bed-feet they stand.*

The police claimed that Collins had told them he had meant to have sex with a woman by force, if necessary. He denied this at the Essex Assizes, although he admitted that when the woman invited him into her bed he "was rather dazed because I didn't think she would want to know me." A trial court convicted him of burglary.

Yes, burglary. It seems an odd and inappropriate charge unless you know some legal history. Reading the law reports, you get the impression that before the days of electric light and fastidiously bolted doors and windows, confusion over who was who in whose bed was an everyday occurrence. It turns out that it was very often the big, very bad wolf in not only grandma's but mother's bed. Sometimes a rapist would climb in right next to the husband and children. Often, a sleepy wife wouldn't comprehend what was what until it was all over but the crying.

A rule grew up around these cases that said you consent to something if you understand the "nature and quality" of what was done to you. That, in part, was why Collins was charged with burglary instead of some specific sexual assault. (Under English statute law, burglary also denoted illegal entry with intent to rape.) The girl knew that he wanted to have sex with her, and she knew what sex was.

In this, she was unlike a girl near her age in the leading "nature and quality" case, *Williams*, known to lawyers as the "Choirmaster

Case." At the Liverpool Assizes in 1922 (when by and large young adults were more innocent than they were 50 years later), Owen Williams was convicted of having carnal knowledge of two of his female singing pupils, aged 16 and 19. The prosecution proved that Williams had undressed the younger girl and earnestly "examined" her with an aneroid barometer — which "was not in working order" — before telling her he was going to make an air passage so she could sing better. He then had sexual intercourse with her, without really putting the young innocent in the picture, assuring her that her parents knew all about it and approved. He even swore to God that he would not harm her.

The court found that Williams had obtained the girl's consent fraudulently. Because the fraud went to the fact of what he intended to do to her, and not to who he was, the court found him guilty of rape and sentenced him to 12 years at hard labor.* When *Williams* came on that afternoon, the chief justice remarked, "It may be that before long persons who are found guilty of this sort of offence will run the risk of suffering the same punishment as that which we have had to deal with this morning." The choirmaster seems to have

---

*Williams's appeal to the Court of Criminal Appeals makes an interesting footnote to the case. According to the London *Times*, the Court of Criminal Appeals heard *Williams* on the afternoon of December 11, 1922. That morning, it had reviewed the case of a man convicted of pimping for a 17-year-old girl. At trial, the pimp had been sentenced to 21 months at hard labor and 15 strokes with the cat o'nine tails. Appealing the corporal punishment, the pimp wanted the court to hear a prison warder testify that he was subject to epileptic seizures.

The court refused to hear the epilepsy claim, while coldly suggesting that those responsible for the whipping might want to consider it. The chief justice emphasized that this was not an endorsement of mercy by the court, and added, "If ever there was a case in which a prisoner deserved corporal punishment, this is it." (The pimp, a married layabout, had picked the teenager up at a dance hall, promising to marry her. He took her from Nottingham to London and after three weeks of cohabitation cajoled her out to the streets, where she earned him ten pounds a week.)

escaped whipping, but the Court of Criminal Appeals affirmed his 12-year sentence.

Cases of this genre obviously concern the most craven sort of breach of trust, and, human nature being what it is, the law reports bulge with them. In other instances, adult women will go to doctors or quack-doctors who obtain putative consent for sex by disguising an assault as treatment. The cases date from the 18th century until as recently as yesterday. In *Doc*, published in 1989, journalist Jack Olsen shows that virtually every woman in Lovell, Wyoming, was sexually assaulted by the town physician — who played on the women's religious piety and innocence, and on their habit (common in our population at large) of equating the family doctor with God and parent. (Like Williams, Doc claimed great therapeutic value for routine "dilation.") In another recent American case, a surgeon sutured closed the vagina of his own ex-wife.

In older examples, market-stall quacks play on simple ignorance and desperation, promising to cure a young woman's seizures by "breaking her string" in the snug of a pub or promising to ease menstrual problems with "dilation." Fortunately, in most of these cases assailants can be convicted of rape, because the fraud goes to what they are doing, not to who they are. On the other hand, the sleeper *au naturel* in *Collins* understood the nature and quality of what Collins did to her. The law therefore said that he might have been guilty of assault, but not of rape. Semantically, and common-sensically, this is asinine: can we reasonably claim that sex with some drunken stranger has the same "nature and quality" as intimacy with a loved one? And beyond this sort of illogic, the "who rule" — the rule that when you have sex with a stranger it is not rape if you consented, thinking the stranger was a familiar — also carries an old double standard. The courts have always said that if the sleeper in *Collins* (to use our ready example) had been *married* and mistaken Collins for her *husband*, Collins would have been guilty of rape. This is an exception to the "nature and quality rule" based not on logic or sympathy, but on the old view of the wife as a husband's property. For the same reason, at one time a husband in three of the United States could legally kill his wife if he caught her in adultery. (See page 149.)

Of course the judges who formulated these rules were men — often old, rigid, sexually frustrated men. In an Irish case from 1878, a woman pleaded that had she been aware that her common-law husband was infected with venereal disease, which he knew about but didn't tell her, she would not have consented to sex with him. When she sued the man for infecting her, the judges said that the consent was valid, and because she was "living in sin" she had no right to complain in the first place. And *plus ça change*, in the late 1980s a Virginia woman attempted to sue her estranged husband for infecting her with genital herpes before they were married. Ruling that fornication was a crime in that state, the supreme court refused to award damages to the woman, even though she had been unaware of her future husband's condition.

The legal shillyshally in the *Collins* case — that sex with an imposter is not rape, *per se* — is even more bizarre when you consider that the law might be willing to cry rape, or something like it, in some situations where the so-called victims are quite clear on who they're going to let do what to them. In the Massachusetts case of *Appleby*, the accused man claimed that he had picked up a male prostitute who, he said, eventually became his live-in "slave." The "slave" begged to be beaten with a bullwhip Appleby used to train guard dogs, and Appleby eventually obliged, because it gave his partner pleasure and made him otherwise sexually pliant. The two later designed a "torture chamber" together. In October, 1975, Appleby beat his partner with the bullwhip and a baseball bat, fracturing his knee. The pair told staff at the emergency ward, as well as a trial court, that the injured man had fallen during an epileptic fit. Appleby was acquitted.

In February, 1976, Appleby was charged with beating his partner with a bullwhip "because of displeasure with a sandwich" the partner had prepared. He was again acquitted, apparently for lack of evidence.

Appleby was finally convicted, and sentenced to eight to ten years in prison, after his "slave" served him some melted ice cream and Appleby simply tapped him with a riding crop. This was at last too much for the supposed masochist, who fled Appleby's house in his underwear and took refuge in a nearby monastery. (Another suggestive aspect of the story is that Appleby refused to let his lover move in with him unless the man promised that they would go to church together every Sunday.) Apparently he was at last willing to testify fully and candidly. The trial court found that although generally the law stays out of the bedrooms (and kitchens) of the nation, in cases of this sort of violence, consent was no defense. The Supreme Court of Massachusetts agreed: "The fact that violence may be related to sexual activity . . . does not prevent the state from protecting its citizens against physical harm."

The same rule had been applied in a 1934 English case, when a 17-year-old girl agreed to be spanked with a cane, only to discover that it wasn't pleasant after all. At trial, the spanker was convicted and sentenced to 18 months at hard labor. The Court of Criminal Appeal eventually acquitted him, but merely because the trial judge had failed to direct the jury to convict only if "the blows were likely or intended to do bodily harm." The judges were evidently loathe to punish a good old public school tradition.

In the *Collins* besoxed midnight rambler case, by the way, the Court of Appeal ultimately acquitted, too, even on the charge of burglary: "Jack" escaped justice this time. If his victim had been able to say that he was on the part of the window-sill *inside* her bedroom before she invited him into bed, he would have been a trespasser, and thus a house-breaker. But because she might have beckoned to him when he was outside the room (under the misapprehension that he was her boyfriend), he was not a burglar.* She had "invited him in." Still, according to the standard criminal law textbook in England, all was not lost:

> *The common law rules relating to [illegal] entry were developed with not a little ingenuity and a fondness for technicality. . . . Collins . . . does seem to involve a rejection of the common law rule that the entry of any part of Defendant's body sufficed. To that extent it has been welcomed for otherwise: Burglary may well . . . vary with the length of a part much more private than the prisoner's foot.*

21 Get thee behind me, silicone

Female plaintiffs have been important pioneers in modern tort law. Two spring to any lawyer's mind. First, and always, comes May Donoghue, the English shop assistant who allegedly found a decomposed snail in her ginger beer while chatting with a friend at Minchella's Cafe in the early 1930s. Although her claim never reached trial, the judicial committee of the House of Lords revolutionized Anglo-American law by holding that the manufacturer of the ginger beer could be liable to Donoghue, never mind that her "contract" for the drink was not with the manufacturer but with

---

*Again, the judges did not consider that if you invite B in thinking he is A, you are not really inviting B in. The court rejected the argument that only the girl's mother, as tenant, had the absolute right to allow anyone into the house.

Minchella, the restaurateur. As Lord Atkin put it, once and for all, manufacturers and distributors were legally close enough "neighbours" to the ultimate consumer that the contractual chain was not broken by the middleman. The consumer could sue all the way up the line for "product liability."

Defining the limit to this principle was the American Helen Palsgraf, who found herself at the end of a cartoonish chain of events in the late 1920s. Two railway guards pushed a man to help him get into a train car as it left a New York station. This dislodged a package of fireworks from the man's arms. The fireworks exploded on the rails and the explosion knocked over a large scale at the other end of the platform. The scale fell on Palsgraf, who proved just as unlucky in court when she sued the Long Island Railway for her injuries and her ruined visit to Rockaway Beach. While the ginger beer bottler had owed a duty to Donoghue, never mind that the middleman, Minchella, actually sold her the beverage, the New York Court of Appeals ruled that the danger of the scale falling on Palsgraf was not apparent "to the eye of ordinary vigilance." And that was all the law could ask of public transportation companies.

In other words, during my parents' generation, these two women helped define the scope of duty in our current law. This development reflected society's anxiety to deal with the complications posed by growing industrialization, and to address public concern that even corporations owed reasonable duties to their fellow citizens. Now, reflecting the values of my own generation, tort law has a new female protagonist. As the *New York Post* has put it, "DANCER GETS 30G IN THE END: BETTER THAN A KICK IN THE BUTT."

Mary Gale was working as an exotic dancer in Hackensack, New Jersey, when she decided that plastic surgery would improve her career prospects. She had a local surgeon round out her breasts from an A to a C cup. He also pumped artificial substances into her lips, after which Gale bought a new chin and forehead. And in 1990, when she was 33 and decided that her rear end was too flat, she went big-time. To obtain a fuller, rounder behind (something which, her lawyer admits, most women in our society would prefer to avoid), she went to Park Avenue in Manhattan, and the offices of Dr. Elliot Jacobs.

A jury seems to have believed, or wanted to believe, that Jacobs did not forewarn Gale that, for her $6,500 (U.S.), he was going to stitch silicone breast implants into her buttocks. Not altogether surprisingly, the result, according to Gale, was that "it looked like I had two tits on my butt."

Reporters who have seen the photographs agree ("Her claims were buttressed by photos taken shortly after the operation that showed what looked like two small breasts protruding from about halfway up her rear end"), but Jacobs testified that Gale gave fully informed consent for the procedure. He told the jury that if she'd been patient for six months to a year, the implants would have "contoured." Gale says she couldn't even sit down right, let alone wave her bathykulpic bottom around in a bar. She looked like a "freak show," she says. So, after just three weeks, she had Jacobs remove the implants.

She returned to bumping and grinding within two months. And although Gale displayed her allegedly scarred behind in public for years and years to follow — during four more years of dirty dancing and subsequent visits to the beach in a thong bikini — she hired New York lawyer Cynthia Matheke to sue over residual scarring, lost wages, and mental anguish. After deliberating for four hours, the jury found that Jacobs breached his duty to explain to Gale the full nature and risks of the surgery.

Apparently the jurors believed Matheke's story that the deep tan on Gale's glutes, in a photo from 1996, was in aid of hiding the scars. They seemed to have rejected lawyer Paul Paley's closing argument for Jacobs that Gale's persistent fondness for letting it all hang out was the equivalent of a "smoking gun" or "bloody glove," showing that there was no residual damage from the surgery.

Taking the historical view, one suspects that May Donoghue and Helen Palsgraf would not have accused their doctor of sneaking falsies into their behinds if that was essentially what they bargained for. In fact, Gale's case puts me in mind of what I call the Chas Defence. Chas is the son of a friend with whom I once practiced law. One day, when Chas was three or four, my friend had to take him to the doctor because he had a tiny styrofoam ball, some sort of packaging, stuck up his nose. When my friend had asked him, "How did that get up there?" his nonchalant reply was, "Some guy put it there."

Well, in Mary Gale's case, the jury believed this. Some guy put falsies in her butt and she had nothing to do with it. Even the *Post*, sensationalist friend to the working girl (or at least working guy), seemed to find this amazing. Besides the "kick in the butt" headline, their assiduous coverage included advisories such as "I DIDN'T KNOW DOC BUSTED MY RUMP: CHEEK THIS OUT" and "STRIPPER CLAIMS BUTTHEAD DOC MADE CAREER HIT BOTTOM." Jacobs didn't keep her "abreast" of the procedure, the *Post* reported, such that she didn't realize Jacobs's "derri-error" until the surgery was "behind her" and she became "the butt of jokes." For his part, Jacobs thought the suit was "asinine." And so on.

Gale has complained that the $30,000 in damages won't even cover her expenses. If the jury as an institution is as wise as some people claim, maybe that's the wisdom here. Ding the doc for not explaining things properly (we've all been there, after all) — in fact, maybe even ding him for making millions by exploiting desperate vanity. Then again, don't give the desperate, vain stripper the millions she was hoping for, because, well, what did she expect, really, ponying up for more plastic surgeries than Frankenstein's monster?

CHAPTER FOUR

TAKING CARE OF BUSINESS

Contracts and Commerce

22 Manhattan ain't worth a hill of beads

The shopworn principle that "the law will not inquire into the adequacy of consideration" does not impress Peter Francis.

Peter Francis is director of the Center for Bead Research in Lake Placid, New York, and as part of this unusual job, he has looked into the contract for the sale of Manhattan Island to the Dutch in 1626. Popular legend has it that Peter Minuit, colonial governor for Holland, bought the Big Apple from the Manhattan Indians for $24 worth of beads. Or, as the *Encyclopedia Britannica* puts it, "To legitimize European occupation of the territory, [Minuit] called together the Indian sachems and persuaded them to sell the entire island for a handful of merchandise — mostly trinkets" worth 60 guilders.

Minuit really was something of a wheeler-dealer and adventurer:

later, he would make a similarly sharp deal on behalf of the Swedish for Wilmington, Delaware, and then meet a nasty end at sea in a hurricane in the West Indies. The authors of the *Blue Guide to New York* figure his consideration for Manhattan at just a little better than a dollar per square foot, although in those days it would have in fact worked out to about $1.40 (U.S.), inflation being pegged at 40 percent on the exchange for a Dutch guilder these last 375 years. Francis does not dispute this figure, although he blames Martha Lamb for putting it about that the amount was in baubles instead of guilders.

Francis says that in 1877, Lamb published a book called *History of New York* in which she claimed that the Manhattan Indians had traded their island with "unfeigned delight" for "beads, buttons, and other trinkets." There was nary a mention of trinkets in documentation before that. Yet, since the publication of Lamb's history, we've all blithely accepted that the deal was some kind of joke: the credulous natives had really been had. It doesn't seem to have occurred to anybody that maybe the gold coins, themselves, had more interest to the Manhattan Indians than their par value at some bank run by more palefaces self-styled as bigshots.

To begin with, in the Manhattan of 1626, the average apartment was not going for the three or four million that Donald Trump or Mick Jagger might pay today. To the Manhattan Indians, Dutch guilders probably seemed more like baubles than beads did. Guilders might have been the yen of the day, but in North America, the *dollar* was *wampumpeag*, literally "white beads," shortened for convenience to "wampum." You didn't leave home without it.

Wampum had immediate, obvious value to the natives because they had to expend valuable time and trouble just to create it — collecting the proper shells, valuing them, polishing them, stringing them. . . . The guilder was just something shiny that somebody else seemed to think was valuable. Canada's recently minted loonie dollar will buy you a cup of coffee here and there, but my American godson keeps the one I gave him in a drawer in Boulder, Colorado, with his Nicaraguan pesos.

Lamb probably could not have known that Anglo-American law is peppered with instances of folks selling or renting things, often real estate, for "a mere peppercorn," and that lawyers do not find it unusual to call such "trifles" "good and valuable consideration." Nor could she have envisioned graffiti and traffic and people living in cardboard boxes over sewer grates, and Harlem, and the 43rd-Street sin strip, and the Son of Sam, and the World Trade Centre bombing. But given all these facts, doesn't it seem, finally, that a deal is only as good as what you make of it?

23 Shlensky strikes out

Is "corporate social responsibility" an oxymoron? CSR, as Wall Street and its lawyers call the concept, assumes that businesses have community obligations beyond obeying the law and "maximizing profits" for their shareholders. In other words, it assumes companies, as separate legal personalities, have ethical or moral obligations: they routinely should go beyond legal norms in environmental protection, worker rights and privileges, product safety and quality, pay equity, and so on.

The same folks who call such responsible citizenship "CSR" like to label *Shlensky v. Wrigley* a "leading case" on corporate morality, never mind that it is mostly about baseball when it was more of a sport than a business, and never mind that the case takes up fewer than five pages, counting the summary, in volume 237 of the *Northeastern Reporter* for 1968.

By way of the Chicago National League Ball Club (Inc.), the Wrigleys — they of the popular brands of chewing gum and the city's Wrigley Building — had long controlled the Chicago Cubs baseball club. And until the 1980s, the Wrigleys were the last holdouts against night baseball. The Cubs could not play home games after sunset because there were no lights at Wrigley Field. The baseball purists — the nostalgists and conservatives — liked it that way. This was baseball as it was meant to be played, on grass, in the sunshine. No Astroturf. No dome. No lights.

William Shlensky, a minority shareholder in the Cubs corporation, was not a baseball purist. In terms of the CSR debate, this put him in what is commonly known as the Friedman camp, after the heavyweight U.S. economist, Milton. Friedman is the modern proponent of the view that CSR is a communist plot. Social activism is for governments, he says, and corporate management has a single fiduciary and contractual duty to shareholders: bring them the highest return possible on their investment.

Obviously, this is hugely polemical. It looks the other way, for example, from the plain fact that multi-national corporations already govern like city-states, with more influence than any ten thousand citizens, and with greater global reach and propaganda power than any government. All the same, Shlensky was of the Friedman camp, and he accused Cubs director Philip K. Wrigley of negligent mismanagement. Wrigley used his control position of 80 percent of the shares, Shlensky alleged, to impose his personal opinions on the other shareholders, to the detriment of their investment. Wrigley, Shlensky said, thought "that baseball is a 'daytime sport' and that the installation of lights and night baseball games will have a deteriorating effect upon the surrounding neighborhood."

Shlensky told the court that this idiosyncratic, social-conscience stuff was costing the shareholders major-league. "Since night baseball was first played in 1935," he pointed out, "19 of the 20 major league teams have scheduled night games." Except for opening days, weekends, and holidays, every major league team but the Cubs played most of its home games after supper time. The night games made it possible, the evidence showed, to attract more spectators. And the Cubs had been operating in the red for several years, attracting bigger crowds on the road at night than they did at home during the day.

Shlensky also showed that attendance at Cubs' weekend games was roughly comparable to that of the White Sox, the other hometown baseball club. But on weekdays, the White Sox' attendance figures, for mostly night games, were much higher.

Of course, it took another 15 or 20 years for night baseball to come to Wrigley Field. In dismissing Shlensky's claim, the First District Appellate Court of Illinois pointed out that there was something relevant the Friedman camp does not like to think about. It is popularly called "enlightened self-interest." It proposes that short-term gain can cause long-term pain. That is, the court was not "satisfied that the motives assigned to Philip K. Wrigley, and through him to the other directors, are contrary to the best interest of the corporation and the stockholders."

The corporation might well have had a long-term interest, the court held, in the state of the neighborhood and the comfort and safety of the Cubs' patrons. So, in legal history, *Shlensky* stands for the proposition that corporate social responsibility and maximization of shareholder profits are not mutually exclusive. At least in our law books, CSR is *not* an oxymoron. In *social* history, it stands against the young fuddy-duddy school of corporate governance, which changed baseball forever from a child's game to big business.

That began to happen just before the *Shlensky* case, which is probably why there *was* a *Shlensky* case. You might peg the change at around the time that I and thousands of other ten-year-olds were cheering Roger Maris on his way to breaking Babe Ruth's homerun record in 1961. The turning point, most sports journalists agree, was television. Television had been using baseball for years as filler on weekend afternoons, and it understandably made a big deal of Maris's record chase. Around the same time, it bought the broadcast rights to the National Football League, and sports were never the same.

During a rain delay in a Saturday afternoon baseball game in 1959, say, the TV networks would stay tuned. Commentator, and former pitcher, Dizzy Dean would pull out his guitar and, over shots of the ground crew rolling the tarp out on the diamond, he lazily would sing "The Wabash Cannonball." When TV bought into the NFL, in order to sell and broadcast more commercials it began to dictate the rhythm of professional sport. Rules changed to make televised sports "more exciting," and often more violent. To attract the Sesame Street Generation and its ever-decreasing attention span, the teams brought in light shows and fireworks and rock music and McDonald's hamburgers. Players hired agents, who began calling their clients "entertainers," "assets," and "valuable commodities." Players' salaries rose astronomically, to the point that a 21-year-old rookie can make ten times what an experienced cancer nurse in a children's hospital earns. A hint of rain, and the "Game of the Week" suddenly left Chicago for sunnier, or domed, climes.

In other words, William Shlensky has won on ultimate appeal, and we purists are still paying the costs. And the question re-asserts itself: is corporate social responsibility an oxymoron?

24 Jesus saves, Moses invests, Solomon shoots

Into just their second season, the Toronto Raptors basketball team lost considerably more games than they won. But they already had accomplished a unique slam-dunk: at about 18 months old, they had made shotgun clauses a household word.

The shotgun clause works like this: Rich offers to sell his shares to Richer for umpteen somolians apiece. Under the shareholder agreement, Richer has only two choices: buy Rich's shares at the offering price, or *sell* his own shares to Rich at that identical price. The same scheme applies if Richer offers to sell first: Rich must buy or sell at Richer's offering price. The agreement holds a shotgun to the parties' heads, absolutely requiring a deal at the offering price. In the Raptors' case, Alan Slaight, holder of 39.5 percent of the Raptors, offered to buy out John Bitove's 39.5 percent stake. Bitove could not come up with the dosh (something between $42- and $65-million U.S., depending on whose sports pages you read), so he lost his entire stake to Slaight.

Whether "shotgun clause" is a felicitous phrase for this arrangement is another matter. Shotgun weddings are common enough, but a shotgun divorce? "Mexican standoff" would be spot-on, if you could say such things these days. "Forced buy-out," which seems both accurate and politically correct, is perhaps not high-plains-drifter enough for men in grey flannel suits sitting amidst the tumbleweeds and chuckwagons at high noon on Bay or Wall Street.

Their lawyers have even more grandiose fantasies about these things. They tend to characterize shotgun clauses as "nuclear deterrents," the ultimate weapon you keep "in your drawers" (no doubt a Freudian slip) to facilitate less obliterative forms of dispute resolution. Yet, presumably because of this dispute-resolution aspect of forced-buyout clauses, a renegade pacifist faction of lawyers has suggested yet another synonym. These peaceniks — law professors, five will get you ten — are prone to call the buyout clause a "Solomon dispute resolution clause."

Of course this invites more conceptual trouble than "shotgun clause." Apparently the peacenik faction is thinking of the famous story of Solomon and the two mothers. In other words, it's the devil quoting scripture.

I first read about Solomon and the mothers in the color comics supplement to the Sunday *Denver Post*, when I was maybe five or six. In that telling, two women come to the king, each claiming possessory title in an infant. Apparently impatient with the idea of investigating priority of registration and what-not, the king summarily calls for a sword — a shotgun being unavailable — so that he can just cut the kid in half and have done with it. One litigant agrees to the scheme. The other cries out that, in the interests of sparing the child, the first woman can take the whole interest. King Solomon decides that this is mother-love talking, and awards title to the woman who disclaims it.

Even in childhood I felt doubtful about King Solomon's trial tactics, because it seemed to me that the kidnapper could just as likely have reacted as the biological mother did: *prima facie* the kidnapper was not a bad person; she took the kid because she *really* wanted it; she was in mortal pain because she had no child of her own. She wished no harm to the child. In fact, she had killed her own baby accidentally. I know this crucial detail now because, in light of shotgun clauses in shareholder agreements, I finally got around to checking the King James version of the two-mothers story. It still sounds uncomfortably like Judge Judy dispensing palm tree justice.

According to the authorized version, the improvised trial-by-sword marks Solomon's first moments on the bench, just after God has given him "a wise and understanding heart." The king describes *himself* as "but a little child," showing in that admission more wisdom than those who think the sword business is such a judicious approach to cross-examination.

King James' mother-litigants are "harlots." Perhaps this was a necessary plot device: if there had been an identifiable father, he could have testified as to whose child was whose, ruining the whole drama of the thing. Harlot I complains that Harlot II accidentally smothered her own child by rolling over onto it in her sleep. Harlot I then tells the king that Harlot II switched babies, so that when Harlot I awoke, she held the dead child in her arms.

We won't get into how harlotry might relate to modern shareholder dealings. But even accepting the conventional view that Solomon's cross-examination by sword is eminently wise, it is hard to see what is Solomonic about a forced-buyout clause. Unlike a shotgun-clause situation, the mothers never had a common interest as "stakeholders" in one baby — that's the whole point of the story.

More specifically, Bitove, whom the popular press characterize as the true, loving parent in this modern song of Solomon, did not sell off his shares in order to save the baby. Yes, he told the press, "When you really love something, you have to be prepared to let it go," but he sold his shares because he had signed a contract — voluntarily, no doubt, and based on independent legal advice — which left him no other choice. No outside authority waved a sword over, or held a shotgun to, his baby's head.

Perhaps in years to come the Raptor case will serve as a footnote to the Bar Admission Course materials on corporate law. A caveat in the existing chapter of the materials the Law Society provided me on shareholder agreements reads:

> *Before one allows a client to sign an agreement containing such a "shotgun" or "Solomon" dispute resolution clause, one should be sure that one's client has the financial means to purchase the interests of the other shareholders in the corporation if this should prove necessary.*

Then again, one can't hold a gun to their heads, can one?

25 A really big beef Bourguignon

At 61, with his carefully trimmed beard, rugged good looks, and woolen vest, André Porcheret seems typecast as a typical Burgundian farmer. In fact, he's one of the most respected winemakers in the world. Which is why it shook the entire sniff-and-spit world when he pronounced one night in the cellars where he worked at Domaine des Hospices de Beaune, "I am not a crook."

Apparently, what he actually said, to the Côte d'Or wine merchants assembled there to taste the 1997 vintage, was, "We are completely open about what we did. And we did not commit fraud." Of course, the authorities beg to differ, but Porcheret says that he based his conduct on the wine merchants' interpretation of French law. French law mandates that you can either chaptalize your wine — add sugar to it to increase its alcohol content — or add tartaric acid to compensate for low acidity in grapes. But you can't do both to the same vintage.

The merchants claimed that they had found a technical end-run: there was nothing to stop vintners from adding sugar to the must (the grape mash before it is fermented), then adding acid to the actual wine of that same vintage. They neglected to tell Porcheret, apparently, about a letter from the authorities in Paris, insisting that this method amounted to a dodge, not a legal distinction: it still constituted illegally using two additives in one vintage. So, Porcheret, already inclined to *le sauçage du vin* (the "saucing" or "improving" of wine) as a trade practice, put sugar into the vats of must, and added tartaric acid when the must had become wine in barrels.

To support his case that this was perfectly legal, he hid nothing; he even recorded *le double sauçage* in the cellar logs as the law required. And because Domaine des Hospices de Beaune produces some very chi-chi wines — the beloved Montrachet, for example — the result was a global *affaire notoire*.

Beyond violation of domestic regulatory law — not to mention the global scandal — there was the little problem of how certain people interpreted European Commission wine regulations. In each distinct "product," the regulations said, acidification and "enrichment" were to be "mutually exclusive." But the larger problem for Porcheret and his peers was that the French could no longer afford to ignore competition from vineyards in California, Australia, and even New Zealand.

They used to have a one-word reaction to the upstart New World vintners: *terroir*, they would sniff, meaning that no one — and especially no *arriviste* whipper-snappers in former British colonies — could ever compete with the special soil and the old vines on it that the French had cultivated lovingly over the centuries. But New World wines, with less strict regulation, have begun to put paid to that doddering snobbery, and if the old Burgundy *domaines* have to pick their grapes a little early, or if there is a drought in a given year, they are increasingly anxious to help the final product along.

Public relations in Burgundy were not assisted by news in the spring of 1997 concerning what some have styled "the Bordeaux milkshake." The former manager at Château Giscours, a prestigious Médoc producer in Bordeaux, accused his ex-employers of mixing milk, acid, water, inferior wine, and maybe even wood chips into its premium Margaux. The château says that perhaps someone with a grudge beefed up their Sirène product with some Haut-Médoc, but that was all. Yet they offered to buy back the Sirène from all purchasers.

Meanwhile, back at the Côte d'Or Winegrowers Association in Burgundy, at least one member said that the old French law on additives was out of date and deserved to be flouted. Or at least of Porcheret and his supporters, he remarked, "I am satisfied with the way winemakers in Burgundy have chosen to interpret it."

Many view old veterans like Porcheret as artists, whose judicious use of additives is part of their craftsmanship. In his encyclopedic

Wine Guide, U.S. wine guru Robert Parker, Jr. laments that the "hoopla" over *terroir* is more about "political correctness" — *terroirisme* — than demonstrable fact. *Terroir*, he says, "is often a convenient excuse for upholding the status quo." Parker, an ex-lawyer whom the French call the Pope of wine (this is meant ironically, and often angrily, among the traditionalists in Bordeaux), sees makers such as Porcheret as "pushing themselves as well as their peers to produce the highest-quality burgundies possible." Inevitably, perhaps, some in the French wine industry grumble that Parker's tasting notes are so influential (they influence wine prices like comments by Alan Greenspan have influenced the financial markets), makers "improve" wines to cater to his biases.

Others propose a compromise: the anti-adulteration rules should apply only to the more up-scale product, not to ordinary table wines. But of course this would not greatly assist Domaine des Hospices de Beaune, with its high-end emphasis on Montrachet, Meursault, and Corton. And *terroir* remains a form of state religion. One sommelier has observed, "Technology can hide defects but it can also rob a wine of its individuality just as plastic surgery can improve a face but also deprive it of its beauty. To abandon concepts of *terroir* is like abandoning art in favour of geometry."

Unlike his colleagues in Burgundy, even the head of the Bordeaux vintners' association has commented that rules such as those founding the French *appellation contrôlée* system give consumers "a well-defined product" and promote "regional authenticity and taste." "It's not the same thing," Philippe Casteja says, "if you add raspberry syrup." Speaking of saucing the wine . . .

26 Some hot tips on being gratuitous

My friend Neil, lawyer to the food-workers' union, has a motto about waiters: never upset a person who handles your food. Generous tipping comes into the equation, of course, if you habitually dine at the same establishment. Tips are bribes and protection money by another name — thank yous, yes, but thank yous for not running the cab over my Samsonites, shaving *too* close to my jugular, sneezing in my pizza....

One theory has it that "tip" is an abbreviation for "To Insure Promptitude," which caveat supposedly was printed on boxes at the doors of ye olde inns and taverns. Considering that service is more or less agreed to be "an extra" in everyday transactions — not a part of the central contract — "To Insure Promptitude" is a compelling etymology. The main contract between restaurant and customer seems to be that the former will simply *feed* the latter. When and how is a collateral matter. Thus, in a Peter DeVries novel a man regularly eats in a cafe where they provide what he calls "same-day service." Israel Shenker seems to have experienced similar customer relations in a kosher restaurant where he interviewed the writer Isaac Singer. It was lunchtime and Shenker found himself gnawingly distracted from what the Nobel laureate was saying by the thought, "Some day my blintz will come."

Not having heard of the "promptitude" etymology, I had thought that "tip" might have come from "tipple": you've had your drink, now it's the waiter's or bartender's turn. Again you pay extra to protect yourself from the server's disgruntlement or envy — and temptation to slip you a Mickey Finn. In French, as a matter of fact, a tip is *un pourboire*, money for the waiter's drink; and in Britain, punters typically tell the server to keep part of the change with "And have one yourself." But the prevalent dictionary opinion is that "tip" comes from thieves' cant of the 18th and 19th centuries, as in "Tip me a wink" if the cops are around. "Tip me a hog" meant "Give me a shilling."

Whether tipping is collateral or at the heart of the contract, it has become *de rigueur*, an institutionalized annoyance. In his stand-up days Woody Allen did a routine about having a Messianic complex. Whenever he took cabs, he said, he tipped big, "because He would have."

In his autobiography *La Bonne Table* the famous restaurateur Ludwig Bemelmans writes that "restaurant law" in Austria once demanded that though customers left three separate tips (for the captain, the waiter, and the busboy or *piccolo*), the captain was entitled to all the tip coins he could grab "within the reach of his outstretched thumb and index finger." For this reason, patrons left three separate stacks of coins, widely spaced, at the edge of the table.

During my own salad days as an advertizing copywriter (when eating large and tipping big were tribal rites), a roustabout art director swore to me that he had seen waiters at one of our regular hang-outs literally extort a tip. The principal of the piece was a mutual acquaintance who had entertained a high-rolling crowd at the downtown Toronto spaghetti house. When he failed to leave the customary 15 percent (my friend claimed), the waiters and busboys circled him and wouldn't allow him to leave. The lawyer in me wants to know whether this was false imprisonment or enforcing a lien on the "chattel" (the non-tipping customer) in the restaurant's possession.

Etiquette maven Eve Drobot has no answer for that, but she tells me that the unwritten law says: Airline crew, no gratuity (it's an insult; but upon deplaning make sure to smile and say goodbye; they feel hurt if you don't); *the maitre d'*, only for good service over a number of visits. (But if your dinner companions imitate the accents of waiters in ethnic restaurants, tell them "in no uncertain terms that you do not wish to be associated with such displays of insensitivity. Show them that you mean it by moving to another table if necessary.") Roving restaurant violinists/guitarists/accordionists, not necessarily (unless you request a tune, of course); pizza delivery boy, definitely. But then, Neil the food-workers' lawyer could have told you all that, while giving you a look which said, "You have to ask?"

27 Hendrix a big star on a different front

Sure, you worry now and again about what will happen to Einstein's brain. You vaguely remember reading that it's just sitting there, in a pickle jar on some scientist's desk, like yesterday's, well, pickles. Next to a half-eaten cheese sandwich or whatever. And then there was that article in *Harper's* about the guy who drove across the country with parts of it sloshing around in tupperware. Einstein's brain! And didn't you clip something from the *New York Times Book Review*, yeah, here it is . . . no, well, something about how somebody claimed that this shrivelled-up, cigarish thing in a box was Napoleon's "private person," as they say over at the Court of Appeal? Wasn't there a protracted exchange of letters about whose private person, or cigar, it might be, or might have been? Yes it is, no it isn't, it's mine, it's his. Ah, the life of the mind!

Whose organ is it? It's a question that has become legally significant in a more popular vein lately, so popular that the question itself has become, "Whose 'rig' is it?" That's what the plaintiff in *Albritton v. Cohen* has called Jimmy Hendrix's private person. A "rig"— not the sort of language one sees in the *New York Times Book Review* re

Napoleon Bonaparte, but still, lately, a legal term of art.* One quotes from the Albritton diaries:

> *We need a ratio 28:28 (a much larger than normal amount of mix) and found this just barely sufficient. He [i.e., Hendrix] has got just about the biggest rig I've ever seen! We had to plunge him through the entire depth of the vase. . .*
>
> *We got a beautiful mould. He even kept his hard for the entire minute. He got stuck, however, for about 15 minutes, but he was an excellent sport — didn't panic . . . I believe the reason we couldn't get his rig out was that it wouldn't* GET SOFT*!*

Obviously Hendrix was a superstar in every sense of the word. His bassist Noel Redding was cut from a different mould. Although he "moulded superbly" and "only got stuck for five minutes, . . . he got panicky and began to get soft." The rest of that particular adventure is too painful to relate.

Talk about making someone a sex object! Cynthia Albritton and her assistant met rock stars during the 1960s and '70s by offering to make plaster casts of their private persons. Manually, and sometimes orally, they would stimulate their subjects into a state of alertness and then plunge them into a flower-vase of alginate, the stuff dentists use for modelling your crowns and bridges. The young women would fill the mould with plaster and, as the plaster hardened, they paid their personal homage to its endower.

One commentator, super-groupie Pamela Des Barres, has offered this perhaps catty observation, professional to professional, on the self-styled "Plaster Casters": "The big drawback with this charming

---

*"A word or phrase used in a definite or precise sense in some particular subject . . . ; a technical expression." *The Oxford English Dictionary*

concept was that the girls had to get intimate with guys they weren't wigged out over, just to further THE CAUSE." Albritton, Des Barres says,

> *was painfully shy and I couldn't imagine her with the alginate and plaster, buried in Eric Burdon's crotch area, but I saw the casts for myself, and was wowed by the artistry involved. For Cynthia it was a science, her true calling in life, the thing she was born to do, and Frank [Zappa] was her mentor, just like he was mine.*

At some point, Albritton had decided to re-cast the sculptures in bronze. Hearing of the *oeuvre* in progress, musician Frank Zappa offered to sponsor her, hoping to mount a major exhibition of the likes of Hendrix, Redding, Paul Revere and all his Raiders, Eric Burdon (of The Animals; you might remember: "We gotta get out of this vase/If it's the last thing we ever do . . .") and, for Canadian content, The Lovin' Spoonfuls' Zal Yanovsky. Indeed, these musician's "rigs" got their names re-attached to them when they went to the L.A. courthouse, presumably all in a row, with high-rolling lawyers referring to them as "the Hendrix," "the Redding . . ." *the Revered?*

But I digress in premature adjudication. Ensconced at Zappa's expense in L.A. during the early 1970s, Albritton had indulged in her art with new vigor, until her apartment was burglarized. She moved the completed bronzes to the office of Zappa's manager, Herb Cohen. After a couple of years, Cohen suggested that the casts' attraction might be wearing off in the public mind, if not in Albritton's hands. He suggested that she abstain for a while, pending a bout of flower-child, free-love revival. So the statues, 25 in all, stayed with Cohen for two decades. When Albritton attempted to reclaim them, Cohen refused to give them back, contending that he had gained ownership of the casts through some sort of legal transaction with Zappa, and that Albritton had abandoned them.

Albritton sued Cohen for $1 million (for conversion, evidently).

This being California, Cohen saw her the $1 million and countersued for another million. The trial lasted some two weeks, with Geoffrey Glass, Albritton's counsel, arguing that "Jimi Hendrix's guitar went for $500,000, his headband went for $26,000, the one-of-a-kind replica of his penis must be worth at least as much." Maybe it was the ambiguity in this argument that led U.S. Superior Court Judge Lillian Stevens to award Albritton just $10,000 for her lost opportunity to display the 25 moulds.

Unfortunately, legal reporting services have not seen fit to publish the reasons in *Albritton v. Cohen*. But evidently Judge Stevens held that the statues were "the progeny of [Albritton's] original casts" and ordered Cohen to return them to their maker.

The legal squabbling over Jimi Hendrix's body did not end there, however. Yet again, the litigation involved women who claimed to know him intimately. In fact, it seemed to involve attempts to prove who had known him most intimately, never mind Albritton's compelling claim in that respect.

If you think that only men experience mid-life crises, you have not heard of Monika Danneman and Kathy Etchingham. When she died on April 5, 1996, Danneman was 50. Etchingham was 49. As former girlfriends of Hendrix, who died in 1970 after mixing a very large quantity of wine with a handful of barbiturates, they had spent the last 26-odd years fighting over who was truest and bluest. And they saved the highest melodrama for the last half-decade. Not long before Danneman died, Etchingham brought a motion for contempt of court against her that turned out to be the *coup de grâce* in what truly had been trial by battle.

In a sense, Danneman suffered the death penalty for breach of a promise to the court. Accounts vary, especially insofar as Danneman and Etchingham could never agree on certain central facts, but the story seems to have gone something like this:

Etchingham lived with Hendrix for two and a half years during the late 1960s. She is said to be the "cute little heartbreaker" and "sweet little lovemaker" of Hendrix's "Foxy Lady." But according to Etchingham, herself, Hendrix was lying when he promised her in that famous song, "I wanna take you home, I won't do you no harm, no." After Hendrix died (when both women were about 25 and Hendrix was 27), Etchingham told a British tabloid that he had been a "violent, hard drinking, drugged-up sex maniac."

Danneman always disputed this. She claimed that she had met the rock star in a Dusseldorf bar when she was a 19-year-old figure-skater. Around the time that Hendrix broke it off with Etchingham, he and Danneman reconnected, and they lived, Danneman said, a very quiet, domestic life in her west London apartment, right until the night that he died.

Danneman insisted that Hendrix had proposed marriage to her, and during the High Court contempt proceedings she wore what she claimed was an engagement gift, a large ring designed in the form of a serpent. Newspaper reports described her as faithfully comporting herself throughout in the manner of the "archetypal rock chick" of the 1960s. Indeed, she remained nunnishly faithful to Hendrix's memory for a quarter century, living more recently in a thatched Sussex hermitage, rendering painting after elegiac painting of rock's lost "Voodoo Chile" as a sort of cosmic traveler, and writing about him to "spread his word."

Etchingham had been somewhat more pragmatic about unsticking herself from the '60s. She married a physician and has two sons. But neither was she altogether unstuck. Her gloss on Danneman's engagement claim is typical of their long-standing rivalry. After winning the contempt application, she told reporters, "Monika Danneman was always trying to show that she was engaged to Jimi while I was going out with him. They were only together the last three days of his life."

In 1994, Etchingham convinced the London police to re-open

their investigation into Hendrix's death. She sent a 34-page *J'Accuse* to Scotland Yard, alleging, among other things, that Danneman had waited up to five hours before calling an ambulance while Hendrix lay dying in her apartment. When the police went public with this, Etchingham advised the *Daily Mail* that Hendrix's "death was all very dodgy. He was in the wrong place at the wrong time with the wrong people."

Etchingham had wanted the inquest re-opened given that the coroner had rendered an "open verdict"— a finding that medical authorities could not determine the cause of Hendrix's death. During the 1994 investigation a doctor who treated Hendrix upon his arrival at hospital, on September 18, 1970, said that the rock star "drowned in red wine," which had stained his body and matted his hair. Apparently this accords with the popular understanding that Hendrix choked to death after regurgitating the wine and drugs. The doctor also said that Hendrix had been dead for some time when his body reached the hospital.

Eric Burdon, Hendrix's friend and fellow musician, has confirmed that Danneman telephoned in the very early hours of the 18th to report that Hendrix was so stoned she couldn't revive him. But the police cleared Danneman of any wrongdoing. In fact, apparently Hendrix was conscious at some point that night or morning. Conventional wisdom has it that his last words were a message on his manager's answering machine: "I need help bad, man."

Following the second police investigation, British Attorney General Sir Nicholas Lyell refused to make further inquiries into Hendrix's death, and Danneman felt vindicated. While her return fire at Etchingham was always less spectacular than her rival's appeals to the down-market press and up-market law enforcement establishment, Etchingham regularly used the legal system as an effective sword and shield.

In a libel action in 1992, Etchingham alleged that Danneman had circulated stories about her, to the effect that Hendrix had bad-mouthed Etchingham. According to Etchingham, Danneman quoted Hendrix as making disparaging remarks such as, "Kathy Etchingham was another girl who I met when I came to London who would cheat and lie for money. When I went on tour I left her in charge of my flat and when I came back I found everything plus Kathy gone."

Danneman denied that she had anything to do with such rumors. Nonetheless, she agreed to pay Etchingham $2,000 plus costs, and undertook not to repeat the libel. In a 1994 book called *The Inner World of Jimi Hendrix*, Danneman wrote that one of Hendrix's former girlfriends had "constructed the most gruesome story of Jimi's death. It was all an invention." Eventually, Justice French of the High Court found that the former girlfriend described in this statement was identifiable as Etchingham to those who knew the Hendrix story, and that the statement amounted to Danneman's repeating the libel.

Although Etchingham's counsel, Charles Gray, Q.C., had sought a jail term for Danneman, the court declined, finding that she was ill and so poor that she was having to sell her Hendrix paintings from the walls of her Sussex "shrine" to the acid-rock virtuoso. However, his lordship ordered Danneman to pay Etchingham's costs of some $60,000. Two days later, the police found Danneman dead from inhaling exhaust fumes in her Mercedes.

Danneman claimed to have devoted her life to Hendrix's memory, and one might say that her death has fulfilled that particular undertaking.

28 The call of nature heard, and reported

During just a single week, the memorable week of September 19, 1994, in the course of my duties in Her Majesty's press corps, I came across three separate stories about toilets and the law in the daily papers. This served to confirm: (1) my long-held suspicion that there should be a separate category for the subject in the official law reports; (2) the law may not belong in the nation's bedrooms, but the loo's another matter; and (3) there's always a market for toilet humor. Consider the following genuine cases from the law reports:

(1) LOO LAW — INTELLECTUAL PROPERTY — INVASION OF PUBLICITY RIGHTS — PRIVACY.

Comedian and talk show personality Johnny Carson sues a Michigan outfit which markets portable toilets under the trade name Here's Johnny. HELD: While the defendant could not get damages for trademark infringement or unfair competition (although famously associated with the comedian, the phrase "Heeeeeeere's Johnny!" was not registered and there was no likelihood that anyone would confuse Carson with the toilet marketer), the toilet man had breached Carson's right to be free from "invasion of publicity rights": *John W. Carson v. Here's Johnny Portable Toilets Inc*, 698 F. 2d 831 (1983), *per* Bailey Brown J., U.S.C.A., Sixth Circ. For more detail, see page 122.

(2) LOO LAW — NEGLIGENCE — PROXIMATE CAUSE — LANDLORD AND TENANT.

The plaintiff Rush (no pun intended) sued a property management company after she fell through a rotted trap door in a privy nine feet, by her measurement (nine inches by landlord's), into the waste below. Rush had no choice, the Supreme Court of New Jersey held, "when impelled by the calls of nature, but to use the facilities placed at her disposal," whose floor was "poorly maintained." While the court "hardly thought this was the assumption of risk" — in other words, the judge doubted that Rush had acted negligently herself in taking her chances using the privy — it was for the jury to determine if walking on the floor amounted to such "contributory negligence." So the court sent the matter on for a full trial. *Rush v. Commercial Realty Co.*, 145 A. 476 (1929).

(3) LOO LAW — NEGLIGENCE — PROXIMATE CAUSE — PUBLIC AUTHORITIES.

In this case, the English Court of Appeal found a district council 75 percent liable after a woman in high heels fell off a toilet-paper roll while attempting to climb out of a stall in a public washroom. There was no handle on the inside of the door, which was seven feet high. The woman's train was arriving any minute, her husband was waiting on the platform, and she could not attract help by waving and shouting.

The council should have inspected the door and repaired it, the court ruled. "It seems to me to be asking too much of the so-called reasonable man or woman to suppose that he or she would just remain inactive" in the circumstances. *Per* Lord Evershed, *Sayers v. Harlow Urban District Council*, [1958] 2 All E.R. 342.

(4) LOO LAW — PERSONAL PROPERTY — 5,300-YEAR-OLD CORPSES — OWNERSHIP — PROOF — FINDERS, CREEPERS.

Lucy the homonid had the misfortune to be disinterred in a time when people named old bones after Beatles' songs. Consider if somebody had dug her up in the '90s and called her after, say, "Enid" by the Barenaked Ladies? Or consider "Otzi the Iceman," who had the misfortune to die on what is currently the border between Italy and Austria.

Thanks to the glacier that was his tomb, Otzi was exhumed in a remarkably preserved state, despite the fact that he was 53 centuries old. The find provoked a dispute over which country "owned" him (while a corpse cannot be property, apparently — see page 59 — someone, somehow, can own it as property.) Supposedly, it was all solved by the medieval equivalent of toilet paper — which is to say, moss. Otzi, it turns out, was carrying the *neckera complanata* variety (exhibit 1A, your honor). Experts say that this moss could only have come from the Vinschgau Valley in what is today's Italy.

As a correspondent to the *Globe and Mail* pointed out, "Even back then, travellers knew in Europe you had to carry your own toilet paper." What one wants to know is, what makes them so sure it wasn't his lunch?

(5) LOO LAW — LABOR RELATIONS — COLLECTIVE GARGLING — NO SIT-DOWNS.

Apparently Gainers Meat Packers in Calgary, Alberta, refused to take anything from its employees sitting down — not figuratively, anyway. Literally, according to the popular press, if the workers had to use the loo other than during a contractually stipulated break, owners Burns Foods would dock their pay.

(6) LOO LAW — LABOR RELATIONS — STILL FLUSH, DESPITE THE RECESSION.

In related labor relations news in Ontario, the Ministry of Labour provoked consternation in the construction industry by defining a toilet as an entity "used for the disposal of human waste."

Only among lawyers would this be controversial, you would think. But what worried those directly affected was that, thanks to a labor adjudicator's report, the definition required employers to use non-recirculating flush toilets, like the ones in our homes, which cost more to operate than do the usual johnnies on the spot (like the ones in our cottages), in which a chemical solution rinses waste into a holding tank (see number one above). That is, the flush kind truly *disposes*. Adjudicator Robert Blair found that because of the holding area, apparently, the non-flush variety did not "remove human waste."

The ministry attempted to find a middle ground by proposing that a flap be interposed between the bowl and the holding tank. The Ontario Sewage and Liquid Waste Carriers Association replied that this "is like trying to convert a Chevrolet into a Rolls-Royce by changing the hood ornament."

In the circumstances, the remark might not bring labor peace, but it could slow down the theft of hood ornaments.

CHAPTER FIVE

THE MORON IN A HURRY

Intellectual Property Isn't Necessarily Smart

29 Dr. Doolittle before the defense

In a courtroom, generally only so-called expert witnesses are entitled to give opinions on subjects not completely familiar to adults of average intelligence. Even the most ardent stamp collector might not qualify as an expert in philately if she could not prove formal training or its equivalent.

Once a court accepts a witness as an expert, the opposing side will still attempt to discredit the expert's qualifications and testimony. One common ploy is to ask something like, "And how much is the plaintiff paying you to say that?" And true enough, expert testimony for pay has become a cottage industry in litigious North America.

Another cross-examination technique is denigration. In 1983, under the headline "Great Moments in Cross-Examination," *Ontario Lawyers Weekly* reprinted the following example, purportedly the transcript of a zoology professor's testimony in a 1921 patent infringement case in Minnesota. However accurate it might be, if nothing else it certainly proves the old maxim, "The art of cross-examination is not the art of examining crossly."

The plaintiff had a property interest in a beaver-trap design, and was claiming that the defendant had breached the patent. Probably only mechanical engineers of very peculiar habits can listen to evidence in such cases without going quietly mad. Near the end of an evidently long and tedious case, the plaintiff called the pedantic, retired professor and had concluded his examination-in-chief by lunchtime. When defense counsel began his cross-examination at two p.m., he was drunk, to the following alleged effect:

> Q. *Professor, you say you are a professor?*
> A. *That's right. That is, a former professor. You see, I retired in 1915. No it was really 1916. Pardon me, I would not want to . . .*
> Q. *That's all right, Professor. Professor of what, Professor?*
> A. *Zoology.*
> Q. *What's that?*
> A. *Zoology.*
> Q. *Yes, but what is zoology? Don't try to evade or quibble.*
> A. *I am not quibbling.*
> Q. *Oh yes you are, yes you are, just like all the so-called experts and so-called experts.*
> THE COURT: *Treat the witness fairly. He isn't trying to quibble. He just didn't understand you.*
> COUNSEL: *I have practiced in this court for 29 years and no court has ever accused me of mistreating any witnesses or any court or any client, directly and indirectly, and beyond that . . .*
> THE COURT: *Proceed.*

Q. *What do zoologists do, Professor?*
A. *They study and sometimes teach animal life. It is a bit difficult to define in a sentence. As in many other sciences there are many varied branches and specialties. It is the study of animals and animal life. I know of a professor of zoology at a school in Ohio who spent 35 years studying one animal. A snail, or rather a snail family. And again . . .*
Q. *What was his name?*
A. *James H. Hertford.*
Q. *Where is he now?*
THE COURT: *What has that got to do with this matter? I am afraid you are wandering a little far afield.*
COUNSEL: *Your honor forgets this is a cross-examination.*
THE COURT: *I didn't forget anything of the kind. Get along with your questions.*
Q. *Answer the question.*
A. *What was the question please?*
Q. *Strike it. We will start all over again. I will try to put my questions in such a simple childlike way — so simple and easy, that even a professor, a dignified, educated, so-called professor who comes to Minnesota in the north woods after spending his life in a schoolroom looking at snails, then telling, oh, he's telling us, as if we didn't know, what beavers would do.*
PLAINTIFF'S COUNSEL: *I certainly want to object to these remarks. These gratuitous . . .*
THE COURT: *Yes, that is very objectionable. Simply ask your questions. You know how. You aren't testifying. Get down to the meat of this thing. This is cross-examination, but you can't abuse any privilege . . .*
COUNSEL: *Very well, your honor. The attitude of this witness, the sneering, contemptuous, supercilious attitude of this witness toward me and the court has so outraged me that perhaps I have lost my temper. I shouldn't have done so. Read the question.*

PLAINTIFF'S COUNSEL: *There wasn't any question. You were starting to make a speech . . .*

COUNSEL: *I deny that. I absolutely . . .*

THE COURT: *There has been enough of this. If you have any questions, ask them or dismiss the witness.*

Q. *So you say you are a specialist, an expert, on beavers and beaver traps and snails?*

A. *I didn't say any such thing, sir. I said I know a great deal about beavers, just as I think I know, or many people say I know, a great deal about many animals. I have lived with them. I have observed them. I have handled them. I have fed them. I was almost going to say that I have conversed with them. They have a sort of language, you know. They are not inarticulate. And the cruellest thing we can call them is dumb animals; and also . . .*

Q. *You say that they can talk?*

A. *Well, there is a sense in which all nature has a language which we who study it can understand.*

Q. *Answer my question.*

A. *What was your question?*

Q. *You say a beaver can talk?*

A. *Please don't try to make me ridiculous. What I said was this: all animals can speak, and by that I mean that they communicate with one another and understand their own language. Even . . .*

Q. *Can you talk it?*

A. *I can answer it this way . . .*

Q. *Answer yes or no.*

A. *Yes.*

COUNSEL: *I want the reporter to get this. This is good. Mr. Reporter, be sure and get this.*

THE COURT: *He is getting it.*

WITNESS: *I was about to say that if one wants to draw an analogy, even plant life has a kind of language.*

Q. *Do you talk that, too?*

A. *As I said before . . .*

Q. *Don't quibble. Answer yes or no.*

A. *Subject to what I have said, I will answer yes.*

Q. *Did you ever talk to a buttercup?*

PLAINTIFF'S COUNSEL: *Now, your honor, this is too much and I . . .*

COUNSEL: *He is your witness, he is your witness. You brought him and you are bound by his testimony. You brought this man here . . . Did you talk to a buttercup, Professor?*

A. *Well, to those who are familiar with them and have learned to love them, some flowers have a certain language.*

Q. *What did the buttercup say to you and what did you say to the buttercup, fixing the time and place as well as you can?*

THE COURT: *You don't have to answer any such question.*

COUNSEL: *Exception to the remarks of the court. Objection likewise.*

Q. *Did you ever talk to a giraffe, yes or no?*

A. *I can't answer that yes or no. I have told you before that all animals have a kind of language which they speak, which we who have training and sympathy and understanding can comprehend, and I have said, too, that I think I can in a sense speak their language, making them understand me, my motives and my wishes, and so on.*

Q. *Then you have talked to a giraffe?*

A. *Yes, with that qualification.*

Q. *And the giraffe talked to you?*

A. *Yes.*

Q. *Did you ever talk to a lion?*

A. *Yes.*

Q. *And the lion talked to you?*

A. *Yes, with the qualifications I have stated.*

Q. *Did you ever talk to a skunk?*

A. *Yes.*

Q. *Well the next time you have a talk with one of those bastards, ask him for me what the God-damned hell is the big idea.*

According to *Ontario Lawyers Weekly*, Judge Morris of the United States District Court in Duluth ruled that this "cross-examination" constituted contempt of court. He sentenced the defense lawyer to 30 days in jail, the paper says, but released him after he had served 17.

30 Johnny's certainly not heeeeere!

In 1976 entertainer Johnny Carson went to court to prevent a Michigan man from marketing portable toilets called Here's Johnny. Litigation ended eight years later, a banner season for trademark and publicity actions against parodists.

Carson found no relief in trademark infringement and unfair competition. But he ultimately was successful under "invasion of publicity rights," an offshoot of U.S. privacy law. The president of the defendant company admitted that he probably would never have called his product "Here's Johnny" if the phrase had not been intimately associated with Carson as a popular television performer. In fact, his advertizing for the toilets characterized them as "the world's foremost commodian." The U.S. Court of Appeals, Sixth Circuit, held that the phrase "Here's Johnny" itself was protected, even though the toilet company had used neither Carson's name nor likeness. In fact, the court went out of its way to advise the defendant that it was perfectly legal to call his outhouses the "J. William Carson

Portable Toilet," the "John William Carson Portable Toilet," or the "J.W. Carson Portable Toilet."

More recently, a young Omaha artist named Franklyn Novak was marketing t-shirts, mugs, and buttons that parodied the Indian-head logo and typography used by the Mutual of Omaha insurance company. Taking off on the Indian head, Novak's design showed an emaciated face in profile with the phrase "Mutant of Omaha, Nuclear Holocaust Insurance." Styling himself an anti-nuclear activist, Novak also sold products that parodied Mutual's sponsorship of the television nature series "Wild Kingdom" — a show at which Johnny Carson poked fun over the years, regularly pointing out that the host stayed well out of harm's way while ponderously describing his assistant's wrestling matches with alligators and pythons. Novak's products depicted a one-eyed tiger illustrating the phrase "Mutant of Omaha's Mutant Kingdom."

Novak apparently did not mean to imply that Mutual had any interest in the nuclear power or weapons industries; as an Omaha resident, he simply found their name and advertizing a useful vehicle to express his views. But the district court, whose decision the appellate court upheld, admitted evidence of surveys in which 25 percent of those asked agreed that Mutual of Omaha somehow "went along" with Novak's shirts. Rejecting Novak's freedom of speech and parody arguments, the United States Court of Appeals adopted the district court's "finding of a likelihood of confusion" (between Mutual and Mutant) and affirmed the permanent injunction it had issued.

Among the cases the court cited to support this finding were *Carson* and *Dallas Cowboys Cheerleaders v. Pussycat Cinema*, a suit by the Cowboy football club against the makers of "Debbie Does Dallas," a film about a cheerleader who takes very personal initiatives to raise money for the local football team. (See page 138.) But the *Novak* court said that *Girl Scouts v. Personality Posters* did not apply to the "Mutant of Omaha" parodies. In *Girl Scouts*, the court had found no infringement in posters that showed a hugely pregnant Scout touting the organization's motto, "Be Prepared." *Girl Scouts* was different, the *Novak* court said, because the Scouts had not presented even "a scintilla" of evidence that the posters had harmed their trademark.

Mentioned in both *Carson* and *Novak*, and again employing survey evidence, is perhaps the most bemusing of the batch, *Jordache Enterprises v. Hogg Wyld, Ltd. and Oink, Inc.* There, a group of enterprising New Mexico women were inspired with the modest idea that blue jeans should be made to fit human beings like themselves instead of mannequins and anorexic fashion models. They decided to market jeans out of their homes for what the fashion industry called the "fuller-figured femme."

They evidently spent a good deal of time naming their product, tossing around "Thunder Thighs," "Buffalo Buns," "Seambusters," "Hippo Hoggers," "Vidal Sowsoon," and "Calvin Swine." But eventually, when they were ready to go public, another parody name won out.

They displayed the chosen logo on a back pocket. Its main feature was a smiling pig, with its hooves over the pocket top, as though it were peeking out. On the pocket itself was stitching that the U.S. Court of Appeals described as heart-shaped, a true but incomplete characterization. The stitching, in fact, was in the shape of a curvaceous, full-figured set of human buttocks — the Venus Callipygia variety. Between the pig and the set of buns was the company name: Lardashe.

One of the principals of Oink Incorporated testified that, at the time the jeans were named, she had never heard of Jordache, the designer jeans maker, and that the name of Oink's jeans was a polite form of her childhood nickname, "Lardass." She also claimed that Ashe was a fertility goddess mentioned in the Bible, but she could not tell the district court where.

The Court of Appeals was unimpressed by this evidence, comparing it to the testimony of a man who ran an outfit called Sears Financial Network. When Sears Roebuck sued him, the man swore that he had named his company in memory of a lost love called Patricia Sears. Certainly Oink's protestations of innocence seemed at odds with a naming process that included Vidal Sowsoon and Calvin Swine as candidates. But the *Jordache* court was willing to look beyond this "credibility problem." It noted with approval such surprising successes as an action by the Steinway piano makers against a "Stein-Way clip-on beverage can handle" — somehow, the court there found it credible that the public would mistakenly believe that the high-class piano people also made beer-can handles — but in the end the judges held that Hogg Wyld and Oink had not infringed the Jordache mark, a horse's head with the Jordache name in block letters.

31 Morons hurrying hither and yon, sometimes in a very bad light

The moron in a hurry was born into the world in October, 1978, in the case of *Morning Star Co-Operative Society Ltd. v. Express Newspapers Ltd*. *Morning Star* was a communist broadsheet. It had only just changed its name from the less cheery *Daily Worker*, and it wanted to prevent the Express syndicate from naming its new tabloid the *Daily Star*. The *Daily Star* was to feature "startlingly large headlines and . . . pictures of nearly nude models." The public would confuse the two newspapers, *Morning Star* claimed.

But as Bernard Levin would observe in the *Times* of London (not, as the court pointed out, to be confused with the *Financial Times* or the *Cornish Times*), Mr. Justice Foster of the Court of

Chancery was "clearly a man who can tell at a glance the difference between the Dnepropetrovsk Dam and a pair of titties." That is, Justice Foster felt that there was little chance the Express chain would or could pass the new tabloid off as the comrade plaintiffs' broadsheet.

Still, his lordship was not above a little vernacular himself, and right in the heart of his judgment, too. Justice Foster first detailed the vast dissimilarities in circulation (*Morning Star's* 21,000 and dropping, *versus* the *Daily Star's* projected 3.7 million), format, marketing (the *Morning Star* generally was sold "by left-wing persons in the factory or at the factory gate"), and price. "These differences," Justice Foster held, "lead me to answer the question whether the plaintiffs have any real chance of succeeding at the trial in the negative. . . . I for myself would find that the two papers are so different in every way that only a moron in a hurry would be misled."

There he was, like Venus on the half-shell or a defective Adam treading on the orchids of Eden, fully fledged in all his pillock glory, mentally challenged yet at least attempting to improve himself by keeping up with the news. This role model promptly disappeared from the law reports for nine years, achieving a great deal less popularity than his cousins, the "reasonable person," that benchmark against which the law measures the conduct of the rest of us mere mortals, and the "officious bystander," whom judges look to when a reasonable person is nowhere to be found — often in business situations. But in 1987 the harried ignoramus returned triumphant in the private prosecution *The Bank of England v. Boggs*, in which the bank charged that J.S.G. Boggs, who called himself a "numeric artist," was guilty of forgery. Boggs replied that in rendering startlingly accurate freehand versions of various world currencies, and then using them in trade for goods and services, he was practicing art, not crime.

It was true that those who made the trades with Boggs knew that the currency was not issued by government treasuries. As well, Boggs altered details of the currencies (for example, he might change the mint's usual phraseology to "This note is legal tender for artists" or substitute his own portrait for the monarch's) and he would sign the change he received in the transaction, then sell it with the receipt to collectors. The "artwork," in other words, was the hand-drawn currency, the receipt, the change, and, as in "performance art," whatever else eventuated in the transaction. One of Boggs' "pieces" included the four shirts he bought with his "money."

The defense argued that not even a moron in a hurry would confuse a Boggs note with a pound note, the prosecution adding the wrinkle, "Yes, but what about a moron in a hurry in a dimly lighted room?" And although an Old Bailey judge summed up firmly against Boggs (and presumably for the mentally distracted rushing through dusky restaurants and department stores), the jury found him not guilty of contravening the *Forgery and Counterfeiting Act*.

Now, if *Morning Star* marked the first appearance of the moron in a hurry, in a dimly lighted English courtroom in 1979, he nearly came out of the closet three years earlier, in Canada in 1976. To see him, as with the little people in Ireland, you have to believe. And you have to keep in mind that, in general, Canadians are rather more democratic, or maybe just nicer, than the British. On the matter of calling a spade a moron, we tend to mince words.

In August 1976, for instance, the Mr. Submarine food chain wanted to stop another sandwich-maker from "passing itself off" as Mr. Submarine at the Canadian National Exhibition in Toronto. The competitor had been at the CNE in two previous years, with a booth using a color scheme similar to Mr. Submarine's (the company having 130 stores in Canada) and displaying the word "submarine" in the same type-style and red shade that the plaintiff used for its name. Justice Willard Estey, of the Ontario High Court at the time, held:

> *The standard to be applied is not that of a person fully familiar with the detailed operations of a plaintiff and therefore capable of at once distinguishing those of the defendant from those of the plaintiff but rather that of a person who has a vague recollection or understanding of the business or product of the plaintiff and who, on being faced with that of the defendant, may well be confused or deceived as to the ownership or nature of the goods or the proprietor of the business in question.*

Screw your opera glasses tight against your eye sockets, squint hard through the foggy prose, and *voilà!*: a moron in a hurry.

In England, the moron in a hurry confuses barenaked tractor propaganda for tittie tabloids, where those admirable exemplars the reasonable person and officious bystander know exactly what they want at the news agents, and what it's called . . . and that its moving parts are not metallic. On the other hand, Justice Estey seems to imply that in Canada the moron in a hurry isn't the exception to be ignored but the benchmark — that in Canada the average person, the man on the Clapham omnibus, or Bathurst 512 streetcar to the CNE, *is himself a moron in a hurry*. If you've ridden that trolley, you might be inclined to the view that Justice Estey has a point.

More recently, Justice J.B. Dea of the Alberta Court of Queen's Bench quoted Justice Estey's *Mr. Submarine* dictum to issue yet another injunction. In *Walt Disney Productions v. Triple Five Corporation*, Justice Dea decided that there was a better than off-chance that the Canadian public would think Fantasyland at the West Edmonton Mall was connected with plaintiff's Fantasylands in California, Florida, and Sunday TVland. The standard, Justice Dea held, just before quoting Justice Estey, "is the person with an imperfect recollection who upon being faced with the defendant's activities may well believe there is a connection."

On the other hand, in *Miss Universe v. Miss Nude Universe*,

Canadian pride is recovered. In that case, Justice Barry Strayer of the Federal Court suggests that in Canada even a moron in a hurry can tell the difference between a pair of titties and, well, a pair of titties in a bathing suit.

Miss Nude Universe, the business enterprise, intended to stage contests in Canadian taverns in which exotic dancers competed to be the most attractive sex-objects in known Creation. Just as Justice Foster seemed to know the difference between the Dnepropetrovsk Dam and the *Daily Star*'s page-three bimbo, Justice Strayer detected a clear distinction between the nude competition and the plaintiff's less revealing enterprise, which attracted millions of dollars in sponsorship, was shown across the world on prime-time television, and required that the contestants be between 17 and 25 as well as "never married and never pregnant."

"Nor are there any special circumstances to suggest," Justice Strayer held, "that *any but the most unthinking* would assume that Miss Universe Inc. had licensed the sort of performances in bars and taverns which may come to be described as Miss Nude Universe pageants."

If you squint hard again through your opera glasses, you'll see that Canada has gone not one, but two better than the British moron in a hurry: not only would a Canadian moron in a hurry be able to distinguish a pair of whatnots from a pair of them in a bathing suit, he could do it while he was hammered out of his toque on good old Canadian brew.

32   The Official Essay of the 2002 Tishe B'Ab™ celebrations

1987: The U.S. Supreme Court holds that the Gay Olympic Games violated the International Olympic Committee's property rights in the word "Olympic." The court finds that, as a trademark, the word is comparable to other protected names such as "Red Cross," "4-H," "Smokey Bear," "Boy and Girl Scouts," and "Little League Baseball."

1988: During preparation for the winter games in Calgary, the organizing committee threatens to sue Greek restaurants for trademark violations of the Olympic name.

Pretty soon, unless you pay me up front, I will sue you for saying the words "Christmas,"™ "Ash Wednesday,"™ and "Tishe B'Ab."™

As of this moment, I claim exclusive linguistic rights in all religious holidays, including rights in related words such as "tree" (as in, but not restricted to, a partridge in a pear —), "Trash Wednesday" (newspapers, garden refuse, and large articles), and words I haven't figured out yet related to "Tishe B'Ab." "Tissue," probably, but maybe I'll give a volume discount for kindergartners singing "B'Ab, B'Ab Black Sheep."

No doubt some of you will balk at divvying up. "How can you justify charging me to say 'Christmas and Ash Wednesday,'" you will want to know, "let alone 'Tishe B'Ab?'" In an outraged tone, you will add, "I don't even know what Tishe B'Ab *is*." And by the time you stop to catch your breath, you will owe me $300. Plus interest.

How can I do this? Until recently, I was an ignorant pauper, posing as a legal columnist in newspapers and on radio, eking out just enough for stale bagels, mouldy cream cheese, and the occasional morsel of Christmas cake™ Then, by the simple act of reading the day's news, I learned of a lucrative way of getting the rights to religious festivals ABSOLUTELY FREE!

Send me $500 today, and I will tell you how you, too, can use legal precedents invented by Olympic™ organizing committees to claim property rights in words at least 20 centuries old!

Yes, for this minimal investment, I will let you in on how, from at least 776 B.C. to very recent times, "Olympic" meant nothing more than "of Olympus,"™ the mountain home of the Greek gods in whose honor the games were held. Helpless to control your astonishment (and glee at your great luck that this VALUABLE inside INFORMATION is costing MUCH LESS THAN AN MBA) you will read that, among the Greeks, the Olympic Games™ were not a time of filing for injunctions, but of commemorating their dead, celebrating their young, and paying homage to Zeus.

Yes, I said "Greeks," not "geeks." Incredibly, they even let slaves and *women* go around using Olympic words without first demanding sexual favors let alone money from them!

YOUR NAME HERE will learn how to take advantage of AMAZING GROUNDFLOOR OPPORTUNITIES to capitalize on the boundless global economic potential of such religious festivals by the very act of commercializing them for others!

Send me $500 TODAY and discover how the progress of civilization has been nothing but the invention of new holidays so that smart people and greeting card companies could profit from them. Use your own eyes and NO OTHER CAPITAL OUTLAY to see how the Olympic Games™ were nothing but the ancient Greek version of Christmas: just as the work-weary among us mark time from Christmas to Easter to Thanksgiving, so did the Greeks reckon on the *olympios*, a unit of four years bounded on either side by the Games.

Learn the STARTLING TRUTH that their failure to license the linguistic rights to this holiday is WHY THE ROMANS CONQUERED THEM!

Yes, because the Greek Empire didn't sue people for profane use of the word "Olympic," the Empire crumbled. It took the Caesars (from Julius to Syd) to show them what was what. The Romans began joining in the Games with the conquered Greeks, who had the "gaul" (pun copyright J. Miller, 2003) to kick up a jealous fit when the Romans started the long and arduous process of commercializing amateur athletics.

"The Greeks charged that the Roman champions had capitalized on their newly gained fame," one account of the early Games says, "by going on tours and accepting cash, or some material equivalent, for making public appearances." Finally, sick and tired of having to justify themselves for simply trying to put a little souvlaki on the table, the Roman athletes rioted at one Olympiad™ "and wrecked about everything that was wreckable in and around the Stadium."

As a result, in 392 A.D., Emperor Theodosius banned the Games as a public nuisance. They were not held again until 1892, and even then, incredibly, they were re-instituted not for financial gain but for the sake of world harmony! Try to buy a cup of coffee with that!

So you see, you will have to act *immediately*! If the liberals or social workers or other commies get in charge of things, or even of THIS ENTIRE COUNTRY, which they may do ANY DAY NOW, they could ban our God-given right to sue Greek restaurants named "Olympus Fine Foods."

Rather than employing thousands in chains of official Olympic shishkebob drive-thrus and balalaika bars, multi-national corporations would be stuck freezing Big Macs in the dark! Santa Claus would be locked in the public domain, everybody's whore instead of YOURS! And the Tishe B'Ab bumper-sticker industry could be open to foreigners!

Let's face it: in this age of the Fourth Empire (Greek, Roman, British, Your Name Here), the really New Testament is the bank book. If you doubt this, consider that in 1986, potentates in Vancouver, B.C., sold a novelty company based in Seattle, Washington, the exclusive use of the (Vancouver) Expo '86 logo — the maple leaf that serves as Canada's national symbol — as well as exclusive use of the word "Canada." Roll on, free trade!

And if you don't think there is pecuniary value in the words "Tishe B'Ab"™ (which in Hebrew means "the ninth of [the month of] Ab and commemorates the destruction of the Jewish Temple in 70 A.D. by Vespasian, Roman EMPEROR, SPORTSMAN, AND GENIUS ENTREPRENEUR who constructed the Colosseum, where, for a very reasonable fee, you could watch lions eat Christian trademark violators), consider that, according to the *Wall Street Journal*, one memorable Tishe B'Ab, producers of a talk show in the U.S. sent Barbra Streisand flowers in honor of the holiday — on the chance that the singer might grant them an interview out of gratitude.

33 Not everybody's smiling when they say "Gruyère"

> *Basically, from the technical point of view, they don't accept the minimum maturation period stipulated by the proposed regulations. . . . There are about 15 such objectors. Several of them are advised by Maître Jost, in Berne. The Gruyère Producers Association deplores the attitude of this lawyer. Jost is using his opposition to the regulations to mount a personal crusade against gruyère.*

Yes, Phillipe Bardet, the director of the Gruyère Producers Association (*L'Interprofession Gruyère*), is talking about Swiss cheese. And, yes, he's accusing a Swiss lawyer of hating it, passionately.

For some time now, Bardet's Swiss association has been trying to get gruyère — "the one without the holes," as some people put it — registered under the *appellation d'origine contrôlée* system. We've seen those words on wine bottles, of course, where they mean that, if the label says *appellation contrôlée St.-Emilion*, for example, the wine is a genuine St.-Emilion. It actually comes from what French law defines as the St.-Emilion region and complies with all laws guaranteeing that it *tastes* like it came from there: it hasn't been mixed with juice from other regions or otherwise had its quality compromised below a certain rigorously enforced standard. Absent fraud, it's the real deal. And, since 1980, although probably most people in the rest of the world don't know it, France has had a similar regulatory system for cheese.

Apparently it was too late for camembert and brie, because they already had suffered the fate that the *appellation contrôlée* system seeks to prevent: everybody and his sister floods the market with a certain product in a race to the bottom as far as quality is concerned — a race, it sometimes seems, to see who can sell the most insipid milk curd at the highest price. In fact, it looks like it's too late for that *other* Swiss cheese — the one most North Americans think of as *the* Swiss cheese — Emmenthal, the Swiss cheese with the prominent holes. (Mind you, just as some gruyère can be a little holey — the proposed regulations go so far as to say that a few tiny holes, four to six millimetres in size, are "desirable" — Emmenthal can be without holes or "blind," as Swiss cheesemakers say.) Eighty-eight percent of Emmenthal is made outside of Switzerland, whereas 74 percent of gruyère is still manufactured there. And Bardet's association is determined that Emmenthal's fate will not befall their beloved *fromage dur*.

Or, rather, their beloved gruyère "pâtes" (rounds of cheese), "smooth and slightly moist . . . velvety, with medium firmness, a modest tendency to crumble . . . [and] a uniform ivorine color that can vary according to the season." That, anyway, is what the regulation demands, and a long, fussy document it is. Gruyère's taste, for instance, must be

> *sustained by a more or less salty note, with fruitiness dominating, by virtue of the coordination of lactic fermentation and the natural milk flavor. It can vary according to the particular quality of the maker's pastures [* le terroir, *the same word that wine producers use for their vineyards and vines].*

And makers are forbidden to use growth activators or hormones to help along the bacteria that creates the cheese.

If you think that stipulating an "ivorine" color is, well, rather Swiss, consider the packaging regulations for gruyère. The "authorized colors" for the text on the label are "Pantone black, Pantone white, Pantone 287c blue, Pantone 032c red" — Pantone being an international inking standard used by art directors and printers. The background color must "coordinate aesthetically with the text," and the word *Gruyère* must be twice as big as anything else.

Because of opposition in Switzerland to the *appellation contrôlée* proposals, the gruyère regulators have agreed to reduce the minimum ripening period from five months to three. But some non-traditionalists have been holding out for a minimum as short as six weeks. And you can't altogether blame them, or their lawyers, for being nervous about the proposal generally. They amount to voluntarily subjecting your business to yet another level of government. Indeed, Bardet seems to be in the traditionalist regulatory camp, and he's frustrated with the delays. "It's simple," he says. "For the *appellation contrôlée* system to take flight in Switzerland, it needs gruyère.... Everything revolves around gruyère. That might seem pretentious, but it's true: gruyère is one of the benchmarks for Swiss cheese."

Could this be a sniper's pot-shot at Switzerland's lesser-known

Etivaz cheese, which has already got its pedigree papers under the appellation system? Maybe so, but time really is a-wastin' for gruyère: the debate has ripened, you might say, and threatens to drag on past its "best before" date. In 2005, the European Union is set to loosen its own regulation of cheese, and then gruyère could be anybody's baby, not just that velvety and slightly moist pâte from strictly-defined Swiss regions.

Meanwhile, Bardet has no time for Maître Jost, the lawyer who he says has no respect for the superiority of gruyère over so many other cheeses. "It's just too much! If gruyère doesn't get its *appellation*, the small makers represented by Me. Jost will have no future, and in some cases might even disappear altogether."

34 Where there's life, there's lawsuits

If ever there was a doubt which sex the multinational breweries usually put their money on, Budweiser's most familiar slogan clears it up: "I'm a Bud man!" The last word is pronounced "main" in Budweiser commercials — *sneered*, really — evidently because plain "man" ain't mainly enough. But for something over 40 years, the Budweiser slogan was ahead of its time in terms of sexual egalitarianism. It was in 1933 that Anheuser-Busch, the Budweiser brewers, first proclaimed (without sneering), "Where there's life . . . there's Budweiser." This seemed to include females.

From 1956 on, Anheuser spent nearly $50 million promoting this slogan, eventually feeling that the public had become so familiar with their product as to call it by its nickname, "Bud." Why the slogan finally fell out of favor probably has nothing to do with Bud turning up in morgues or war zones. Bud and life parted on the whim, probably, of some advertising guy in search of a fresh 50 million from the brewery. And maybe, in its crackerjack southern way, the Chemical Corporation of America had a little to do with the slogan change, too.

Early "Saturday Night Live" television shows featured a parody of high-pressure TV commercials in which Dan Ackroyd hocked a dessert topping that was also a floor wax. As far as the Chemical Corporation of America was concerned, a floor wax that could do double duty was not necessarily a joke. During the 1960s, Chem. Corp. was marketing a product called Freewax. It was a combination floor wax and insecticide.

The primary market for Freewax was the southern U.S., where Chem. Corp. had been promoting it with the line, "Life on floors ... Death on Bugs." But somewhere along the way, someone in their marketing department did decide that a joke could sell Freewax, serious though the exotic product was. In the summer of 1960, TV viewers in the distribution area for Freewax began seeing a commercial featuring the sort of party-time atmosphere common in beer commercials even today, including Budweiser commercials — an atmosphere that linked lagers and ales with blue-eyed virility, burgers and pizza (no quiche), and scoring in more ways than one. The slogan accompanying this Freewax beer-style commercial was, "Where there's life ... there's Bugs."

Athough most consumers were likely to share more of life with bugs than with beer, Anheuser-Busch won a permanent injunction against Chem. Corp. on the basis that the bug slogan could have created trademark confusion — "the impression" that Chem. Corp.'s "advertizing had some connection with" Anheuser-Busch. When Chem. Corp. appealed, the court felt "an instinctive reaction" that Chem. Corp. was making "a brazen and cheap effort ... to capitalize on the goodwill created by the tremendous advertising expenditure" by Anheuser. The Freewax commercial, the court said, seemed "to fairly reek with unfairness and callous indifference."

Beer and blondes are more commonly associated in advertizing than beer and bugs, of course (making another broad hint at the real target market), and the cases say that the blondes can be as trademarkable as the beer slogans. Such, anyway, is the idea advanced in *The Dallas Cowboys Cheerleaders v. Pussycat Cinema*.

U.S. courts have cited the *Dallas Cowboys* as standing for the proposition that freedom of speech can co-exist with protection of trademarks. But the Dallas cheerleaders were worried less about freedom of speech than about how people might confuse them with the star of *Debbie Does Dallas*, a film distributed by Pussycat's proprietor, Michael Zaffarano, in the late 1970s. According to Judge Van Graafeiland of the U.S. Court of Appeals for Southern New York, *Debbie Does Dallas* was

> *a gross and revolting sex film whose plot, to the extent that there is one, involves a cheerleader at a fictional high school who has been selected to become a "Texas Cowgirl." In order to raise enough money to send Debbie . . . to Dallas, the cheerleaders perform sexual services for a fee. The movie consists largely of a series of scenes graphically depicting the sexual escapades of the "actors." In the movie's final scene Debbie dons a uniform strikingly similar to that worn by the Dallas Cowboys Cheerleaders and for approximately twelve minutes of film footage engages in various sex acts while clad or partially clad in the uniform.*
>
> *Defendants [Pussycat Cinema] advertized the movie with marquee posters depicting Debbie in the allegedly infringing uniform and containing such captions as "Starring Ex Dallas Cowgirl Cheerleader Bambi Woods" and "You'll do more than cheer for this X Dallas Cheerleader."*

In footnotes, Judge Van Graafeiland noted that 1) the Dallas

Cowboy Cheerleaders were also known as the "Dallas Cowgirls"; 2) Bambi Woods "is not now and never has been a Dallas Cowboys Cheerleader"; 3) whether the movie was obscene was none of his judicial business. All the same, he could not agree with defendant Zaffarano, of Pussycat, that the uniform the Dallas cheerleaders wore was purely functional and "generic." The Cowboys had a common-law (that is, unregistered) trademark, Judge Van Graafeiland ruled, in the "particular combination of colors and collocation of decorations of the uniform" — white vinyl boots, white shorts, a white belt decorated with blue stars, a blue bolero blouse, and a white vest decorated with three blue stars on each side of the front and a white fringe around the bottom.

In affirming the Cowboys' injunction against Pussycat, his honor concluded that "it is hard to believe that anyone who had seen the defendants' sexually depraved film could ever thereafter disassociate it from the plaintiff's cheerleaders."

35 Miami J'yce counsel on the lookout for synteresis

James Joyce spent seven years writing his *magnum opus Ulysses* and finally published it in 1922. When his estate's copyright expired in 1991, the only authorized *Ulysses* in print was the 1986 edition, based on literary archaeology performed by German scholar Hans Gabler and his computer. Scavenging for every available clue to Joyce's seven-year writing delirium, Gabler "restored" material to the 1922 edition from manuscript and proofs. In all, he made some 5,000 changes, claiming that they were based on Joyce's original creative intention.

It is an assertion that has caused a good deal of teeth-gnashing, even among the usually pacific readers of the *New York Review of Books*. Behind it lies the ever-widening controversy over whether Gabler's *Ulysses* is legally a "derivative work" — a new *magnum opus* that attracts a whole new copyright, assuring the Joyce estate continued royalties and copyright control. The two disputes mixed explosively in the winter of 1988, literary politics coming face to fist with the law at the University of Miami. Joyceans from across the world had convened there for an academic pow-wow called, after its subject's punning penchant, "Miami J'yce."

The most unlikely participant was probably William Dunaj (pronounced Duh-NAY), a Florida specialist in intellectual property whose clients have included real estate magnate Markborough Properties and the Hudson's Bay Company. Dunaj carried no brief to talk about stream-of-consciousness or literary Dublin. He was on hand to troop the colors for academic freedom.

Dunaj says that in anticipation of the conference the trustees of the Joyce estate had threatened to sue anyone who so much as *mentioned* the author without their approval. The university's counsel and staff therefore had asked him to address the symposium on what was legally safe for Joyce scholars to handle — what was "fair use." Clive Hart, a Joyce expert and one of the trustees, assured the symposium that the estate's bark was worse than any intended bite. He promised quick approval of most requests. In turn, Dunaj assured Hart that, outside genuine copyright matters, this was like Hart's promising to let the sun rise. "He said they were not trying to stifle debate, and I basically said, 'Well, good, you don't have a right to stifle debate.'"

More lately, Joyce scholar and intellectual property lawyer Robert Spoo has claimed that Joyce never managed to copyright the first edition of *Ulysses* in the U.S. at all. Because that edition, published in Paris in 1922, was banned from the U.S. as "obscene," Joyce was unable to fulfill the requirements of the 1909 *Copyright Act*.

"Under our copyright law in effect in 1922," Spoo recently told me,

> a foreign-based author writing in English was required, upon publication of the work abroad, to deposit a copy in the Copyright Office within 60 days of foreign publication, and thereafter to reprint the work in the States within another four months. Failure to comply with these requirements meant that the work could not acquire a U.S. copyright. This was our much-criticized 'manufacturing clause,' so called because it was designed to protect the interests of American printers and book manufacturers.

The Joyce Estate and Random House, the first U.S. publisher, "appear to reject this argument," Spoo elaborates,

> but after more than two years and several invitations to come forward with a counter-argument, neither the estate nor its lawyers have offered anything more than reiterated assertions that the 1934 edition is in copyright here. Random House has published three principal editions of Ulysses over the years: 1934, 1961, and 1986 (the Gabler edition). My view is that each of these texts is a derivative work in relation to the original 1922 edition and the early serial versions of Ulysses chapters appearing in the Little Review in the U.S. between 1918 and 1920 (also in the public domain here as a result of the natural expiration of their copyright terms).

In Spoo's view, the Random House works:

> enjoy only a thin derivative-work protection that prevents a user from copying them in whole or in substantial part — that is, in excess of fair use. Of the three Random House texts, Gabler's probably has the strongest claim to a derivative-work copyright because

> his edition famously incorporated 'fresh' manuscript material never before used in a Ulysses text.
>
> My campaign has been for recognition that, whatever the status of these derivative texts (and I have no desire to challenge any thin protection that they may enjoy), the 1922 Paris edition of Ulysses is in the public domain in the U.S. and therefore freely available for anyone to use here.

In a 1998 piece in the *Yale Law Journal*, Spoo elaborates:

> Whereas the illusion of American copyright once helped to compensate Joyce for the privations he had suffered at the hands of protectionism and piracy, today that illusion serves only to sustain an extra-legal monopoly that controls the availability of Ulysses and dictates the forms in which it may appear.

A new wrinkle, Spoo notes in an article he wrote for the 1999 *Joyce Studies Annual*, is added by the Internet. Spoo invites us to imagine that someone in Canada publishes a public-domain *Ulysses* on the Web. Readers in Montana and England, "places where this edition is arguably protected by copyright," download it. Parties to the infringement lawsuit? Where? Why? According to whose law?

As far as the Gabler edition is concerned, Dunaj does not see how it creates a new copyrightable work at all. "All they have done is try to go back as scholars and find out what Joyce intended to do the first time. There's no creation in that. If they're doing what they say they're doing as scholars, they're not *trying* to create" a new work, but to make the old one accurate. "That's the whole point. It's the antithesis of creation to try to find out what *was* created." Dunaj likens the *Ulysses* controversy to a case he wrote about three decades ago in his master's thesis on copyright. In the 1909 *Aeolian Piano* case, the U.S. Supreme Court held that a piano-roll was not capable of copyright. Even though there existed no other way of recording music at the time, the piano rolls were not "creative works" but "essentially the work of an engineer working from the sheet music." "My feeling about the new *Ulysses*," Dunaj says, "is that the editor did the same thing: we have now an engineer, not an author, going back and trying to find out what James Joyce intended to publish in the first place."

Such revisions have become a cottage industry. Hart himself has co-written a "repair kit" to the Gabler *Ulysses*, even though he was one of its sponsors. And Boston Joyce scholar John Kidd has weighed in against Gabler's 5,000 changes with 20,000 of his own. Most controversial is Gabler's inclusion of a passage concluding "Love, yes. Word known to all men." Many readers feel that these few words make the entire massive and difficult book more comprehensible and "human." They accept Gabler's view that Joyce's typist left them out in error (the original manuscript being lost, Gabler discovered the love passage in a manuscript Joyce had copied out in his own hand to sell for pocket money). Despite the supposed significance of the lines, Gabler feels that Joyce didn't notice their omission in the page proofs. For many years, much ink was expended on whether it was love that was known to all men, or death (the passage being associated with the dead mother of a central character in the book), or, in one case, "synteresis" (conscience), which struck one Joyce expert as a word "unknown to all men."

Still, at "Miami J'yce," Hart declared that *Ulysses* should represent what Joyce managed to do, not what we speculate he wanted to do. His repair kit deletes the love passage, just when everyone was beginning to think they could use it to make sense at last of *Ulysses*. Of course, obfuscation is what keeps both academics and lawyers in business.

Academic Hart was a hard act to follow, but Dunaj upstaged him, inadvertently. Because the lawyer had been invited to speak only on general fair use issues, he was unaware of the controversy about the newer *Ulysses*. He had not heard accusations from the conferees that the Joyce estate had rushed the Gabler edition, which even they now said was inaccurate, to try to get a new copyright. He had not heard the bitter fights about whose *Ulysses* was Joyce's *Ulysses*. So when one professor coyly asked "if someone added a little bit, say about love," would that make a new copyright, Dunaj innocently inquired if the love passage was part of Joyce's original 1922 intention. As Brenda Maddox put it in the *New York Times*, "It is not often that a question from a copyright lawyer brings down the house."

36 Igpay Atinlay oesgay to ourtkay

Iyay on'tday etgay isthay isnessbay boutyay Apsternay andyay Igpay Atinlay. (Translation: I don't get this business about Napster and Pig Latin.)

Napster, of course, is the cyberspace middleman that provides a website where visitors can trade MP3 music files. Although Napster itself does not supply the files, courts in the United States have found that it could well be infringing copyright vicariously and by contributing to infringement. In response, and pending full trial of the issues as I write, Napster has agreed to block certain recorded music titles, in an attempt to stop downloading without payment of royalties to the copyright holders who assert it.

A Toronto firm has designed software that uses a variation of Pig Latin to help would-be infringers circumvent the blocks. Apparently the message goes out that Jane in Pugwash, Nova Scotia, is looking for something like "Ancingd EenQ," and because Napster has blocked only "Dancing Queen," the request gets through to Nelson in Harare, who is willing to share his ABBA files. I'm no Bill Gates, but can't Napster simply use a similar program to block Pig Latinate versions of blocked titles?

The legal issues are somewhat more vexing. Sheldon Burshtein, an intellectual property expert at the Blake Cassels law firm in Toronto, can't see how the Pig Latin software would be an infringing use in itself. "If you sell someone a crowbar," he says, "and he uses it in breaking and entering somewhere, selling the crowbar doesn't constitute breaking and entering." Canadian law does not include what U.S law calls vicarious and contributory infringement (aiding or abetting an infringement without actually performing the infringing act, rather like the driver of the getaway car). However, in this country it is unlawful to authorize infringement, which includes countenancing and approving an infringement, Burshtein explains. My own non-specialist answer to that is, if the "rowbarkay" is sold (or given) intentionally for the specific use of breaking and entering, it's an infringing crowbar: the seller has countenanced and approved the infringement. After all, a "housebreaking instrument," as the criminal law calls it, is a screwdriver by another name.

In this respect, I would be surprised if our law is much different from that in the U.S. As Judge Robert Beezer has said in affirming the interlocutory injunction against Napster at the Ninth Circuit Court of Appeals, service providers are not "liable for contributory infringement merely because the structure of the system allows for the exchange of copyrighted material." However, as District Judge Marilyn Hall Patel held in the court below, Napster probably infringes because it "has actual knowledge that specific infringing material is available using its system" — a restatement of the ancient common law principle of *scienter:* if you know something fishy is going on and turn a blind eye, you're not off the hook.

Which brings us back to legal Latin. Pig Latin originally was "Dog Latin," said to have become popular with "Dog Greek" among young scholars messing around with mongrel ("doggerel") versions of what they learned in school. There is some case law precedent for the use of Pig Latin as thieves' cant — as a villain's method, that is, of trying to hide what he was doing from the coppers — particularly in the United States. And Pig Latin came up about ten years ago in intellectual property law proper when a Vancouver man sued director George Lucas for supposedly appropriating "his furry creatures" called Ewoks.

The plaintiff, Dean Preston, said that he developed the name and concept while playing around with the song title "I Walk Alone," giving it a cockney twist in the second person — "'E Walks. . . ." George Lucas of course used furry Ewoks in his *Star Wars* sequel, *Return of the Jedi*. He testified that he developed the characters from the related Wookiee creatures in *Star Wars*: "It is a moving around the letters of Wookiee," Lucas told the court.

> *I took the end of Wookiee, the 'ie' off Wookiee, and put it at the head, like Pig Latin, and then started, when I said it phonetically, it sounded like Ewok which is very similar to Miwok which is the Indians that sort of inhabited the area where I live and where my studio is. Matter of fact, there was a Miwok village just outside my office. So I thought that was a nice, nice sort of reverberation of the idea and eventually took the 'i' and one of the 'os' out and it was Ewok.*

Preston's lawsuit failed.

Then there is the recent U.S. case in which at least the dissent seems to view the use of the words "Pig Latin" itself as a way to circumvent the law. At issue in *Lenz Hardware v. Wilson* was whether Wilson had defamed the vice-president of Lenz Hardware in a "penny-saver ad" in a community newspaper. Wilson ran a competing hardware store in St. Johnsville, New York, population 1,800. His ad featured a "compare and save" list of items, showing the cost at

Lenz for each item, and the lower cost at Wilson's own store. The bottom of the ad read: "No Coupon Necessary at St. Johnsville Hardware. We have friendly, fast service. We Speak English, Plumbing, Farming and Dabble in Pig Latin."

Myong S. Daley, Lenz's vice-president, claimed that "We speak English" was defamatory of her because she was of Korean origin. The majority of the Supreme Court of New York Court dismissed the case on the ground that there was no connection in the ad between Daley and "We Speak English." However, dissenting Justice Peters wrote that "the majority should have found relevant the population of the community . . . and the limited area where the advertizement was circulated." In other words, given the setting, the ad was a poke at Daley.

They aren't teaching Pig Latin as a first-year law subject yet, but then, who'd heard of information technology law — or Napster — eight or nine years ago?

CHAPTER SIX

ALL IN THE FAMILY

Family Law

37 Before his passion had time to cool

> *Neither can he be thought guilty of a greater Crime [than manslaughter], who finding a Man in Bed with his Wife, or being actually struck by him, or pulled by the Nose, or filliped upon the Forehead, immediately kills him.*
>
> HAWKINS, A TREATISE OF THE PLEAS OF THE CROWN, 1716, CHAPTER 31, SECTION 36.

"It used to be in the United States, that if you came home and found your wife in bed with the postman, it was perfectly okay to get your shotgun and blow the heads off the both of them."

Professors of criminal law like to impress their students with the "unwritten law of adulterous provocation." It is seldom part of the curriculum; usually, it is just one of those subjects that seems to present itself off-the-cuff, a professorial ploy to keep lectures interesting, something the students can regale friends and family with over dinner. In some classrooms, the unwritten law is limited to the southern United States or to Texas. In my case, at a Canadian law school, the entire U.S.A. (with the possible exception of Alaska and Hawaii) was implicated.

My professor probably had heard the same story in slightly different language from his own professor of introductory criminal law. Rather than gustily losing their heads, perhaps the lovers were "filled full of lead," or the husband treated his wife to a shotgun divorce. In a leading textbook on criminal law, La Fave and Scott note, "In the adultery situation there is a popular belief that it is not the crime of voluntary manslaughter, but rather, no crime at all for the enraged husband to kill his wife's paramour."

Although the unwritten law, or at least the common law, has always recognized the provocative nature of adultery, only exceptionally has it altogether excused killings provoked by marital infidelity. In 1716, William Hawkins stated the law as it still exists in many jurisdictions: if a spouse discovers *in flagrante* adultery and gets the irresistible urge to attack, he (and now she) will be guilty of manslaughter and not murder. In other words, there was still a punishable homicide.

In Hawkins' day, even lawyers viewed such a crime as very much the least blameworthy form of homicide. As the 18th-century legal historian Blackstone says in his discussion of provocation:

> *So also if a man be greatly provoked, as by pulling his nose, or other great indignity, and immediately kills the aggressor, though this is not excusable, se defendo, since there is no absolute necessity for doing it to preserve himself; yet neither is it murder, for there is no previous malice; but it is manslaughter. But in this, and in every other case of homicide upon provocation, if there be a sufficient cooling-time for passion to subside and reason to interpose, and the*

> *person so provoked afterwards kills the other, this is deliberate revenge and not heat of blood, and accordingly amounts to murder. So, if a man takes another in the act of adultery with his wife, and kills him directly upon the spot, though this was allowed by the law of Solon as likewise by the Roman civil law (if the adulterer was found in the husband's own house) and also among the ancient Goths, yet in England it is not absolutely ranked in the class of justifiable homicide, as in the case of a forcible rape, but it is manslaughter. It is however the lowest degree of it: and therefore in such a case the court directed the burning in the hand to be gently inflicted, because there could not be a greater provocation.*

With "such a case," Blackstone is referring to the 1683 prosecution of John Maddy, who brained Frank Mavers with a stool upon surprising him in bed with Mrs. Maddy. The Court of King's Bench accepted a plea of provocation and convicted Maddy of manslaughter instead of murder. Then, accepting Maddy's plea of clergy,* the judges released him after directing "the executioner to burn [his thumb] gently [to mark the fact that he now had a criminal record], because there could be no greater provocation than this."

A fearsome problem with any law that would excuse homicide for in-the-act adultery is that it might *encourage* adultery: a spouse might suspect adultery, for instance, but say nothing or even facilitate a tryst so that he can do away with the illicit lovers. To answer this and similar problems, the common law has held that discovering your spouse in the act of adultery will not by itself support a defense of provocation. On any plea of provocation — arising from adultery or from anything else — the accused must have killed, as Blackstone suggests,

---

*A plea for mercy, generally for those who were literate. Burning the thumb recorded the fact that the convict had used up his share of the state's forbearance. See page 178.

"on the sudden and before his passion had time to cool."* The accused cannot facilitate the compromising circumstances based on knowledge or suspicion of past adultery. And, as Blackstone suggests, provocation is never a "complete" defense; it merely reduces a murder charge to one of manslaughter or "unpremeditated homicide."

Generally, the "unwritten law," or "honor defense" as it is occasionally called, imposes no such explicit conditions. Most dramatically, it supersedes 16th-century tendencies to leniency toward cuckolds and makes adulterous provocation a complete defense.

The legendary unwritten law of adulterous provocation finds its counterpart in the law books, but mostly as a written law, on the statute books of three of the United States. At one time, in Utah, New Mexico, and, yes, Texas, legislation provided that if one discovered his spouse *in flagrante delicto*, killing at least the interloper was "justifiable homicide."

Article 1102 of The Texas *Penal Code* provided that

> *a homicide is justifiable when committed by the husband upon the person of any one taken in the act of adultery with the wife; provided the killing take place before the parties to the act of adultery have separated.*

In *The Law of the Land*, Charles Rembar compares this to the Anglo-Saxon *infangthief*: "A man who had been attacked and injured had the right to kill whoever injured him, a notion the great state of Texas has conserved for the benefit of cuckolds."

Bizarre to say, by virtue of this provision a Texas husband (not a

---

* Section 232(2) of the Canadian *Criminal Code*, a fairly clear summary of the British-American common law, directs that a "wrongful act or insult that is of such a nature as to be sufficient to deprive an ordinary person of the power of self-control is provocation enough . . . if the accused acted on it on the sudden and before there was time for his passion to cool."

wife) could get away with murder on discovering *in flagrante* adultery, but not with "mere" mayhem. In 1922, a Texan named Sensobaugh caught his wife and her lover in compromising circumstances. He "pulled a gun" on the man and tied him up, specifically telling him that he didn't want to kill him. Instead, he cut off the man's penis with a razor, for which mercy the Dallas County Court convicted him of criminal assault.

Sensobaugh appealed, claiming that article 1102 provided him a defense. If you could kill someone for having sex with your wife, why couldn't you simply make a gelding of the same rogue stallion? The Court of Criminal Appeals admitted that if only Sensobaugh had annihilated the lover, or at least cut off his genitals with the intent to make him bleed to death, the law would probably have held him blameless. But this was a case of cold-blooded forbearance, a fate for Sensobaugh, if not the lover, worse than death. The appeals court affirmed his fine of $300 and jail sentence of 60 days.

In jurisdictions lacking a complete statutory defense to adulterous provocation, juries have occasionally moved beyond *Maddy's Case*, more or less imposing the legendary unwritten law, finding an avenging cuckold not guilty even of manslaughter. The same year that *Sensobaugh* reached the law courts, Kentucky law professor W. Lewis Roberts went so far as to propose that, as rather frequent democratic expressions of "the popular will" in the southern U.S., jury acquittals in "unwritten law" cases ought to be recognized as binding precedent — as modifying the common law.

The state of Georgia seems to have granted Prof. Roberts' wish, for a time, in the sense that the local courts interpreted statutory criminal law so as to make adulterous provocation a complete defense, in the mould of self-defense: "A killing to prevent the beginning or the completion of an adulterous act," one court ruled in 1948, "is justifiable homicide under the law." The statute did not provide the defense explicitly, and even the judicial or "unwritten" law did not permit the killing of the wife: "Killing the lover to prevent adultery could be justifiable homicide to protect the marriage," another Georgia court said as late as 1977, "though killing the spouse could not be justifiable because it would terminate the marriage." The Georgia unwritten law was nothing if not "logical."

In the 1977 *Burger* case, the cuckolded husband had spied on his wife and her paramour for some time. Waiting one day until they were engaged in flagrantly compromising behavior, he shot both of them. The court called his plea of justifiable homicide an "absurd and dangerous" judicial creation, and concluded:

> *In this day of no-fault, on-demand divorce when adultery is merely a misdemeanor, and when there is a debate raging in the country about whether capital punishment even for the most heinous crimes is proper, any idea that a spouse is ever justified in taking the life of another — adulterous spouse or illicit lover — to prevent adultery is uncivilized. This is murder; and henceforth, nothing more appearing, an instruction of justifiable homicide may not be given.*

But lately it has become debatable whether North American common law continues to heed this caution. In some situations there seems to be an increasing tendency to permit a "cooling-off period," or at least a quiescent gap that does not count against accused who kill long after actual provocative events, but are said to be "provoked" into irrational homicide by a course of past wrongs.

The recent *Menendez* case has become notorious for this: two brothers admitted killing their parents after premeditation and planning, but won mistrials by blurring provocation with self-defense and "temporary insanity," complaining that long-term abuse by the parents had driven them to desperate measures.

A related but more sympathetic trend involves the abused spouse who kills her sleeping or incapacitated husband. Although abuse is not manifest just before the killing, the husband's chronically brutal nature might convince the trier (or a sentencing judge) that, psychologically, for the abused woman there is no "cooling-off" period; there is no gap to bridge between the abuse and the homicide. Again, defense lawyers characterize such cases as transcending provocation explicitly, to become self-defense or temporary insanity situations. Because of the inference that the woman couldn't help going to extremes, despite the outwardly quiescent gap, the cases have an "I just snapped" feel about them.

Unfortunately, abusers can use such defenses, framed in terms of "dissociative states" or "temporary insanity" — and sometimes apparently aimed at exploiting folk belief rather than working justice — as readily as those they bully. Prosecutions in our age of talk-show psychotherapy have featured claims that consumption of sugary junk food or incessant nagging catalyzed a killer's ruminations on betrayal into homicidal psychotic breaks. Given that such pleas are offered not in mitigation of admittedly wrong behavior — not as evidence of provocation, *per se* — but as evidence of a complete defense to homicide, they can seem to be attempts to "make true" unwritten or borderline law, dressed as science.

Fortunately or not, defenses at this extreme have not enjoyed much success. The fact that they sometimes have been given folk names — the "Twinkie defense," the "Jewish-American Princess" defence — and have incorporated popular psycho-social trends, demonstrates how folk belief and the law can mingle rather freely. But it also betrays the skepticism the defenses encounter in some quarters, as, indeed, desperate appeals to mass ignorance or prejudice.

In any event, 25 years after *Burger* it seems inconceivable that anyone in the U.S. or Canada would raise adultery as a complete defence to homicide. As the court there suggests, it is inconceivable that Burger himself raised it in 1977.

38 If you're not pregnant, it wasn't adultery

I don't know when I first heard the word *adultery*, but I think I understood it to be something nasty right away. The clue, probably, was the context, the way it was said (muttered? snarled? whispered?). I at least took it to mean what it seemed to say: that only adults could do it.

I may even have heard Woody Allen's adultery routine at the time, the one about how a lawyer told him that in order to get a divorce there had to be a flagrant act of illegal connection. He volunteered. His wife, however, beat him to it, he said, although she claimed later that she had been "violated." She sued, Allen added, when he remarked in public that it could not have been a moving violation.

In any event, I, child, did not understand that *adultery* was closer to *adulterate* (corrupt, spoil) than *adult*, an honest enough mistake, especially considering that even people who were committing it claimed that they didn't know what it was.

In 1948, for instance, there was the *Barnacle* case. Mrs. Barnacle accused her husband of adultery and obtained a divorce decree, at which point the king's proctor (a Crown lawyer) discovered that at the time of her petition she herself had been shacking up with a lover. The court berated her solicitor for being too tactful with her, but you have to wonder what the poor sod was supposed to do with a client who thought she wasn't committing adultery unless she got pregnant in the process.

The trial judge, Justice Wallington, fumed that it was high time that solicitors laid it on the line for the self-professed naive client. He, himself, was weary of hearing men of the world, "well-educated and well-informed businessmen of 40 and upwards," who thought it was adultery only if the woman was under 50 — the obverse of my childhood philology that only adults qualified. Sometimes the definition was significantly less restrictive, at least in the experience of the king's proctor. He testified that he had also heard people swear that adultery was "getting a girl in trouble," "drinking with men in public houses," and possible only after sunset.

A jury in an 1836 lawsuit for criminal conversation — an action in which the wronged spouse sues his partner's lover — refused to believe that adultery could take place on a public pathway during daylight, not to mention in a library under circumstances carefully sidestepped in the case report. But when the case was appealed, the reviewing court could not restrain itself from ordering a new trial, considering that the defendant lover, a lawyer, had been found hiding in a closet in the plaintiff husband's house, coming and going at odd hours (sometimes with his boots off), and spending half an hour in a stable with plaintiff's wife.

Four years before *Barnacle*, Justice Wallington himself refused to believe that adultery was possible in the cab of a truck. He declined to grant the husband a divorce based on the wife's adultery. When the husband appealed, Lord Greene, the Master of the Rolls, took exception to Justice Wallington's conclusion that because the alleged adulterers disappeared from view they had ended up on the cab floor. Lord Greene agreed that anything approaching genuine adultery would have been impossible down there, but added that the learned trial judge perhaps should have resisted falling back "on his own knowledge of the layout and dimensions of the cabs of lorries." "Their disappearance from view," his lordship wrote of the impugned couple, "was clearly consistent with their bodies being supported in a semi-recumbent position by parts of the seat next to the driver's seat." Considering the couple's "long history of passionate intimacy, . . . there was no element of unfamiliarity or reluctance to contend with. . . . They could have overcome such inconveniences as existed." Therefore, Lord Greene could not, himself, believe that the wife had gone to the truck merely to ask the defendant to stop spreading rumors about them, and then passed the time of day discussing chickens and tomatoes with him.

In another English case six years on the other side of *Barnacle*, Justice Karminski played it even safer. "Nobody yet attempted to define adultery," he observed, "and I do not propose to rush in where wiser men have not." All the same, "manual satisfaction" — masturbation — was not adultery, his lordship held, no matter how offended a wife might feel about what her husband and his mistress were doing.

These two lines of judicial embarrassment merged, as it were, as late as 1984, when a woman in Toronto was charged with performing an indecent act by masturbating a man with her breasts in the front seat of a truck. But the prosecution was obliged to withdraw the charge when the judge found that even this was impossible. "The only way she could perform an act of masturbation," he lectured a skeptical assistant crown attorney, "is to use her hand."

"Well, your honor," the prosecutor replied, "in my respectful submission, the hand and the breast are just two different parts of the body and the act of masturbation could take place using either."

The judge admitted that there was some sense to this, but then considered the evidence that the woman had draped herself over the man, who had lain on the seat and rubbed himself against her. "There is nothing in the information read to me that indicates that she [the accused] performed any act," the judge decided, "except being there."

In a groundbreaking 1958 case, the Scottish Court of Sessions refused to believe that artificial insemination could be adultery. The presiding judge, Lord Wheatley, thought that to hold otherwise would father nightmarish extrapolations of its own. Ronald George Maclennan had not had "access," as the court puts it, to his wife Margaret Euphemia from May 31, 1954 on. All the same, she had a child 14 months later, on July 10, 1955. But when Ronald sued on the ground of adultery, Margaret denied it outright. She had been inseminated artificially, she said, with the seed of someone she didn't even know, and that was not adultery at law. Undeterred, Ronald replied, "Adultery is adultery, including with a syringe."

Reviewing the authorities from Moses to the *All England Law Reports*, Lord Wheatley disagreed. His lordship held that "the idea of *conjunctio corporum* seems to be an inherent concomitant" of adultery. "The idea," Lord Wheatley added, "that adultery might be committed by a woman alone in the privacy of her bedroom, aided and abetted only by a syringe containing semen, was one" — unfortunately for a lonely Scottish Sessions Court judge — "with which the earlier jurists had no occasion to wrestle." Still, precedent showed that a woman could be impregnated by "alien" seed without committing adultery. There were, for example, two English cases where the courts annulled marriages for non-consummation, despite the fact that children were born of the relationships. In the first case, the wife had become pregnant by artificial insemination with the husband's semen. In the second, penetration had been frustrated, but not fertilization.*

Yet while "unilateral adultery is possible," Lord Wheatley decided, "as in the case of a married man who ravishes a woman not his wife, . . . self-adultery is a conception unknown to the law" — even with a consenting syringe. Otherwise, Lord Wheatley wondered, where a physician assisted the artificial insemination, was he to be a co-respondent (and therefore subject to an action for criminal conversation)? Was the donor an adulterer? What if the donor died? Then, Lord Wheatley said, the woman would not only be an adulteress, but a necrophiliac.† No, his lordship said, adultery was not simply adulteration of the genetic line, but "the physical contact with an alien and unlawful sexual organ," a formulation that makes you think E.T. had some fun before he went home.

---

*The law even has a term of art for such an event: *fecundation ab extra*.

†For the associated legal problems in such a case, see page 75.

39 From the frying pan into the feminist fire

One mild Saturday one recent November a group of women paraded up Dundas Street in Toronto near the Eaton Centre, pulling a donkey they had made out of styrofoam and plywood. The donkey carried a mannequin, a man mannequin, riding backwards, and the women carried signs: "WIFE ASSAULT IT'S A CRIME!" "We will NOT be BATTERED."

Banging pots and pans with spoons, the women, members of the Ontario Association of Interval and Transition Houses, chanted an explanation: "There is a man in this place, has beat his wife, has beat his wife. It is a very great shame and disgrace, to all who live in this place. It is, indeed, upon my life." They later added that, to dramatize the need for stiffer sentences in family violence cases, they were staging a "charivari," a European practice (they explained) of the 1840s which humiliated wife-beaters by loudly exposing them to community scorn. One of the women told a reporter that today, "when men are convicted, they get very light sentences. It's not a deterrent; in fact, it's probably the opposite."

It is true that by the mid-19th century, British and North American law was beginning to recognize, groggily, that women might be human beings, with individual feelings, needs, and aspirations. But I have been unable to find a usage of *charivari* in English to describe the public humiliation of a woman-beater specifically.

Although it may originally have been simply onomatopoeic, like *hurly-burly*, the origin of *charivari* is uncertain. French settlers seem to have brought it to Canada, where it is more commonly pronounced and written *shivaree*. Canada exported it to Louisiana with the expulsion of the Acadians. In these parts, it usually describes the noisy callithumpian band (of pots and pans and so on) that serenades newlyweds on their wedding night. The earliest usage given in the *Oxford English Dictionary* is a definition from a 1735 dictionary:

"Mock Music, that was given to a woman that was married again immediately after the Death of her Husband."

Hence the general belief that the charivari was aimed at *women* who remarried in "indecent haste" (although it is hard to say what is decent about waiting a polite interval while you and the kids starve to death). When a second marriage was given this treatment in early Canada, the happy couple found peace only by buying it — paying off the revellers in money or refreshment.

In the late 1700s, John Long wrote in his *Voyages and Travels of an Indian Interpreter*, an account of his adventures in Canada,

> *generally, either when the man is older than the woman, or the parties have been twice married . . . they beat a charivari, hallooing out very vociferously, until the man is obliged to obtain their silence by a pecuniary contribution, or submit to be abused with the vilest language.*

By 1958, the practice had become so rowdy in Edmonton that the town council passed a bylaw forbidding it.

Still, the term *charivaris de poêlles* ("frying-pan serenades") was recorded as early as 1611 in a French-English dictionary, which defined it as, "The carting of an infamous person, graced with the harmony of tinging kettles, and frying-pan musicke." Presumably this could have included men who assaulted women, but that would not often have brought infamy at the time. A supplementary usage given by the OED comes closer to describing the Toronto parade: "A serenade . . . of incongruous or unpopular marriages, and of unpopular persons generally."

There is certainly long precedent for parading malfeasors around on lower mammals, a practice occasionally used in lieu of the pillory, the ducking-stool, or tarring and feathering. A tenancy in Somersetshire in the middle ages specified that the widow-tenant held the manor only until she married or "was found incontinent."

Remarriage was evidently a more grievous offense than fooling around (as the early use of *charivari* suggests) insofar as she could pay penance for any incontinency and take her land back if:

> She come into the next Court, riding astride upon a Ram, and in open Court do say to the Lord, if he be present, or to his Steward, these words: "For mine Arse's Fault take I this Pain, Therefore, my Lord, give me my Land again."

Jackass-parading could also be a form of consumer protection. In the 14th century, tradesmen who indulged in sharp practices were sometimes led through the street on the animals, with their faulty wares, and sometimes urinals, strung from their necks. Town records tell of bakers taking a humiliation-ride wearing a necklace of their underweight loaves.

As little as 15 years ago, in New Delhi, more than 50 men were paraded on donkeys for having brawled in the streets on New Year's Eve. Some were made to display signs that said, "This is going to be the fate of bad characters in 1986."

Of course, animals have made asses of humans more directly. In *Beastly Law*, British barrister Fenton Bresler quotes a story of Sir Walter Scott's about a trespassing cow in Forfarshire. The cow allegedly had drunk some homebrew that had been set out on a porch to cool. When the brewer sued the cow's owner, the presiding judge held for the cow. Because the cow was *standing* when it drank, the drink was *deoch an dornis* — a "stirrup cup," the libation traditionally offered travelers "at the start of a journey, for which no charge could be made without violating the ancient hospitality of Scotland."

Whether a charivari, or callithump of whatever description, has any effect in the streets of a big city in modern times is another matter. Even on a Saturday near Christmas, when the jaded natives give the Eaton Centre over to less cynical visitors from the suburbs and beyond, hardly anyone took any notice of Toronto's styrofoam donkey and his human accompanists.

40 Aren't your in-laws really your bylaws?

One day a poor man approached a rabbinical court with a problem: "I live in one room with my wife and children," he complained, "and now all my in-laws have moved in. I can't stand it any more. I'm going crazy."

"Do you have goats?" the rabbi asked. The man nodded, puzzled. "Bring them in the house."

A week later the man returned. "Rabbi," he said, nearly in tears. "I did what you said, even though it sounded *meshuggeh*. I brought my goats into the house, into the *house* I brought them, and now it's a worse nightmare than ever."

The rabbi nodded. "Bring in your ducks, too."

"But, rabbi, three ducks, two goats, eight people . . ."

A week later the man came back, desperate, and the rabbi said, "All right, put out the goats." The man returned the goats to the field and reported that things had improved but were still difficult. "Very well," the rabbi advised. "Put out the ducks."

The man put out the ducks and a day or two later he ran all the way to the rabbi's house to tell him what a genius he was to solve the problem of the in-laws.

This of course is an ancient version of that folk headache cure, hitting your thumb with a hammer. But it also sums up the overcrowded feeling you get about acquiring in-laws. Yet more people in your business and you can't tell them to shut up! More intimacies pushing up the pressure in your little universe, chafing and bumping until it threatens to explode and stick to the heavens, like the corned beef your mother-in-law made in the pressure cooker. How, exactly, did these people get to be your relatives "in law"? You married your spouse, after all, not the whole family tree.

According to canon law (church law, which of course preceded secular law in our legal system), you did marry the whole family tree. In canon law your in-laws were tied to you by marriage — "affinity" — in the same way that you were tied to your own family by blood, or "consanguinity." Because at marriage man and woman became one flesh (the man's), the relatives of your spouse became, in law, your own next-of-kin. To consort with them sexually was to commit incest.

It was this law which Henry VIII altered so that he could marry Katharine of Aragon, his brother's widow, making himself an ecclesiastical outlaw. You could say, in fact, that the amendment was the beginning of the Reformation. But why "in-law"? Why not "mother-*at*-law" or "father-*by*-law"?

The law is very loosey-goosey about its use of prepositions. The phrase *at common law* always grates on the ear today, for example, when what we mean is "under common law" or "by the common law." Perhaps people used to say things such as, "There's no remedy for that at the courts of common law" — as distinct from the courts of equity — and eventually they shortened this to "at common law." The trouble with such an etymology is that you'd think they also would have said "at equity," an expression you don't hear.

Attorney-at-law makes a little more sense. If you said "attorney-*in*-law" in my family before I went to law school, people would think you were talking specifically about the only lawyer we'd managed to produce, second cousin Herbie Galchinsky. We were all dignified by association, *in-law*-wise. A phrase rang constantly through my childhood, almost as much as "Push up your glasses": "Your cousin Herbie, he's a big-time lawyer." And sure enough, today Herbie's a judge.

"Attorney-*by*-law" would sound like maybe you became a lawyer by peerage — you didn't even have to go to law school to get your bar accreditation, they just, you know, *Crowned* you. And there's the chance of confusion with *bylaw*, which originally had nothing to do with prepositions.

Today *bylaw* generally means a sort of side or minor law, or law made by a sort of by-the-way government. Small potatoes. But it comes from the Danish — which is to say pre-Anglo-Saxon — *byrlog*, *byr* meaning "town or community." *Byrlaw* made its way into English to describe the town and market laws that were made by custom, outside the common law courts, and enforced by byrlawmen. Yet the ambiguity of *by* itself is ancient. In 1607 English lexicographer John Cowley defined *byrlaws* as "Laws made *obiter* or by the By, orders made in court leets or courts Baron, by common assent, for the good of those that make them, farder than the publique law doth binde."

This does not mean, of course, that bylaws cannot have pretensions. For many years, a sign on the outer wall of Christ Church Meadow in Oxford advised:

> *The meadow keepers & Constables are hereby instructed to prevent the entrance into the meadow of all beggars, all persons in ragged or very dirty clothes, persons of improper character or who are not decent in appearance & behaviour: & to prevent indecent, rude, or disorderly conduct of every description.*
>
> *To allow no handcarts or wheelbarrows, no hawkers or persons carrying parcels or bundles so as to obstruct the walks.*
>
> *To prevent the flying of kites, throwing stones, throwing balls, bowling hoops, shooting arrows, firing guns or pistols or playing*

games attended with danger or inconvenience to passersby; also fishing in the waters, catching birds or bird-nesting, or cycling.

To prevent all persons cutting names on, breaking or injuring the seats, shrubs, plants, trees or turf.

To prevent the fastening of boats or rafts to the iron palisading or riverwall & to prevent encroachments of every kind by the riverside.

Under the Anglo-Saxons, *inlaw* also had ambiguous currency. Sometimes it was the opposite of *outlaw*, a term in flippant use today but which was of extremely serious import in merrie olde Englande. Outlaws were literally beyond the protection of the law, "frendlessmen" who could be killed on sight. So it's true that Robin Hood's merry men could not have been very merry. Then again, they didn't have to put up with all those goats and ducks.

CHAPTER SEVEN

IN LAWS AND OUTLAWS

Lawmakers, Lawbreakers

41   Will this red Robin keep bob-bob-bobbin' along?

It took more than 600 years, but according to a headline in *The Times*, "Sheriff of Nottingham banishes Robin at last." Actually, though, the sheriff was not exactly committed to the idea. Also, Robin Hood has always been "banished," of course, and even the Nottingham First consortium was only thinking about killing him off for good. But this was one trial balloon destined for slings and arrows.

The consortium is a group of Nottingham businesspeople, professionals, and councillors, and their research has told them that Robin Hood is "out of date." Their chief executive has gone so far to confess that,

> As a child I never liked Robin Hood. I am afraid I always preferred

> the Sheriff of Nottingham. I even preferred Dr. Who. The Daleks were much more plausible than the Merry Men. Men in doublets and tights simply do not project the right image for a modern, vibrant city. Nottingham is the headquarters of Boots, you know . . .

Boots being the British-based pharmaceutical multi-national.

Another Nottingham First member has suggested that if a German electrical concern, say, wanted to locate in Nottingham, the symbol of an inveterate thief, poacher, and murderer on the city crest — and everywhere else in plain sight — might give the Germans the wrong idea. Indeed, apparently it is the new economics which threatens to eradicate Robin and the crumbled utopian communism for which he stands.

When pollsters asked ordinary folk all over the planet to free-associate on the word "Nottingham," all they heard back was "Robin Hood." Nottingham First considered this a bad thing. Never mind that the local council was Labour-controlled. Taking from the rich isn't what it used to be. Just ask Tony Blair. The sheriff, Roy Greensmith, a former Nottingham councillor who is now the town's mayor, suggested that Nottingham natives Torvill and Dean, the ice dancers, would have been more appropriate representatives of modern Nottingham. But his Labour-leaning heart was not really in any scheme delivering the *coup de grâce* to his old nemesis. Perhaps centuries of contention had bred a grudging respect between the two, as with an old married couple.

Sheriff Greensmith loved kitting himself out in his medieval sheriff's gear, complete with jeweled sword. And it could only have been regret wafting up between the lines when he observed, "The legend of Robin Hood is of a person with a soul and a civic conscience, a man who robbed the rich to give to the poor. That is rather out of fashion these days." Never mind the 1.5 million tourists who throng the city each year on the strength of Messrs. Hood et al.

Never mind that this highwayman with a social conscience has been a part of English culture since the 14th century or earlier. (The first written reference to him appears in *Piers Ploughman*, circa 1377.) Never mind that the Yorkshire town of Barnsley probably has a better claim to Robin and his merrie men, anyway.

The earliest versions of this renowned *Ur*-Marxist have him growing up in Barnsley, which is some 50 miles from Nottingham. A Yorkshire correspondent wrote *The Times* to point out that "the most precise map reference for him in the earliest known ballad has him raiding traffic on the A1, not far from Wentbridge." Meanwhile, Lincoln has been making a more specious claim as Robin's haunt, the local chamber of commerce seeing green in more than his "Lincoln green" tights. But of course Robin really was a no-land's man. His predatory view of regional clerics, sheriffs, and landlords put him outside the law of any jurisdiction — beyond all British law's *protection*, which is what "outlaw" meant before Hollywood gave us Clint Eastwood. As Charles Rembar has written:

> Law is shelter, and the sentence of outlawry was exposure. The outlaw was like the nonperson of some modern states, except he was not merely shorn of privileges; if it pleased the one who found him, he might be murdered, and his murderer had done well. Outlawry was defenselessness, the outlaw's state of life was dread. The merry men of Robin Hood could not have frequently been merry.

And sure enough, the earliest ballads show that they were not. Rather, they were self-righteous, rather in the way of the robber barons they plagued. Robin (like Marx) was something of a messianic figure, devoted to the Virgin Mary but otherwise not a lady's man. Maid Marian was Friar Tuck's moll; only much later was she associated, in tarted-up tales, with the ringleader. In the quasi-epic "A Gest of Robin Hood" (circa 1500), Robin instructs his followers not to interfere with the lower orders or even decent knights and squires:

> *'Thereof no force,' than sayde Robyn;*
> *'We shall do well enowe;*
> *But look ye do no husbonde harme,*
> *That tilleth with his ploughe.'*

Instead, it is bishops and archbishops his gang is to "beat and bind," and "'the high sheriff of Notyingham, / Hym holde ye in your mynde.'"

To save a similarly pious knight from losing his land to an unscrupulous monk, Robin puts up £400, with the knight pledging "Our Lady" as security for the loan. Robin then refuses repayment on the basis that he, himself, has already taken twice the debt from the divine, and thus the Virgin has discharged it. The financing seen to, Robin kills the Sheriff of Nottingham, just when they seem to be getting along. Disguised as an abbot, the king himself pursues Robin, who treats His Disguised Majesty to a dinner of his own game.

Robin is nobbled, but only briefly. Today, bad guys start out with petty thievery; in those days (as the law reports attest), the equivalent was poaching game on feudal estates. Everyone gets pardoned, but Robin can't abide the terms of the release — working in the king's service. On the pretext of making a week's pilgrimage, he gives in to that freelance, call-of-the-wild, be-your-own boss urge that has always defined him, and goes AWOL for 22 years.

But of course he has stayed in the heart and mind of world culture ever since. Or, as one modern acolyte says of Nottingham First, "They have gone crazy. Robin Hood is Nottingham. He is one the best-known figures in world history." In fact, less than a year before Sheriff Greensmith "banished" Robin, he showed unbridled enthusiasm for him as a local means of production. He told the *Independent*:

> *The Sheriff was a wicked character, no question. He was there to do*

> a job for King John, and he did it very well. Hundreds of people went out to live in the green woods because they couldn't stand any more of the floggings and the torture, and the fact that their homes were destroyed and taken from them.
>
> It is not a proud legacy, but it is one that we carry quite happily these days, because of the importance it has for the city. The legend brings in an awful lot of money.

Notice how this has the definite modern ring of down-sizing and debt-restructuring so dear to today's lords and ladies. So the smart money stays on Robin, who is going to get his hands on it one way or another.

42 Francis Bacon goes cold chicken

Did the Rosenbergs really spy for the U.S.S.R.? Was Lee Harvey Oswald a communist, Mafia dupe, lone fanatic, or all of the above? And was that really Jimmy Hoffa window-shopping with Elvis last week at the West Edmonton Mall? The common law does not answer a lot of the questions it raises — not even such historic ones as, did Sir Francis Bacon really die trying to figure out how to refrigerate fresh chicken?

Much has been made of the sordid end this famous jurist, essayist, and philosopher suffered in the 1620s. A lot of the interest in his demise seems to be simple *Schadenfreude*. Bacon was the first Queen's Counsel of all time, under Elizabeth I, as well as attorney general, keeper of the seal, and lord chancellor to James I. More than any other lawyer, Sir Francis is responsible for the establishment of the courts of equity, which softened the rigidity of the common law by applying principles of everyday fairness or, to some minds, loosey-goosey non-principles that amounted to palm-tree justice. And then, of course, some people, who can't have read his essays or sundry pronouncements, think he was Shakespeare.

Aside from sometimes being the Bard, he is best known, probably, for having been bounced off "the woolsack" (the lord chancellor's seat) after he was caught taking bribes to fix cases in Chancery. In mitigation, it must be said that Lord Chancellor Bacon gave all the appearance of wanting to get caught, taking money and gifts to fix the cases and then deciding against the would-be bribers. This amazing *chutzpah* inspired a flood of complaints, even from litigants whose bribes had paid off. Bacon put the situation best himself in perhaps his most famous dictum, although he probably didn't really intend self-reference at the moment: "A popular judge is a deformed thing, and plaudits are fitter for players than magistrates."

Despite, or maybe even because of, his disgrace, it remains curious that he's so little-mentioned in law books — compared, say, to his contemporary and famous adversary, Lord Coke, the champion of the no-nonsense common law courts and their official view that not even the sovereign was above the law. Their high-stakes competition sometimes got embarrassingly personal, in the manner of a low-stakes cock fight. Coke won the "girl" they were both after (Lady Hatton), competed against Bacon for the favors of Queen Elizabeth (who appointed Coke chief justice and attorney general), and engaged in mudslinging with Sir Francis when the two lawyers argued cases in court.

> COKE: *Mr. Bacon, if you have any tooth against me, pluck it out, for it will do you more hurt than all the teeth in your head will do you good*

BACON: *Mr. Attorney, I respect you; I fear you not, and the less you speak of your own greatness, the more I will think of it. [Here he added some other similar expressions with an insolence which cannot be expressed.]*

COKE: *I think scorn to stand upon terms of greatness toward you, who are less than little, less than the least.*

BACON: *Mr. Attorney, do not depress me so far; for I have been your better, and may be again when it please the Queen.*

As Charles Rembar has observed, Bacon was much the better lawyer than Coke, and he was certainly the wilier politician. Coke was braver and more principled, standing up to James I, insisting on the primacy of the common law courts over the sovereign supremacy as vested in equity. And history has shown Coke's view to be the more democratic, now that equity and common law are one. "Equity" in Coke's and Bacon's day did not have the same populist ring it has now, of course. It meant freedom from common law strictures, but it was basically a power-play by establishment toffs to entrench royal prerogative. In any event, as Rembar says of Bacon v. Coke, and the parallel battle of equity v. common law courts, Bacon's opportunistic advice to James "that the other courts must yield to equity's injunction remained the law after the opponents of the Stuarts triumphed, and it remains the law today."

Many say that Bacon was the best mind of his time. This ignores the fact that Shakespeare was in his way as much of a philosopher and scientist. And, *pace* the literary revisionists, Bacon was no poet. But what a formidable fellow was Sir Francis — politician, writer, jurist, scientist, "the wisest, brightest, meanest of mankind" all at once, as the poet Alexander Pope would later put it — really the sort of person we mean when we say "Renaissance man."

As with Bacon's "popular judge" dictum, many of the wise words he's remembered for make ironic reading given his disgraced end. "A wise man will make more opportunities than he finds." "If a man look sharply and attentively, he shall see fortune; for though she be blind, yet she is not invisible." Then again, "Great riches have sold more men than they have bought." And: "There is no vice that doth so cover a man with shame as to be found false and perfidious."

Some say that Sir Francis arranged for his rival Coke to be chief justice of King's Bench to clear the way for his own ascent to the attorney-generalship. Or, as he put it himself, "All rising to great place is by a winding stair." And: "If a man would cross a business that he doubts some other would handsomely and effectively move, let him pretend to wish it well, and move it himself in such sort as may foil it."

The epigrams tend to show, in part, why Sir Francis might not be remembered as Lord Coke, or even as William Blackstone is. As a lawyer, he made a great scientist, his truer interest. Coke, Blackstone, and Bacon all were ambitious. But Coke was a lawyer's lawyer, and Blackstone could seem a toadying buffoon. Sir Francis, on the other hand, was calculating in his ambition, somehow standing away from the fray while in its midst, with an always-adjudicating eye. Until his final days, he lacked the human touch.

Until his final days. At last, he proved prone to basest temptation. He was shamed into pleading guilty before a special commission, which fined him £40,000 for taking the bribes, a breathtaking sum for the day. Chief Justice Coke declared him permanently "incapable of any office, place or employment in the state or commonwealth."

There is a story that, a few years after his fall from the woolsack and out of grace, Sir Francis "caught cold," fatally, like someone in a second-rate farce, while performing an impromptu experiment in poultry refrigeration. Bacon had long been interested in thermodynamics. Several of his biographers report that this interest was in full flight when he was out driving on All Fool's Day in 1626 with the king's physician, Sir John Wedderburn. There had been a recent snowfall which, the story goes, gave Sir Francis an idea. He stopped at a cottage in Highgate and bought a hen, which the vendor slaughtered for him. Sir Francis helped her eviscerate it, the story says, right on the spot.

If this is true, it makes that old Rumpole of the Bailey joke much less clever: Mrs. Rumpole: "Is that you, Rumpole?" Horace Rumpole: "No, Hilda, it's the lord high chancellor, come to read the gas meter." In any event, after the cottager and this particular former lord high chancellor gutted the bird, together they stuffed it with snow, the theory being this would preserve it as well as salt would.

Bacon was wet and cold, the story continues, from tromping around in the snow, shopping, and stuffing chickens. He took a chill. As he got sicker, he was put up at Lord Arundel's place, there being a surplus of rooms thereabouts, seeing how the master had taken Bacon's place in the Tower lately. (Who says prison overcrowding is a modern phenomenon?) Despite being in the company of the king's own physician, Sir Francis was tucked into a damp, chilled, disused bed, wherefrom he wrote his absent host a letter, bragging that the chicken experiment — "touching the conservation and induration of BODIES" — had been a great success, although it was about to kill him.

Which, they say, proved prophetic. Apparently Sir Francis was too far gone by the time he might have turned his refrigeration experiment into a nice bowl of chicken soup, and he died on Easter, 1626. History does not record whether he had time to participate in the butchering, preservation, and curing of the seasonal ham. Renegade biographers, smelling something foul in the chicken story (snow or no snow), think maybe he did. They suspect that the disgraced Sir Francis didn't die in 1626 at all, but fled to the Continent, using the chicken story as a cover-up. Of course, the people who say this are often the same people who say Francis Bacon was really William Shakespeare, or vice versa.

One of these conspiracy theorists, Alfred Dodd, takes the famous reference to Bacon's death on the "day on which was commemorated the resurrection of our Saviour" as a hint that rumors Sir Francis had died were greatly exaggerated, and that he was "reborn" in foreign parts. Dodd agrees with another renegade that the successful experiment mentioned in the letter was actually "the induration of his own body by opium. As seemingly dead he was most probably shown to the caretaker" at Lord Arundel's.

The whole idea of traveling with the physician, this theory goes, was to try a narcotics experiment. In other words, Bacon was not only a bent judge, he was a dope fiend, too, the Timothy Leary of Jacobean times. Upon recovering, the theory concludes, Sir Francis hied himself hence to start a new life, as Shakespeare, apparently, or as a Renaissance Elvis — or history's first refrigerator salesman.

And they say you can't retrain dismissed senior executives! Granted, the bit about stuffing a chicken with snow on All Fool's Day is almost too good to be true. Modern medicine holds that you don't catch cold by *being* cold. Colds are viruses, and you can catch one quite nicely in warm, moist, close environments. In that skeptical spirit, perhaps, under the entry for Sir Francis in the index to his Bacon biography, Dodd puts quotation remarks around "death" — suggesting maybe that was Sir Francis you saw with Elvis at the West Edmonton Mall last week, not Jimmy Hoffa.

In any event, as Charles Rembar has wondered, assuming that there is some truth to the chicken story, this is one common law mystery that remains a burning — or maybe freezing — issue: exactly how ironic was Bacon's end? Was the refrigeration experiment that "killed" him as successful as he thought? Was it bronchitis that finished off the disgraced lord chancellor, or a spot of fowl gone foul?

43   Is that a tattoo on your wee thumb, there, Father Ted?

It is rudimentary Freud that, but for a strong will to overcompensate, the policeman would be a murderer. The more extravagantly sanctimonious you are, the profounder your inclination to sin. Still, we profess shock when televangelists defraud their flocks, and we blink in disbelief no matter how many times we hear of priests and Christian brothers fumbling in the dark with choirboys or students. If they can't control themselves, what hope is there for the rest of us?

So keen is our need to believe in human perfectibility that clerics can get away with murder, or at least fraud and hypocrisy. Indeed, our common law would still languish in the Dark Ages had the king not made a nervous peace with medieval ecclesiastical courts through such concessions as "benefit of clergy." Under clergy, as it was familiarly known, a man in holy orders would be tried first in the king's courts, but could then "plead his clergy," asking to have his ultimate fate decided by canon law. (The privilege was not open to women.) Ecclesiastical courts were inevitably more lenient; and where the secular courts regularly hanged even petty thieves, canon law recognized no capital offenses, not even murder.

As our original "scholars," clergymen were allowed to prove their status simply by reading from the Bible, usually the first verse of Psalm 51, which came to be called "the neck verse" by virtue of its saving so many — the numbers of the redeemed being greatly expanded once laymen who could read or mumble patches of the neck verse from memory were granted its refuge.

Although a prisoner could plead clergy on arraignment, before any determination of culpability, the neck verse seems to presume guilt. Perhaps that helps explain why it made the common law courts uncomfortable. Caught with his pants down today, a blubbering televangelist might still resort to it: "Have mercy upon me, O God, according to thy lovingkindness: according unto the multitude of thy tender mercies blot out my transgressions." But one view holds that clergy stopped juries from compassionate cheating: when they knew that a petty criminal could get mercy by clergy, they were more likely to convict. Today, that same argument is made for repealing the death penalty where it is still on the books. But another view is that clergy spurred lawlessness. A law passed in 1512, for example, under Henry VIII (clergy-baiter *ne plus ultra*), excoriated those who "little regard the punishment ... by the course of the common law ... but bear them bold of their clergy." As well, it denied the privilege to

> *persons hereafter committing murder or felony in any church, chapel or hallowed place, or of and upon malice prepense rob or murder any person or persons in the king's highway, or else rob or murder any person in his house the owner or dweller of the house, his wife, child or servant then being therein and put in fear or dread by the same.*

But so strong was the influence of the church that those "within holy orders" were excluded from the new restrictions.

Eighteen years later, King Henry's *Acte for poysonyng* made murder by administration of noxious substances high treason without benefit of clergy, the mandatory sentence being "execucion by deth by boylynge." The penalty, as well as the law, seem to have been inspired by the doings at the house of the Bishop of Rochester, whose cook, Richard Roose, a chef of "moste wyked and dampnable dysposicyon, dyd caste a certyne venym or poyson into a vessell replenysshed with yeste or barme." The adulterated drink killed rich and poor alike, the Bishop having served his leftovers to local indigents. In response, the *Acte for poysonyng* was mercilessly specific, requiring that "the said Richard Roose shalbe therfore boyled to deathe" — in, according to Sir Robert Megarry, "the pot in which he had compounded his noxious brew" — "without havynge advauntage of his clargie."

In a chapter-length discussion of clergy in his *Commentaries*, William Blackstone strongly approves of the many limitations that Henry VIII imposed on the benefit, calling it an "ill use which the popish ecclesiastics soon made of that pious respect" which "Christian princes" had accorded "the church in its infant state." Eventually, even where clergy was extended to laymen, it applied only to first offenders, who were branded on the "brawn of the thumb" as personal custodians of their own criminal records. (The brand meant they had used up their one free bite.) But Blackstone credits clergy only insofar as it evolved into a statutory mitigation available to all offenders, rich and poor, literate and illiterate.

Still, the gentleman scholar was no democrat: where he depicts the ecclesiastic tribunal as a tired old farce, he alludes without direct criticism to the later "benefit of peerage," virtual pardons available to all members of parliament and peers. Whether literate or not, such potentates could win mercy even for housebreaking, highway robbery, horse-stealing, and robbery of churches. While peerage was unavailable to repeat offenders, no record was kept by way of branding, and where under clergy offenders could still be liable to imprisonment, peers walked free. "And those men who could not read, if under the degree of peerage, were hanged" — the death penalty for illiteracy. Despite reform to "clergy" pleas, justice remained open to all, just like the Ritz Hotel — even when there wasn't one. And *plus ça change.* . . .

Fallen evangelists such as Jimmy Bakker have luxuriated in exile, promising self-resurrection, while Jimmy Swaggart refused to abide by the ruling of the General Presbytery of the Pentecostal church, which suspended him for two years and banned him from the airwaves for one year after he admitted vague indiscretions — indiscretions described in news reports as "paying a prostitute to pose naked." Swaggart relied on the benefit of clergy accorded him by the

Louisiana branch of the church, which commanded him to abstain from preaching for only three months. He did not fall back on the 51st Psalm, although the neck verse, not to mention verses nine and 13, might appeal. Addressing God, verse nine reads, "Hide Thy face from my sins, and blot out all mine iniquities." And verse 13 promises, "Then will I teach transgressors thy ways; and sinners shall be converted unto thee."

Of course the church has also supplied sanctuary in the most material sense. Before surrendering himself to the tender mercies of Uncle Sam, General Manuel Noriega, the deposed Panamanian dictator, took sanctuary for ten days in the Vatican nunciature in Panama City. Under the rules of our own common law, he could have strained the church's hospitality for four times as long, after which the nuncio might have starved him into the tropical streets.

The nunciature is one of the last places on earth that concretely reminds us how political asylum can connect with religious sanctuary or absolution — escaping mortal responsibility for mortal acts that might also be sins. The early Greeks had many such sanctuaries, including one for slaves at the tomb of Theseus (who slew the Minotaur), and a sanctuary for debtors at Diana's temple in Ephesus. The original idea, of course, was that no holy place should be violated by mundane matters, especially matters having to do with material goods and unpious bloodshed. There was also a belief, some commentators say, that an accused person's curse uttered in holy places could have supernatural power against even the forces of good.

Biblical Jews could seek sanctuary at the temple, as well as at the altar for burnt offerings. Six cities offered asylum to anyone who committed murder accidentally, the killers otherwise being subject, under the *lex talionis* (law of "eye for an eye"), to death themselves. Ironically, three of these "cities of refuge" are war zones today: Hebron, Shechem in Samaria, and Golan. Early Christians converted the sanctuary of the Furies at the Acropolis into a church, as a memento of Paul's conversion of Dionysius.

Under Saxon and Norman law in England, a fugitive could gain sanctuary in a church simply by touching the sanctuary knocker on the door. Once inside, the fugitive had to agree to submit to trial or abjure the realm — swear to exile himself as an outlaw and not return without the king's permission. Under King Alfred in the ninth century, the fugitive had ten days to make up his mind. After the Norman Conquest, sanctuary was extended to at least 40 days. The Norman legal commentator Bracton suggests that in some cases sanctuary could be indefinite. Other writers say that if the church wanted shut of a recalcitrant guest, it simply refused to feed him. But history reveals no example of a medieval Noriega raiding the bishop's cupboards in a desperate ransack for Communion wafers.

In the late 1300s, upon being accused of murder, a rogue named John Bentley took sanctuary in a church near Winchester. Townspeople collared him in the churchyard and locked him in the stocks, then led him to the Winchester gaol. Bentley's lawyer seized the opportunity to create a legal distraction, skirting the murder charge to argue that Bentley's right of sanctuary had been infringed. According to English legal historian R.G. Hamilton, no record survives of the fate of this argument.

In his *All Jangle and Riot*, Hamilton also tells the story of Isabel of Bury, who in 1321 was involved in a fracas with the clerk of All Hallow's Church. When the Clerk ordered Isabel to leave for "causing a disturbance," she stabbed him to death. Then, acutely aware of the scene of the crime, she claimed sanctuary in the church (this being long before the days of Henry VIII and his stern view of church murders). Finding itself somewhat in the position of a latter-day Panama City nunciature, All Hallow's refused Isabel sanctuary and the king's men hauled her off to Newgate Prison. On arraignment, like

General Noriega after her, she stood mute, so the court ordered an inquiry into whether she was handicapped — deaf or mute "by visitation of God."

Hale's *History of Pleas of the Crown* gives examples of such inquests as early as the reign of Henry III (1216–1272), in which those who could supposedly hear and speak but obstinately refused to plead were hanged. As late as 1769, Blackstone recorded that those found obstinately mute were liable to the torture of *peine forte et dure*.

An accused "stands mute" if on arraignment she refuses to answer, if she answers in an illegal way (as by exceeding the lawful number of jury challenges), or if she pleads not guilty but refuses to elect a mode of trial. Originally this meant choosing trial by ordeal or by jury. Blackstone advises that electing trial by God and the holy church, in no matter what spirit of piety, counts as standing maliciously mute. So, according to Lord Coke, does cutting out your own tongue.

Punishment of the obstinate by *peine forte et dure* was practiced at least as early as Edward I, who succeeded Henry III in 1272. Originally, the term ("strong and hard punishment") signified incarceration in a dark, cold cell where the accused, not convicted of any crime, was slowly starved to death on bran bread — today's health food, as Charles Rembar has remarked — and polluted water. By the time of Edward, it signified that the prisoner

> *be sent to the prison from whence he came, and put into a dark, lower room, and there to be laid naked upon the bare ground upon his back without any clothes or rushes under him or to cover him except his privy members, his legs and arms drawn and extended with cords to the four corners of the room, and upon his body laid as great a weight of iron as he can bear, and more. And the first day he shall have three morsels of barly bread without drink, the second day he shall have three draughts of water, of standing water next the door*

of the prison, without bread, and this to be his diet till he die.

Procedure dictated that the mute prisoner receive a stern three-part warning of the punishment and be allowed time to meditate on it. According to Hale, the "penance" torture was usually resorted to only after the court tried to make the prisoner plead by tying his thumbs together with whipcord.

When prisoners died as a result of the penance, their estates were not subject to escheat (forfeit to the Crown). To protect their heirs and assigns, prisoners who felt sure they would be convicted would sometimes choose the torture instead of risking escheat after they were hanged. (The Crown could not claim the estate because the accused had never pled and his guilt remained unproved. Originally, the law held that a prisoner would be broken with stones or iron until he did plead — or "answered" — but in practice the breath was crushed out of him before he could manage it.)

Blackstone, in his characteristically apologist way, assures us that the *peine forte* "was intended as a species of mercy to the delinquent," because he died faster than if he were starved to death. In a passage of inadvertent black comedy, he writes, "Thus tender has the modern law been of inflicting this dreadful punishment" that it allowed benefit of clergy before ordering the *peine forte*, even though the prisoner "is too stubborn to pray it." The great commentator does not add that to obtain benefit of clergy, generally the prisoner was required to prove that he could read from Scripture. In other words, a deliberately mute prisoner was allowed clergy only if he were a clergyman — automatically entitled to it without opening his mouth.

Blackstone also wishes us to understand that the *peine forte* is of a kinder, gentler nature than the rack because the rack was "a species of trial in itself" where *peine forte* is "only used to compel a man to put himself upon his trial" — never mind that the result was death (and often untrue confessions) in either case. In any event, standing mute made pleading guilty look like a picnic — which odd state of affairs legislation in the Anglo-American system has reversed. Usually, where an accused refuses to answer a charge, a court will enter a plea of not guilty on her behalf. But in some jurisdictions, even today this applies only to those who are "mute of malice." A startling example arrived by fax in the office of the *Lawyers Weekly* a few years ago, from the publisher's office in Adelaide. The accused was charged with two counts of assault. His references to "answer" are probably replies to the arraignment, in which the court clerk would ask, "How do you answer [plead to] to this charge?":

> IN THE CENTRAL DISTRICT CRIMINAL COURT ADELAIDE, *Monday, 5 May 1986*
> BEFORE HIS HONOUR JUDGE GRUBB
> *May Sessions No. 204/1986*
> *Charge: Assault occasioning actual bodily harm.*
>
> MR. SMART *for the Crown*
> PRISONER UNREPRESENTED
> *While the charge is being read, the following is said by the prisoner: Shut up, fucking poofter. You poofter, thank you.*
> HIS HONOUR: *You just keep quiet. We will have a word with you in a moment.*
> PRISONER: *Fuck to you. All right, you poofter. All right, I fuck you. That is answer.*
> HIS HONOUR: *You understand . . .*
> PRISONER: *Yes, I fuck you, too. Stuff that. Fuck the Queen, fuck Australia, fuck America. All right.*
> HIS HONOUR: *It is said that you assaulted . . .*
> PRISONER: *Fuck the English, America, fuck the colony. All right.*
> HIS HONOUR: *If you don't shut up . . .*
> PRISONER: *Fuck the judge, too. That is not true.*

HIS HONOUR: *Do we assume this is a plea of not guilty?*
MR. SMART: *Yes, I think we can assume that.*
Plea: Not guilty.
PRISONER ARRAIGNED ON SECOND CHARGE.
PRISONER: *I fuck you, answer you, stuff you, poofter. Is that enough for your answer?*
HIS HONOUR: *That is no answer, but I take it it is a plea of not guilty. In view of the outrageous outburst from the accused I assume that the torrent of language from him is a plea of not guilty to each count. Remanded for trial. Has someone been imprudent enough to grant a bail agreement?*
MR. SMART: *I hesitate to ask him.*
PRISONER: *Fuck you.*
HIS HONOUR: *He has a very limited vocabulary. It is unfortunate. Perhaps you would do better in your own language. Do you wish to ask for bail?*
PRISONER: *You ask yourself bail. Now ask me.*
HIS HONOUR: *I don't have to ask.*
PRISONER: *Fuck the bail. Fuck Australia.*
HIS HONOUR: *I take it then you don't wish to seek bail.*
PRISONER: *Stuff that.*
HIS HONOUR: *No application for bail. The accused is remanded for trial in custody.*
PRISONER: *Fucking bastard, poofter.*
ACCUSED REMANDED IN CUSTODY FOR TRIAL.

In Britain, if a jury finds an accused mute because she might have a physical disability or mental problems, the court must order a hearing on her fitness to plead. As recently as 1989, a muteness hearing was held in York. There, a man tried under the style *The Queen v. Anonymous* was charged with two minor offenses but refused to speak. Police officers didn't believe he was dumb because they had overheard him talk in what they took to be an Irish accent. But their efforts to identify him failed.

Mr. Anonymous somehow conveyed that he did not want a legal-aid lawyer. A psychiatrist appointed by the court found him to be mentally ill, possibly schizophrenic. A jury quickly assessed him as mute by visitation of God, and a second jury declared him unfit for trial. He was then remanded to state psychiatric care until he was able to stand trial, if the Crown decided to proceed.*

But 670 years earlier Isabel of Bury had been in immediate peril of being crushed to death with stones. Informed that if she persisted playing dumb she could not challenge the jurors, she pled she had

---

*Another recent British muteness case is *R. v. Paling*, in which the defendant was a barrister accused of attacking several policemen in a courtroom. Originally, he was charged with attacking a traffic warden and a police officer on the street. The Crown brought an indictment against him on these two counts, and on his fourth or fifth appearance in court, the trial got under way.

The traffic warden was called to testify, and during his examination-in-chief, Paling "got up to his feet and was told to sit down." The report doesn't say, but there seems to have been the feeling that he was about to have another go at the warden. A police officer in the room tried to restrain Paling, who punched the officer in the stomach and screamed, "Fascist bastards! Fascist pigs!" It took two officers to subdue him, after which the trial continued.

During an adjournment, Paling got his licks in on police superintendent Forder. In the hallway outside High Wycombe Magistrates' Court, Paling came up behind the policeman, remarking, "Here is the brilliant Inspector." When Forder turned, Paling kicked him in the groin. Forder fell, and when Inspector Elliott attempted to help him, Paling kicked Elliott in the leg.

With these rather more exciting crimes to prosecute, everybody pretty well forgot about the traffic warden, and Paling was arraigned anew. He refused to plead, and a jury found him mute of malice — "not surprisingly, in the circumstances," the Court of Appeal would later remark. He was then convicted of assaulting a police officer, assault occasioning actual bodily harm (on Inspector Forder), and common assault. The trial judge sentenced him to three years' probation on the condition that he submit to medical treatment and pay the Crown's costs up to £500. Paling appealed without success on the ground that he should have been allowed jury challenges on the muteness hearing.

stabbed the beadle in self-defense. When this failed, she at last decided to plead not guilty. She was hanged the next week.

General Noriega met a less conclusive judicial fate, of course, but even during his time at the nunciature, he could have countered arguments by U.S. lawyers with the common law. The lawyers evidently maintained that Noriega could not claim political asylum at the nunciature because he was a criminal fugitive, not a political refugee. Under ecclesiastical and common law, and insofar as the nunciature could be said to be a religious place, there was no such distinction for purposes of sanctuary.

Then again, perhaps, like Isabel of Bury, the general stood accused of such shocking crimes that ultimately the nuncio would have been obliged, for both political and ostensibly moral reasons, to hand him over to secular authorities. For the Panamanians certainly have paid a price to free themselves of "Pineapple Face," heavier than those of common law precedent. In his *Foul Bills and Dagger Money*, Hamilton quotes the law reports on John of Craumford, who —

> *fled to the church of Bamburgh and admitted he was a robber, and promised to go into exile in the presence of William of Bamburgh, then the coroner. He had no possessions. [Normally, anyone who abjured the realm was obliged to forfeit his goods to the Crown.] The evidence of the whole town accused him of robbery, wanting him arrested, but he managed to escape to the church, . . . ; so the town will be fined. And the 12 jurors concealed the matter, so they will be fined.*

England had its counterpart to the biblical cities of refuge — 22 cities by one count. Fugitives were sequestered in them in return for fealty to local lords. Henry VIII exercised control over these by limiting the number to seven. In 1623, James I abolished sanctuary for those accused of crimes. Those facing arrest in civil matters could claim the right (or privilege) as late as the 18th century. Under French law, fugitives could claim church sanctuary until the period of the revolution.

44   When it's Sunday in Fiji, it's Saturday in, uh, Fiji

When you've studied a map of the world, you may have noticed that the international date line looks like an electroencephalogram for Rasputin. *Now he's dead. Now he isn't. Now he is. Now he isn't.* Logically and by design, the date line should be dead straight, north to south. It was created as the 24th meridian, to run along the 180th degree of longitude. At that location, it is supposed to designate the 24th time zone or hour — the point at which the date changes for travelers crossing it.

The earth was divided into these 24 sections in the late 19th century, as technology began shrinking the planet down to a global village. In 1883, U.S. and Canadian railroads became the first to use time zones. A year later, delegates to a conference in Washington, D.C., decided to expand the idea globally. They chose the Royal Observatory at Greenwich, England, as ground zero. Every 15 degrees of longitude from there marked a new time zone, one for each hour in the day and each $1/15$ of the earth, delineated by a meridian.

The meridians are aligned to designate the point at which the sun in that zone reaches high noon. So, when it's Sunday in Greenwich (and Punkydoodles Corners, Ontario), it should be Saturday in Tongatapu, Tonga, at exactly the opposite side of the planet, 180 degrees east. The fact that the mathematics break down is all to the blame of a shopkeeper who broke the *Lord's Day Act*.

Or at least that's how they tell it in the South Pacific, according to William F. Buckley. In one of his obstinately self-indulgent books recounting his obstinately self-indulgent sailing adventures, Buckley describes meeting in Fiji "an obstinately literal historian of the area" whose explanation for the sudden swerve of the date line, as though it were repelled by the magnetic field of New Guinea and Australia two time zones away, was drawn from the annals of legal loopholes.

The historian claimed that a merchant on one of the Fijian islands owned a shop that straddled the date line. The shopkeeper evidently did not share the local proclivity for Methodism, for he "got around the sabbath laws by selling from the eastern end of his shop on the western Sunday, and from the western end of the shop on the eastern Sunday." Hence, the historian said, the local panjandra moved the date line so that all of Fiji would be in the same time zone.

Of course, the sneaky merchant's actions were firmly in the great legal tradition Fiji adopted during its colonization by Britain. Not long after the global time-zone system was set up, English food sellers were trying to avoid the *Sunday Observance Act* by similarly technical ruses. Because the act said that you could sell traditional Sunday dinner fare like beef and mutton on Sunday, a fish-and-chips vendor argued in court that his French fries were meat — at least for the poorer classes, whose budgets did not run to actual animal flesh. Lord Alverstone, the chief justice of the Court of King's Bench, bought the argument, remarking that it "would be ridiculous to say that, although a man may cook mutton, he must not cook an eel pie." A man who urged the same case for ice cream sandwiches was not so lucky. Justice Thomas Horridge admonished him that "there is nothing in the term 'ice cream,' as there is in the term 'mutton chop,' which would make it necessary for us to say that ice cream fell within the exemption." French fries, but not ice cream, were "meat" in the larger sense of "foodstuffs" that you could sell of a Sunday.*

While other Lord's Day agnostics have mounted the battlements of freedom of religion and expression with varied success, it doesn't seem to have occurred to anyone that maybe God wouldn't care so much what day we set aside for the spirit if on that day we devoted as much time and energy to His Cause as we did to trying to circumvent statutes concerned with It. But the state does seem just as presumptuous in God's defense, attempting in a way reminiscent of the pre-Galileo Vatican to tell the earth how and when to turn. Whether the Fijian shopkeeper story is gospel or canard, it demonstrates that local governments have found it carnally convenient to homogenize their real estate.

Fiscal convenience definitely seems to have inspired the other deviations in the date line, in the Bering Strait and Bering Sea. The line swerves east so that all of eastern Siberia is on the same work schedule (Ivan Denisovich might have got out a day earlier, otherwise), and then dips congruently west to do the same favor for the Aleutians. By extension, it would seem that the wow in the date line in the South Pacific simply assures that, no matter what Fijians do on Sunday, none of the 300 islands will inhabit a legal twilight zone.

Because the Washington agreement left it up to local governments to decide where zone boundaries should run, politicoes can send us back to the future to suit the most fantastic government schemes. Newfoundlanders are still trying hard to forget their mysterious maritime experiment with what Fijians call "coconut time," dubbed "double-daylight savings time" by Newfoundland's government, in a plan that had a lot of groggy islanders catching their pants in the dark on fishhooks, two hours ahead of their usual work schedule. Pretty

---

*The French fries and ice cream cases are discussed at greater length in my *Naked Promises*, pages 57–59.

much to a voter, the locals agree that the idea was so insuperably preposterous, it took all the humor out of pub jokes about "Newfie-time."*

And even if moving the date line ended sabbath fence-sitting by Fijian shopkeepers, it has served to muddy the waters just a little bit to the east of Fiji, on the old "Saturday side" of the line. According to travel writer Arthur Frommer, "never on a Sunday" has a pointed meaning in Tonga: "The Seventh Day Adventist church in Tonga," Frommer says, "which celebrates the sabbath on Saturday, declared that since the International Date Line arbitrarily swings around Tonga, Sunday is really Saturday."

45 Norma Rae as the Queen's enemy

The labor relations use of *strike* seems to have become common currency in the mid-18th century, evolving from the sense of striking down sails or scaffolding at work sites. From those meanings, it was a short stretch to "downing" or striking tools and services. But what if the workers' group is a loose coalition of independent truckers, employed by different firms? Can they "strike" in the legal sense? What if they blockade a highway to protest government policies on trucking and incursions by foreign competitors? Does this make them the Queen's or public enemies?

---

*Because Newfoundland sits east of the rest of Canada, it is common to hear on mainland radio and television broadcasts, "Nine o'clock eastern time, 9:30 in Newfoundland."

These were the central questions in *Fishery Products International v. Midland Transport*, a case decided a few years ago by the Newfoundland Court of Appeal. Fishery Products had contracted with Midland to truck fresh fish from Newfoundland to Montreal, Hull, and Toronto. When the three shipments hit Quebec, the drivers discovered that independent truckers had blocked Highway 20 at Drummondville to protest taxes, American competition, and regulatory hassles. Two of the Midland drivers decided to stop in Manseau, Quebec, and wait for the blockage to clear. The third stayed in line and, because of a break in the road block, he was able to deliver his fish without trouble. The loads in the other two trucks failed inspection.

The bill of lading for the fish included the standard *force majeure* or "act of God" clause: "The carrier shall not be liable for the loss, damage or delay to any of the goods described in the bill of lading caused by an act of God, the Queen's or public enemies, riots, strikes, a defect or inherent vice in the goods, . . ." To avoid having to reimburse Fishery Products for the spoiled cargo, Midland contended that this particular *bloc Québecois* was a strike and that the "strikers" were the Queen's or public enemies. And the trial judge agreed. He held that a strike could include a "concerted cessation or stoppage of work which prevents innocent carriers, such as Midland, from performing their contract of carriage." This encompassed work actions directed at a government instead of at any particular private employer.

The trial judge also noted that the *force majeure* clause tacked "or public enemies" onto the usual phrase, "Queen's enemies." This suggested, he thought, an intention to extend the trucking company's protection to "illegal acts by a segment of the public against the interests and rights of the state." Anyone who unlawfully prevented legitimate users from passing over public highways was a public enemy, never mind the extravagance of the phrase.

The Newfoundland Court of Appeal agreed that "strike" could include a "cessation of work for political reasons," but it ruled that the word presumed an employer-employee relationship which didn't exist here. Independent contractors were not employees in the usual labor relations sense. On the trial judge's reasoning that such people could "strike," Justice Margaret Cameron wrote for the three-judge appeal panel, "'strike' could include the blocking of highways by parents protesting the fact that their children must leave their community to go to school, or any social issue." Although they would be acting simply as citizens and parents and not as any really organized group, such as a collective bargaining unit, they would be included in "anyone" who unlawfully blocked the roads.

The public enemies issue was more historically resonant. Justice Cameron looked to the definition in *Black's Law Dictionary*, where "public enemies" were nations or subjects at war with the U.S. "Term however does not generally include robbers, thieves, private depredators, or riotous mobs," says that authority. Her ladyship did not quote the balance of the definition, although it suggests why the trial judge found that the truckers would fall within it:

> *The term has acquired, in the vocabulary of journalism and civic indignation, a more extended meaning, denoting a particularly notorious offender . . . or a social, health, or economic condition or problem affecting the public at large, which is difficult to abate or control.*

By this accounting, the fish truckers might not have been Public Enemy Number One, but they affected fish eaters at large, were difficult to control, and could well incite civic indignation, especially after a couple of really hot days. To support a different conclusion, the Newfoundland appeal court looked back to a case involving another "Midland" transporter, before the Irish Court of King's Bench in 1923.

In *Secretary of State for War v. Midland Great Western Railway*, the Irish court held that before you can have public enemies, "there must be war." The war could be internal, such as the Confederates against the North or the Provos against the Orangemen, but "public enemies" did not include common criminals or even rioters, "however much they may in a sense be at war with society." So, by strict legal definition, Al Capone would not have been public enemy number 100, let alone public enemy number one. Public enemies were enemies of the government in the larger sense, the Irish court said. "Local outbursts do not amount to rebellion."

All of this, by the way, was over a typewriter. The Secretary of State had sent the machine, worth £20, to troops in Sligo. Rebels (republicans, evidently) stole it during a raid on the Sligo station. The court held that the railway was not responsible for the loss of the typewriter, finding that *force majeure* exclusions for "the Queen's enemies" existed in the common law from the time of Shakespeare. It was during the reign of the first Elizabeth that land carriage of merchandise began in the common law world.

As the Irish court mentions, "public enemies" is, generally speaking, not an extension of the category of common law public foes, but a synonym for "the Queen's enemies" taken from U.S. law. Ostensibly everyone in the revolutionary U.S. was once the Queen's enemy, and therefore, locally, a public friend. For Uncle Sam, celebrated rebel against the British sovereign, the Queen's enemies could not be commensurate with public enemies. Thus the "or" in the bill of lading, acknowledging the two separate categories of enemies — the Queen's *or* public enemies. And of course, Canadian trucks commonly operate in the U.S., so truckers would want the *force majeure* to apply across the continent, even down south, where the Queen's enemies might be the public's friend.

46 We the kinder, gentler nation

Next to the weather, the thing Canadians like to complain about most is the constitution. All the same, there was Peter Russell on "The National" newscast one night, with his very own documentary about it. The expert on Canadian constitutional history introduced his subject by saying that he routinely asks his students if they know how the U.S. constitution begins. A large percentage of the students can recite, "We the people." Then, he asks how many know the first words of the Canadian constitution. Apparently, during his 30-odd years of teaching, not one student had been able to recite, "Whereas the Provinces of Canada."

I fell asleep at that point, but my wife tells me that Prof. Russell went on to explain how much the two preambles say about their respective countries. And at first blush, I supposed Prof. Russell had a point . . . which I take to be that the spirit of effusive nationhood is greater in the United States. Canada, spiritually speaking, has always been a loose, pragmatic and ambivalent federation of special interests, a sort of shuddering, geophysical embodiment of utilitarianism.

But I don't know that the preamble to the U.S. constitution is really all that poetic.

> *We the People of the United States, in Order to form a more perfect Union, establish Justice, insure domestic Tranquility, provide for the common defense, promote the general Welfare, and secure the Blessings of Liberty to ourselves and our Posterity, do ordain and establish this Constitution of the United States of America.*

To me, this is a slightly sentimental lawyer's idea of poetry (assuming a sentimental lawyer is not an oxymoron), and not that much of an improvement on certain sections of the *Construction Liens Act*. As a citizen of both countries, my blood does not stir for the U.S. preamble any more than it does for the rather majestic:

> WHEREAS the Provinces of Canada, Nova Scotia and New Brunswick have expressed their Desire to be federally united into One Dominion under the Crown of the United Kingdom of Great Britain and Ireland, with a Constitution similar in Principle to that of the United Kingdom:
> And Whereas such a Union would conduce to the Welfare of the Provinces and promote the Interests of the British Empire. . . .

My first impulse in answer to Prof. Russell was to blame the relative mundanity of the Canadian preamble, if any, on the British. Put it down to my immigrant's pride in my adopted land. I didn't want the Fathers of Confederation to carry the can for that split infinitive in the first bit, not to mention that oddly prurient "conducing union." But then I thought, No, it is quintessentially Canadian not to talk in hyperbole, to be practical-minded, to dream of the possible, including conducing once a week, usually right after "Hockey Night in Canada" on Saturday.

Also, of course, there was Professor Peter Hogg looking over my shoulder, in the shape of my somewhat neglected law school copy of *Constitutional Law of Canada*. While originally, Prof. Hogg writes, the *British North America Act* (which was the Canadian constitution until 1982, when the government of Pierre Trudeau added the *Charter of Rights and Freedoms* and renamed the statute the *Constitution Act, 1982*) derived its authority from Westminster, "the Act was drafted by Canadians at conferences held in Charlottetown, Quebec, and London; only at the very end was the Colonial Office brought into the discussions."

Prof. Hogg says that "it is perfectly understandable why Canada lacks a document which contains ringing declarations of national purpose and independence." The *B.N.A. Act* was not meant to enshrine all the obligations and rights of Canadians. It was *meant* to be *à la mode anglaise*, British constitutional law being drawn from several different sources. For example, Prof. Hogg notes, unlike the U.S. constitution, the *B.N.A. Act* does not establish a Supreme Court; it merely makes it possible for the federal government to enact a statute setting up the court. In the spirit of Canadian pragmatism, the act leaves room for maneuvering among the federal government, the provinces, and (until patriation in 1982) Britain. Prof. Hogg has little time for those who "feel that the lack of [a U.S.-style] document is a reproach to Canada's nationhood." Such thinking is not nationalism, he says, but "probably at bottom a desire to copy the United States; and the idea that a new constitution could somehow be manufactured which would be more Canadian, more legitimate and more inspiring is unhistorical and naive."

Of course, since 1982 the constitutional fault-finders have complained that when we did get a second kick at the can, we just went merrily Whereas-ing off again in the *Charter* — "Whereas Canada is founded upon principles that recognize the supremacy of God and the rule of law . . . ," appended to which, it has to be admitted, is something that sounds like a shopping list for the Civil Liberties Union.

True enough, the *Charter* says a lot about us and our modern habit of insisting on "rights" without thinking about the profounder meanings and consequences of that insistence. Compared to its parent document, as well as to the U.S. constitution, the *Charter* reflects the development from commonwealth thinking to "I Want Mine." I have never liked it much, partly for its ambivalence, partly because in the end it may accomplish the opposite of what it sets out to do. Sometimes I think it looks a lot like the servant who enslaves us. Prof. Hogg himself has told me that he is only just learning to warm to it.

In any case, one could play this keeping-up-with-Uncle-Sam game all day, and at the end merely come up with the historical lesson that we, the people, have only just begun — just at the moment when various regional separatists would rend us asunder. Also, unlike many Americans, we're not all blustering rhetoric, and neither do we feel as imperially arrogant as some Brits do. We're betwixt and between — not a people of grand words, but a people of quiet deeds.

Consider: I can well remember Richard Nixon's "I am not a crook," but I haven't the slightest idea what Pierre Trudeau said upon deciding to resign as Liberal leader. I do recall, though, that he did something quintessentially Canadian on that occasion: he went for a solitary walk in a snowstorm, to think things through.

47 Her Majesty, Robbie the Pict and one *heavy* political football

Is it an *inter vivos* gift from Her Majesty, or restitution to Robbie the Pict, following unlawful conversion 700-odd years ago?

The Stone of Scone, a 182-kilogram slab of drab sandstone about the size of the seat on an armchair, supposedly started life as Jacob's pillow. It is said that, while sleeping on it, the patriarch dreamed about angels on a ladder to heaven (Genesis 28:11: "And he took of the stones of that place, and put them for his pillows . . ."). From that context, the Stone came to represent a sanctified place, where Heaven and Earth communed. Legend has it that the pharaoh's daughter then carried the Stone from Egypt to Ireland. After a lot more meandering around as a sacred relic, in a triumph for internal rhyme the Stone ended up in medieval Scone, in Perthshire, Scotland.

Scotland crowned its monarchs as they sat on the Stone, but that all ended in 1296 when Edward I converted it to his own use and spirited it to England. In 1308, the stone was installed in Westminster Abbey, where it sat for the next 489 years under the coronation chair, surrounded by metal railings and burglar alarms. Abbey authorities instituted the latter precautions after Scottish nationalist students repatriated the Stone in the dead of night, in 1950, using a borrowed Ford Cortina. A Unionist government in Scotland facilitated the return of the Stone, or a facsimile of it, to Westminster in early 1951.

I say "facsimile" because some claim that the real Stone has always been in Scotland, and others say that the Stone which was returned to England in 1951 is an impostor. Supposedly the real thing groans when a genuine monarch sits on it (as well it might), but nobody's heard it do that for a while — perhaps because of all the caterwauling over where it belongs.

In any event, Queen Elizabeth II was crowned while sitting just above the putative Stone, and — on the English assumption that the British Crown has legal title to it — Her Majesty acceded to its return north of the Tweed. Prime Minister John Major announced this in Parliament, only to be accused by Scottish nationalists of trying to buy them off with a rock.

Ian Hamilton, Q.C., a fervent Scottish nationalist and in 1950 the ringleader of the students who repatriated the Stone to Scotland, expressed muted satisfaction. Just how muted became clear when he published an article in *The Times* addressed to "you English" about the possibility of a referendum on Scottish nationalism. "Does no one tell you," he wondered rhetorically,

> how much we hate the Tories? Or do you really think that the return of that old relic, the Stone of Scone, will win a vote? I may have helped to steal that old stone in my younger days, but it was never meant to be used as a voting gimmick. We're all daft up here, but not as daft as that.

Other Scots think that the whole business is a load of old codswallop. Edinburgh resident Jim Brunton wrote in the English newspaper, *The Independent*: "Better by far to take the thing up in a helicopter and drop it into the deepest part of Loch Ness. With luck, it might brain the Monster and so kill two Scotch myths with one Stone."

The delight of Robbie the Pict, however, seems unalloyed. In fact, he takes credit for the return on the theory that the English had in fact converted the Stone to their own use without lawful right.

Robbie is occasionally described as "Scotland's most famous freedom-fighter." Some years ago, he legally changed his name to Robbie the Pict, to protest the section of the *Immigration Act* that changed the status of Scots from British subjects to British citizens. More recently, he has been driving around with a plastic replica of the Stone of Scone strapped to the roof of his car — when his license isn't under suspension: in 1991 he was convicted of "failing to display a road tax disc" as part of his refusal to "recognize" government authorities. He decried the suspension as the "road traffic equivalent of being a political prisoner."

In 1993, Robbie reported the theft of the Stone, 697 years earlier, to the Chief Constable of Perthshire. He followed up that unrecent complaint with three dozen or so letters to members of the British Parliament, staking a claim to the Stone for the homeboys. As well, he offered a reward of £250,000 (mostly of other people's money) for its safe return. Her Majesty has not yet claimed the reward. As for the assertion that the Stone at Westminster might have been a fake, Robbie is sanguine. He told Gillian Bowditch of *The Times*: "There might even have been a double switch if the monks sold Edward I a dummy in the first place. It's quite amusing if they've had a cess tank lid on ceremonial duty for centuries."

Meanwhile, several British scholars have shouted into the political maelstrom that the accession of James VI as James I merged the histories and politics of England and Scotland, such that it makes no more sense to return the Stone than to send the Elgin marbles back to Greece. Speaking of which, just an hour after Prime Minister Major announced the planned return of the Stone, he received a fax from the Greek minister for the European Parliament: "I sincerely hope you will show the same sensibility for the Parthenon Marbles, which were stolen 200 years ago from the Acropolis of Athens by Lord Elgin."

As he awaited the return day — on November 30, 1996, St. Andrew's Day — Ian Hamilton predicted imminent sovereignty. In his book about engineering the repatriation of the Stone in 1950, he wrote nostalgically of a rhyme his mother recited to him when he was a boy:

> *Unless the fates shall faceless prove,*
> *And prophets' voice be vain,*
> *Wherever the sacred stone is found,*
> *The Scottish race shall reign.*

48 Minding their please and queues

In 1837 the British essayist Thomas Carlyle credited the French with bringing order to public gatherings by spontaneously creating neat line-ups, *queue* being French for "tail." But now, some Britons blame "the Continent" for the demise of patiently waiting one's turn, just as they see "Europe" generally as causing western civilization to crumble. At the stroke of midnight, January 1, 1994, London Transport's Queuing By-law died in its sleep. It was 56, and continues to be deeply mourned by those who write letters to newspapers.

The by-law was born into a less selfish world, in 1938, almost exactly 100 years after Carlyle wrote, "That talent … of spontaneously standing in queue distinguishes … the French People." Some British lawyers say that the queuing by-law was meant to condition people for the greater discipline and flexibility required for the war against Hitler. Others think its original purpose was to control unruly football (i.e., soccer) mobs at trolley stops. What it actually said, insistently for almost six decades, was that whenever six or more people waited for a trolley car, they had to stand "in lines or queues in an orderly manner" no more than two abreast. The fine for failure to comply was £2. This amounted to a week's wages in 1938.

Now London Transport has put the old law down because, like the horse in the knacker's yard, it has served its purpose long since. The British, after all, queue by predilection. But some of the locals have not proved so sanguine about this alleged national *politesse*. Jonathan Sale, a correspondent for *The Independent*, observes that modern Britain is plagued with "queue-jumpers" and that Paris remains "the best place to wait in line." And he's talked to the experts. No kidding. There is a science called "queuing theory," and its practitioners at the University of Minnesota have informed Sale that we spend five years of our lives in lines, "as opposed to a mere 12 months that is wasted in looking for things we've lost."

The war era of the queuing by-law's youth was what Sale calls "the golden age of queuing," given that "civilians joined any stationary line in the hope that it led to a shop actually selling something." "Queue-jumping," his research shows, did not enter the language until 1959.

Last September, a commuter in one London bus line told the *Times of London*, "Nobody knows the law exists so it's a waste of time. You always get people jumping queues wherever you go." Indeed, just as London Transport was doing away with the by-law, the busy Victoria bus station implemented what *The Times* calls "an airport-style boarding system, to avoid what have become unseemly battles to get on to coaches." The station's managing director told the paper that the situation at Victoria had become survival of the nastiest. "Those who were in their school scrum make it first into the coach; the old and infirm are last." An interviewee from the London Regional Passengers' Committee (they're serious about this stuff over there) added, "In the morning you see people piling out of Charing Cross station and it tends to be a case of everyone — and their elbows — for themselves."

But it wasn't one of the madding crowd who blamed the global village for such pushiness. David Worthington, a queuing theorist who teaches at university (what else would a queuing theorist do?), told Sale that queue-jumping might be related to the Europeanization of Britain: "You could formulate a hypothesis that we are adopting EC patterns of behavior." In fact, the Londoner in the street, albeit a Russian immigrant, remarked to *The Times*, "It's normal politeness to wait your turn and to form an orderly queue. Only foreign people seem to have manners over here."

I once took a jurisprudence course in which spontaneous queuing served as an example of what was "not law." We were discussing legal philosopher H.L.A. Hart at the time, so I suppose the point was something like, "People recognize that queuing is the done thing, but there is no formal recognition that this type of social ordering is meant to have legal effect or consequences. There is no state sanction, no rule of recognition." In other words, despite how strongly we feel about queuing, it's mere custom.

But perhaps that's precisely what makes us so angry when somebody violates the tacit Queuing Code. We feel more miffed at that breach than when somebody breaks a commensurately petty law. Even my jurisprudence instructor admitted that he happily ran red lights *like everybody else* (the telling words, of course), but was ready to bash someone who butted in front of him while he was waiting to get in to see *Presumed Innocent*. The queue-jumper — or, better, the "butter-inner," a juvenile term befitting juvenile behavior — has not simply violated the law, she has violated something more sacred in countries with British and French traditions: a sense of fair play. Indeed, the British jurisprude John Rawls has said that justice itself resides in the idea of fair play.

The queue-jumper is villainous to us precisely because he *doesn't* behave like everyone else. In fact, experience suggests that maybe we *do* want our non-statutory, or "folk," Queuing Code to have the legal effect of London Transport's late, lamented by-law. Maybe there is an attached "rule of recognition" of the "Queuing Code" as actual law, to use Hart's lingo.

Not long ago, thousands of North Americans from hundreds of backgrounds stood in the winter cold for as long as 12 or 14 hours, waiting outside a General Motors plant for a chance at a necessity of life — a job. Not surprisingly, the crowd was quite prepared for the folk Queuing Code to have legal effect in that situation. Queue-jumpers — butter-inners — were escorted from the scene, by the local constabulary. Hip-hip-hooray, I say, with all those non-queue-jumpers. I, for one, have always preferred Rawls on law — justice as fair play — to Prof. Hart, from the land of the cowboy and every Amurrican for him- or herself.

49 It's an ill windfall that blows no tax break

Garden Bay is a busy fishing port not far from Vancouver, near New Westminster, British Columbia. One February day 34 years ago, Bill Cameron, a salmon fisherman, spied a waterspout from the bay shore, then the flash of something muscling and whipping against the surface of the water. After a few moments, it happened again, fountain spray pulsing up from the water, followed by pure kinetic energy cutting the bowline. None of the fishermen had ever known killer whales to enter this southerly bay, but there it was.

The men put to sea and secured the bay's mouth. They hitched their salmon nets to logs and drove the luckless whale into this artificial "herring pond." When the Vancouver Public Aquarium caught wind of the catch, it offered them $5,000 for the whale. Two months later, during a bowling banquet, the fishermen noticed an entire pod of killer whales in Garden Bay. Using their proven herring-pond technique, they captured several whales and sold them to various aquaria.

Altogether, Bill Cameron made about $8,000 as his share of this brief stint as an accidental whaler. And when the Minister of Revenue wanted him to pay income tax on that amount, he demurred: the money was not income from his business, he insisted, it was an accident, sheer serendipity, to which he had applied his equipment and wits. It was a non-taxable windfall.

Cameron and his fishing buddies, in other words, got paid not to be whalers, like the farmers who get paid by commodity boards not to farm (to control supply and demand). And sure enough the *Income Tax Act* (ITA) goes along with this non-joke, making the same argument by being silent about it. Tax lawyers put it this way: the state taxes income only if it derives from a source defined as such in the law — generally, as an office, employment, business, or property. If there is no such source, as far as the revenuers are concerned it's capital that appeared magically in your hands. It just happened to you, lucky you.

And, yes, the tax lawyer's term for such manna from heaven is "windfall." In the 1992 case of *The Queen v. Rumack*, Justice James K. Hugessen of the Federal Court of Appeal writes that this legal usage derives "from the old rule whereby, as between the remainderman and the tenant for life, timber trees blown down by the wind were required to be sold and the proceeds invested as capital." Because the "remainderman" got the interest in the land after the life tenant used it (the remainder interest), the law didn't want to tempt the tenant to hoard all the profit from timber that fell accidentally or accidentally-on-purpose. So, it forced the tenant to invest the money as shared capital. In the sense of a lucky eventuality, "windfall" has been in use from at least the early 16th century.

And in both senses, it applied to the accidental whalers in Garden Bay. When fisherman Bill Cameron appealed his tax assessment on the whale sales, the Crown argued that Cameron had been conducting a form of his regular salmon-fishing business: he and his associates had used their boats, nets, and sea smarts to engage in a profit-making venture. Yet A.J. Frost, the Tax Board member hearing the case, held that salmon fishing was not whaling. Although the salmon fishermen certainly had used their equipment and sea knowledge, the first catch was largely fortuitous, and the second somewhat less so, but still extraordinary. If there had been a third round-up, Frost admitted, the Crown *might* have had an argument worth listening to, but until then, Cameron et. al. were purely accidental whalers, at least from a tax, or rather tax-free, point of view.

Windfall is a concept that has not come easy to revenuers. In 1955, the Anglo-Oriental and General Investment Trust in London decided that it would give 22 of its loyal employees a special Christmas gift — a tailor-fitted suit, overcoat, or raincoat, or combination thereof, to a value of £15. S.A. Rogerson, a clerk at Anglo-Oriental, went to the designated tailors to be fitted for a suit, and on delivery the tailors billed Anglo-Oriental £14.5s. Then, anxious to share in the seasonal spirit of give and take, the Inspector of Taxes assessed Rogerson for the full amount his employer had paid for the Christmas present.

The trial judge did not buy poor Rogerson's argument that the suit was a mere gift, not a taxable benefit. The tax inspector admitted it wasn't a bonus, because Anglo-Oriental had paid Rogerson a Christmas bonus in cash, which he had declared on his tax form. And yes, the suit seemed to be of a lower quality than Rogerson's other suits; it would wear out rather more quickly. Come to that, it might have zero resale value in his hands, not only because it had been fitted specifically to him, but "because his employers would have been displeased if he had sold it." So the trial judge gave Rogerson a break to the extent that he would be taxed at the suit's second-hand value — a tidy £5, everyone agreed.

This held up on appeal — when the Crown failed to convince the Court of Chancery that what Rogerson got was not a suit, but £14.5s dressed up as a jacket and trousers. But the point here is that Her Majesty prefers taxpayers to receive property as profits, perks, or consideration because taxpayers do not have to share mere gifts and serendipity — windfalls — with the Crown.

The Canada Customs and Revenue Agency has come to use the term formally by virtue of the leading 1982 case, *The Queen v. Cranswick*. The taxpayer there, J.E. Cranswick, had rather more luck than Rogerson enjoyed with his Christmas suit. Cranswick held shares in Westinghouse Electric, the Canadian subsidiary of the U.S. appliance manufacturer. In 1976, Westinghouse Electric sold some of its assets for $6 million less than their book value. To keep shareholders from rebelling, they offered to buy back their shares at $26 each or, if the shareholder preferred, Westinghouse would pay the shareholder $3.35 per share owned. Cranswick accepted the $3.35 on each of his 640 shares, so that Westinghouse paid him $2,144. When Revenue Canada purported to tax Cranswick on that amount, the Federal Court of Appeal held that this was impossible: there was no "source" for the money within the reach of Canadian tax law. The payment did not arise from the shares; it was not a dividend, certainly, but an extraordinary payment that he could not have set out to earn from the shares. The payment was a windfall.

The CCRA has based its Interpretation Bulletin IT-334R2 on *Cranswick*. The bulletin says that "a particular receipt" has the look of a windfall where the taxpayer did not make an organized effort to get it, and had no "customary or specific expectation" of the receipt.

Rumack, where Justice Hugessen traced the history of "windfall" as a legal term of art, represents a wrinkle the law developed to cope with the modern burgeoning of lotteries and other games of chance. In 1994 the federal Standing Committee on Finance recommended that all lottery and gambling winnings of more than $500 — no matter how unsystematically acquired — should be taxed, after taking into account the taxpayer's losses in the gamble. But, to date, Parliament has not acted on this recommendation: the ITA still deems lottery prizes as "acquired" at a cost equal to their fair market value. Presumably, this would be the treatment on any windfall: there's no tax payable on the windfall capital itself, only on anything earned by using or disposing of it. That, in fact, is why in 1992 Marion Rumack had to pay tax on her winnings of $1,000 per month for life in the "Cash For Life" lottery. The charity running the lottery had bought an annuity on Rumack's life, and she received her $1,000 per month out of that. So the court said she had to pay tax on anything beyond the capital which the charity invested in the annuity. That is, during the relevant tax year, the charity's capital investment of $3,845 provided Rumack that year's $12,000 in prize money. She owed Revenue Canada tax on the difference — $8,155.

Justice Hugessen noted that, even had Rumack received her total prize as a lump sum (at a capital value of $135,338), she would have had to pay tax on any gain she made by investing it. But his lordship did not consider that Rumack could have spent all the capital very quickly, just as she easily could have spent the entire $1,000 each month. What if she had been out of work, say, or wanted to pay off a mortgage all in one go?

Now of course, sometimes a taxpayer does not want an apparent windfall to be characterized as such: insofar as a windfall has no tax consequences, you can't deduct anything you spent to acquire it. On the other hand, when you lose money trying to acquire income from a source, the ITA allows you to reduce your taxable income by some or all of the loss. So, in 1974 a federal bureaucrat went to the tax review board to prove that his "hobby" of car-racing had become a vocation once he started spending 80 percent of his salary on it; despite only losses to that point, he successfully argued that he had a reasonable expectation of profit through prize money. And for showing similar professionalism, a hunter for pirate's treasure on Oak Island, Nova Scotia, could deduct losses incurred for his explorations, upon demonstrating that he was searching in an area where there really was a chance of recovering some of Captain Kidd's doubloons or early vintage bottles of rum.

Everyone loves a potential tax loophole, of course, and researching this subject put ideas in this taxpayer's head. I have been a runner for many years, and I had been thinking about road-racing again, competitively. It had occurred to me that, at 50, I might be old enough finally to win something, if only a distant third place in the old shufflers' category. In other words, if I were lucky, the rest of the competition would have gone to fat, given up, or died.

But my age really told on me when, instead of considering how unlikely victory might be, I started worrying about the tax consequences of the prize money. I went so far as to imagine the argument — a sort of anticipatory *esprit de l'escalier* — that I would have on the telephone with my regional tax office.

"It's about my assessment," I argued several hypothetical times with the Revenue Canada representative. "I'm a lawyer, although not a tax lawyer," I admitted, just in case. "But I happen to know that windfalls are not taxable, and there's an amount that you're taxing me on here, and it was a windfall."

"If that's the case, sir," the representative said with unnerving hypothetical kindness, "I'm sure we can correct the record. What kind of a windfall was it?"

"Well, see, that's why it's upsetting. It was such a piece of luck." I felt a moment of hypothetical doubt about whether it was luck versus pure athletic prowess. "I mean, I'm pleased to say," I permitted myself a chuckle, feeling myself warming to the representative, "I'm happy to say that I got it for winning a race. A ten-kay race."

"You mean like at a country fair or something?"

"No, a ten-kilometer road race. You know, where they block off the streets and you get maybe a t-shirt and a bagel for your $20 entry fee, and you run in a race in the city streets? And I'm in the 50- to 60-year-old division, see, so I guess the competition's a little thinner there, and so, lo and behold, I won. Just third place, but I surprised even myself, after all these years of running. 500 bucks. Persistence pays, I guess, eh?"

"So, you're a regular runner."

"Well, yeah. I run five or six days a week. Have done for, I don't know, 12, 15 years, although of course sometimes you kind of give it up for a while, especially during the winter. But on and off, yeah, mostly on, for many years."

"So it wasn't a windfall."

"What do you mean? Of course it was a windfall. I've been running in these races for 15 years, and it's the first time I've ever won."

"But you just said yourself, sir, that you train for the races, and that you've been competing for 15 years. That's an organized effort, sir, with some expectation of an enforceable claim. To put it in the vernacular, see, you are working at it. You are applying skill and effort. That makes it taxable income — income from a business or profession."

"I'm telling you it's a fluke, man," I said dubiously, grudgingly enjoying the suggestions of skill and enforceable claims.

"You're not doing yourself justice, sir."

This completely flummoxed me, even in my own fantasy world. Whatever you called that $500 prize, they were going to take away nearly half of it, the only thing I'd won in my life, a whole $500 after I'd slogged my guts out through 15 years of heat prostration and shin splints and plantar fasciitis and pulled groin muscles and strained hamstrings and chondromalacia patellae and, one godforsaken winter, even a frostbitten willy ("You'll never have children," the doctor joked, wiggling it, and I almost fainted), and *I'm* the one doing the injustice. "I'm going to appeal this," I threatened. But then, I realized that I would look like a terrific ingrate. Unfazed that I nearly flunked gym in grade school, Revenue Canada had certified me as a winning professional athlete.

So, feeling ironic pride in the possibility of such an assessment notice, in real life I called my accountant, Rubin, to get his view. "Theoretically," Rubin advised, "you could turn your running into a business. Then, surely you would generate more expenses than revenue, create a loss, and trigger a refund."

Rubin was taking the car-racer, pirate-treasure-hunter view, I saw. He was making me a beautiful loser, in the allowable deduction sense, instead of an accidental winner in the non-taxable windfall sense. In tax law, after all, sometimes losers are winners, and vice, depending on how the wind blows, versa.

50 Gentleperson usher of the black hockey stick?

If they'd listened to Walter Robinson, the whole thing would have been solved by installing a doorbell. Instead, the prime minister appointed a new gentleman usher of the black rod.

In fact, 47-year-old Mary McLaren was the first female gentleman usher in Canadian history. Her best-known duty was banging on the doors of the Commons with her black rod — a cane of ebony topped with a miniature lion's head — to summon members to the senate chamber for the opening of Parliament. The tradition began in Britain, where the gentleman usher is also sergeant-at-arms and royal attendant. The Commons members were hoping that the usher would derail Charles I's scheme to arrest several members of Parliament.

The Canadian government explained that it intended to expand McLaren's role beyond door-knocking and senate administration, presumably because people like Walter Robinson, director of the Canadian Taxpayers Federation, thought that her salary of $73,400 to $86,400 per year was not in keeping with modern fiscal realities. Robinson had told a reporter for Canadian Press, "We don't want to be paying people 75 grand a year to knock on a door for a throne speech. Buy a door bell!"

New Democratic Party leader Alexa McDonough remarked that women would have been more impressed if McLaren used her rod to cudgel the government into dealing with issues such as employment equity, child care, and the much-vaunted social safety net. McDonough said "prod the government," to be precise, which formulation steers one toward the other euphemistic dust-up engendered, pun intended, by McLaren's appointment.

In French, McLaren's honorific had traditionally been translated as *le gentilhomme huissier de la verge noire*. A few days before she assumed that position, however, the prime minister's office purported to change her title to "Usher of the Senate" (*le huissier du Sénat*), thus overcoming the gender problem in both languages, not to mention The Sex Problem. As the old joke on Parliament Hill had it, *le gentilhomme huissier de la verge noire* gave new meaning to the phrase "honorable member." In French, *la verge noire* means "black rod" as well as "black penis." And, despite what you might have read elsewhere, *verge* is not slang for "penis," the way *rod* is slang for "penis" in English. As *le Petit Robert*, the French language authority, puts it, *verge* is perfectly correct French for *"l'organe de la copulation (chez l'homme et les mamifères)."*

Still, senate Progressive Conservatives resisted the name change. Opposition leader John Lynch-Staunton complained of political correctness run rampant, remarking that "when a member of a visible minority is named to the position . . . we may have to use 'white rod' or 'off-color rod,' 'no-color rod' or 'neutral rod.'"

Of course, McLaren is no gentleman — strictly speaking, not only a man, but a man of noble birth — and to say otherwise is to consign her to the mini-hell suffered by Henry, clerk to Rumpole of the Bailey: according to Rumpole's biographer, John Mortimer, when Henry's wife became town mayor, tradition demanded that Henry be called "the lady Mayoress." Indeed, the law reports indicate that historically "gentleman" — like "lady Mayoress" — was no mere honorific, but a term of art.

A gentleman was less than an esquire but more than a commoner. Under the 1745 *Act more effectively to prevent cursing and swearing*, offenders "of or above the degree of gentleman" were subject to a fine of five shillings per offense, where day laborers were liable to pay a single shilling. Consequently, when in the pages of *Uncommon Law* Albert Haddock swears more than 400 times on one occasion and is subject to a fine at the gentleman's rate, he pleads in mitigation that "he is not a gentleman when he is playing golf."

This defense itself has common law precedent. In the early days of the 18th century, a defendant named Battersby denied that he owed a debt to the man who sued for it under the name "Edward Nash, gentleman." The court obligingly dismissed Nash's lawsuit: despite a bond documenting Battersby's debt to Nash, it was a complete defense "that the plaintiff is no gentleman." The court relied partly on *Messor v. Molyneux*, where the justices refused to admit an affidavit into evidence because it had been sworn by a lawyer whom the affidavit referred to as "gentleman" instead of (properly) "esquire."

Ultimately, the Canadian senate saved McLaren from the fate of Henry, the lady Mayoress. It reached a compromise in both official languages. McLaren is to be known officially in English as the Usher of the Black Rod. In French, "Rod" is now to be translated as *bâton*, like the sticks carried by cops and hockey players of both sexes. *Traduttore, traditore.*

51 Mozart as specific and general deterrence

They don't expect that Mozart will prevent murders, but he has discouraged vagrancy at shopping malls and, never mind the contradiction, the music "really does make a nice ambience." That's what a spokeswoman for the Toronto Transit Commission says. To combat loitering and violence by young people at the Kennedy subway station in Scarborough, Ontario, the commission is playing classical music over the loudspeakers. This isn't the only security measure the TTC has planned for the station, where a teenager was stabbed to death not long ago: for example, the commission has installed more and better lighting. But the Debussy Deterrent gets all the press — largely, of course, because it has disturbing, well, overtones: to begin with, don't we want our kids to *like* "L'après-midi d'un faune"?

The commission did not invent the Debussy Deterrent. (I would have called it the equally alliterative Dvorak Deterrent, but Antonin makes even adults run for cover.) Government agents in Panama and in Waco, Texas, have tried to drive holed-up "perps" crazy by blaring recorded music at them, some of it "popular." And for about a decade the Seven-Eleven convenience store chain has scared off the occasional hangabout by playing anything-but-rock outside its U.S. franchises. Finding that Beethoven isn't always annoying enough, they have experimented with Montovani and country-and-western — surely the musical equivalent of pepper spray.

Edmonton, Alberta, officials and citizens groups have employed the Debussy Deterrent to fight drug-dealing and vagrancy in Beaver Hills House Park, and in 1993 a business association played classical music recordings to "clean up" the Monument Square area of Portland, Maine. Two years later, Jeri and Ernie Foppiano did the same to clear the street in front of their bar in Stockton, California. Jeri explains, "We thought about all different types of music, like Greek or Chinese, something we don't care for ourselves. Then somebody suggested the Beethoven and Bach."

In fact, the Foppianos claim success through Vivaldi, opera, and Liberace, played "loud on lousy speakers," technology the TTC perfected long ago in its stations and subway cars. The Foppianos' regulars have brought in CDs to aid the cause, an act of self-enlightened charity which Toronto strap-hangers might want to emulate for our cash-strapped transit authority. But the guy who ran the boarding-house across the street from the Foppianos' bar did not agree that the music discouraged undesirables. "It doesn't help at all," he told a reporter. "They start dancing to it."

Indeed, the Debussy Deterrent could backfire in Toronto, too, and not just because we want teenagers to think of "Air on the G-String" as a decent thing. One recalls *The Dawn of the Dead*, the 1978 movie featuring teenaged zombies wandering around a shopping mall while muzak played incessantly in the background: the mindless vagrants weren't *leaving* the business district, they were *haunting* it, to full orchestral accompaniment.

Also, young vagrants aren't stupid, necessarily. Battered day after day by the "Toreador Song," they will discover, eventually, that it comes from an opera about young vagrants — a secular passion-play about loitering with intent and everything that follows: sex, drugs, and rock-and-roll. Bizet could become their idol. Already, everyone knows that *Carmen*, a.k.a. Sex and Violence at the Cigarette Plant, can melt any quantity of heavy metal. *Amadeus* portrays Mozart as a sex-mad rebel who is much more interesting than James Dean. And don't get me started on *La Bohème*. I mean, these days don't all the kids call that particular opera *Rent*, and sleep on the winter sidewalks to get a ticket for it?

52 It's part of *Nature* for lawyers to fight lyrically

You have to wonder if the editors of *Nature* feel they've been scooped by a night at the opera.

It all started, apparently, in 1993, when Fran Rauscher, a psychology professor at the University of Wisconsin in Oshkosh, reported that university students performed "spatial-temporal reasoning" better after they listened to Mozart's *Sonata for Two Pianos in D Major*. This spawned books and CDs boasting of the "Mozart Effect." Mozart, the pitch went, "makes you smarter." When he was governor of Georgia, Zell Miller sponsored a bill that sent new mothers home from the hospital with a tax-funded, classical music CD, *Build Your Baby's Brain Through The Power of Music*. Colorado followed

Miller's lead, and Tennessee began presenting new parents with vouchers redeemable for the classical music recording, *Listen, Learn, and Grow*. Not to be caught Bach-handed, the Florida legislature passed its own "Beethoven Babies Bill," requiring state-run daycare centres to play classical music every day.

I think that it was Oscar Wilde who said Wagner was better than he sounds. And I have a running debate with more than one friend that Mozart is more "Musical Joke" than "Magic Flute." Dying young (my argument runs) doomed him to eternal immaturity, which is probably why he is so lauded in our society, as it worships adolescent self-regard above all else. Mozart wrote some pretty nice stuff, but he could never resist showing off. So I have to admit that I experienced a little *Schadenfreude* — the German for sadistic pleasure fits so snugly, here — when Kenneth Steele, another psychology professor (at Appalachian State University in Boone, North Carolina), reported on his attempts to duplicate Rauscher's Mozart Effect.

Steele played one of his student test-groups the Mozart sonata, the second group a Philip Glass (melodic modern) piece of the same length, while a control group heard nothing for the same period. The differences in test results, Steele says, were negligible. Following in his footsteps, three different research teams reported in *Nature* that they had similar non-results.

Keith Humphrey, who conducted the research at University of Western Ontario, told the *National Post* that "you will improve your spatial-temporal reasoning by performing tasks of spatial-temporal reasoning, not just by listening to Mozart." In other words, the students improved slightly in the tasks because they had already done them once, BM (Before Mozart). Which brings us back to the scooping, or the alleged scooping, of *Nature* at the opera — by a tax lawyer, no less. Details are sketchy pending trial, but here's what the alleged victim, Alexander Weaver, yet another lawyer, alleges.

Weaver, 44, was taking in *La Traviata* at the Lyric Opera of

Chicago when someone started rattling a candy wrapper behind him. He shushed the would-be candy-eater, who was or was not tax lawyer John Gaggini, 49. Gaggini says the shushing startled him out of a doze, making him involuntarily tap Weaver on the back of the head. Weaver says the tap was a deliberate slap, which is why he called the cops. Now, Gaggini stands charged with misdemeanor battery and faces a maximum penalty of a year in chokey.

If Weaver's story is accurate, all we can say (resisting the opportunity to pun on the legal repercussions of hitting sour notes) is, obviously, listening to classical music does not make you smarter.

We won't even mention the rock music enthusiasts who sent Rauscher threatening letters about the Mozart Effect. But perhaps *Nature*'s next foray into musicology will feature laboratory refutations of William Congreve, the countryman of Wilde the Wagner-phobe who claimed that music has charms to soothe the savage breast. *Nature*'s scientists might like to start at the Lyric Opera in Chicago. Mind you, the Associated Press has quoted an employee of that outfit as remarking, "The only thing I can tell you is that this is very unusual. Slapping incidents are very, very rare among opera patrons."

And one is at least glad to know that, when they are not engaged in black-tie fisticuffs, the Windy City's lawyers are vocal supporters of the arts. In my experience, the same holds true of Toronto, my home town, where I have been in the same symphony audience as several prominent lawyers, including the former attorney general of my province and the current dean of my former law school. The preponderance of the evidence, in other words, is that, even if classical music doesn't make you smarter, the smartest people listen to it.

53 Thirty days in Hell to firmer thighs

"Scarcely-veiled torture," one penologist called it, although the irony has hit me only some $3,600 later. Mind you, nearly $500 of that is Her Majesty's share. Where she used to take her toll in servitude on the treadmill, now the sovereign gets it through goods and service taxes when you buy one. Voluntarily.

Maybe it was the return of the harder Canadian winter, when exercise outdoors sears the lungs, bleeds the sinus cavities, takes the feet from under you and deposits your backside on bone-shattering black ice. Or maybe it just seemed more fun to watch Judge Judy while I performed cholesterol's daily penance. For whatever reason, my household succumbed to the post-holiday guilts and bought a motorized treadmill, the modern version of what used to be considered hard penal labor.

Apparently a highly celebrated industrial engineer invented the thing in its expressly punitive mode. While designing windmill sails in the early 1800s, William Cubitt created the first "prison tread-wheel." Her Majesty installed one in Bury St Edmunds Gaol in 1819, and they began to catch on with penologists like post-Christmas weight-loss schemes.

Sadists, of course, liked them long before we modern masochists started using them as part of our desperate, hamster-going-nowhere efforts to keep up with the Joneses. Australia's most notorious penal colony, Moreton Bay, employed treadwheels to particularly brutal effect in the 1820s and '30s, but even then they were seen as "improving" and humane, as substitutes for relentless floggings. In his highly-entertaining history of Australia, *The Fatal Shore*, Robert Hughes writes that the prison treadmill "stood for progress — the rationalization of punishment. It was a more philosophical instrument than the cat." And when you read there of prisoners flogged so often that the bones in their backs were permanently exposed, you get the drift. Still, one pauses to recall Lord Ellenborough's description of transportation of convicts to Australia as "a summer airing by an easy migration to a milder climate."

Hughes also notes that, back in cold London, whence the courts regularly shipped their bad 'uns to the fatal Australian shore, the Archbishop of Dublin recommended hard labor at the mill to free convicts of their sins: "With each additional step they took on the treadmill they would be walking out of prison." The treadwheel taught discipline, the reformers believed, habituating the lower orders to their natural, menial lot at the bottom of the food chain.

The treadwheel at Moreton Bay, which the convicts called "the everlasting staircase" and "the cockchafer" ("because the stiff prison clothes scraped one's groin raw," Hughes explains), at least had a practical purpose. Fifty convicts at a time trod its 40-foot boards to grind corn for their keep. But the mill we saw in *Wilde*, the film in which Stephen Fry plays reckless Oscar, apparently was more typical. Their feet in heavy shackles, prisoners, walled off from their fellow convicts and staring at blank wallboard, silently turned a wheel for some four hours per day, to no real practical purpose. *Black's Law Dictionary* includes an entry for "tread-mill, or tread-wheel" that describes this Cubitt design more precisely:

> *An instrument of prison discipline, being a wheel or cylinder with an horizontal axis, having steps attached to it, up which the prisoners walk, and thus put the axis in motion. The men hold on by a fixed rail, and, as their weight presses down the step upon which they tread, they ascend the next step, and thus drive the wheel.*

A sort of sail was attached on some prison roofs, to add resistance. Apparently authorities were to let the prisoners rest every 15 minutes, but medical experts had set their thrice-weekly "goal" at the equivalent of 1.4 miles of climbing, in a futile attempt to escape Hell.

I try to go at least five miles per session on our mill, and Judge Judy can be hell, but of course the comparisons stop there. I am better fed and clothed than most transported miscreants, and I exercise free will whenever my family, employers and governments tell me that I can. By contrast, "any chance of escape, no matter how thin," Hughes writes of Moreton Bay in remotest Queensland, "was preferable to life in this Georgian snake pit where even their turds were inspected for undigested kernels of stolen corn" — stolen, of course, before they could be treadmilled.

And although I metaphorically flagellate myself if I don't try hard enough or if I escape the mill's custody altogether for a day or two, no one else cudgels or flogs me for it. By comparison, no inmate escaped Moreton Bay, Hughes says, and those fugitives who survived the bush "walked or were dragged back . . . , half-dead from exhaustion, to face 100, 200 or even 300 clawing strokes of the cat and be loaded with 20-pound irons for the rest of their sentences." When the merciless Patrick Logan was magistrate there, on top of all this he illegally increased the would-be escapers' sentences by three years.

Yet no doubt the ghosts of Moreton Bay find "passing strange" the modern treadmill craze, at as much as $6,000 out of one's own pocket. What their contemporary advocate Sydney Smith says of the old prison treadwheels can apply to the modern voluntary versions. Never mind the attempts to distract you with pre-programmed workouts and read-outs on your calorie count and heart rate. "The labour of the treadmill is irksome, dull, monotonous and disgusting to the last degree." Judge Judy, or *Midnight Express* and *The Birdman of Alcatraz* on video, can ease the monotony. But one way or another we're still paying a high price for our indulgences.

54 Feeling less than flush, they blame Canada

The low-flow toilet seemed like a good idea in 1992. Even George W. Bush thought so, when all of North America was briefly being green. Environmentalism was fashionable, at home and on the hustings. But when the toilet clause of the U.S. *Environmental Policy and Conservation Act* took effect in the mid-'90s, "Not in my en suite!" became the battle cry of the republic.

The idea was to make the low-flow toilet the benchmark, as it were, by requiring that all new homes and renovations use the 1.6-gallon instead of the standard 3.5-gallon flush. But the citizenry found that they were obliged to flush twice and three times, and where was the conservation in that?

On September 10, 1997, Representative James Traficant — a Democrat, yet! — officially called for the repeal of the low-flow provision: "Mr. Speaker," Traficant said in Congress,

> *a flush is not a flush. The old standard toilet flushed away 3.5 gallons of water, so Congress in its inimitable wisdom passed a new law that said all toilets in America must use only 1.6 gallons of water. Since then, Americans are flushing . . . like mad, wasting more water than ever, recklessly trying to remove all of that void. . . . The American people, Mr. Speaker, are a flush away from a major movement. . . . If Congress can repeal prohibition, Congress can repeal this toilet.*

A black market developed. People bought old, high-flushers at wrecking yards and garage sales. Los Angeles homeowners double-hired plumbers to replace brand new low-flushers with the 3.5-gallon outlaw models as soon as the building inspector left. John D. Wagner of *Homeowner* magazine reported that one New York City property manager "saw 70 high-flow units mysteriously disappear from the junk heap overnight when he was overseeing a bath upgrade in an apartment building." And according to the *New York Times*, Wagner wrote, "some people are even taking their old toilets with them when they move. One woman said that her almond-colored toilets are 'going with me whether the next bathrooms I have are purple, yellow or black.'"

"Get the government out of bathrooms!" scofflaw Americans still shout, obliviously paraphrasing Pierre Trudeau on a different room, while, perversely, just like Robin Williams on a recent Academy Awards show, blaming Canada. In November, 1998, under the heading "The Maple Leaf Menace," journalist Dave Barry began spreading the Canadian conspiracy manure.

We were luring Americans across the border, he said, with our freeholds on 3.5-gallon high-flushers. In a sort of reverse rum-running, law-abiding Americans were falling prey to "Canadian toilet cartels headed by greed-crazed Canadian toilet kingpins who will stop at nothing to push their illicit wares on our vulnerable society."

Now, no less an authority than *Time* magazine insists that these rumors are true. According to *Time* correspondent Stacy Perman, Veteran Plumbing and Supplies of Windsor, Ontario, just the other side of the Detroit River from Michigan, reports that American high-flow business has increased its revenues by 20 percent. "And here's the best part," Perman gloats, clearly from the Canadian perspective. "Most of the outlaw commodes sold in Windsor are made in the U.S. by companies like Kohler and American Standard. The high-flush models can still be produced for export, so long as they are not resold in the U.S. And thanks to NAFTA, they are duty free."

In the result, a Republican congressman from Michigan, Joe Knollenberg, is doing his patriotic best to coax business back across his border, consolidating legislative support to sink the low-flow provision.

The truth seems to be that the controversy has forced manufacturers to make better low-flows. Supporters of low-flows claim that, now, one flush does it nine out of ten goes, saving billions of gallons of water. I own two low-flows, myself, actually, voluntarily purchased in the last three years, and as I've mined just about every other aspect of my personal life in my writing career, I might as well add that being green leaves us flush with pride about two tries out of three. Oh, Canada!

CHAPTER EIGHT

SOME OF MY BEST FRIENDS ARE BALD, DEAD WHITE GUYS

Human Rights

55 Go up thou, bald head

I started balding when I was 19. There was a bald spot at the top of my head that grew only very slowly — reverse-glacially, really, scooping out my follicles the way a glacier slowly scrapes away at the earth. It grew so gradually that for several years, I didn't think about it. It didn't occur to me that friends and acquaintances found it amusing or that strangers would decide that I was not worth meeting because an above-average quantity of testosterone coursed through my veins. I hadn't the slightest idea that people considered involuntary hair loss a handicap, a repulsive deformity. As it turned out, people are even more prejudiced about hair status than they are about color, race, and brassiere-size.

For some years after I hit 25, hardly a day went by that someone didn't merrily inform me that I was bald, even though there was still sufficient hair on my head that I had pretty much forgotten about the peach-fuzz patch on top. Then I read of a psychology experiment in which the subjects were shown close-up photographs of people they had never met. The subjects were asked to rate these strangers on how much they would like to get to know them. Based on appearance alone, nobody wanted to know the bald guys.

By the time I finally had refined a response to those who insisted on reminding me that my head was showing, it was too late. In my 40s, people expected me to be bald. So I waited in vain for the day when someone displayed a prurient interest in my semi-nude cranium. My unexecuted plan was to unbutton my shirt and suggest that they would be even more fascinated by the rest of my body — which, incidentally, has more hair on it than most barbershop floors. At least then the oglers would have had a really good reason for snubbing me.

Of course, hair-status prejudice signifies the end to civilization as we know it. Clearly we have wandered so far astray of our natural heritage that there is no return. We eat plastic food, we live in plastic environments, we breathe plasticized air, and now we don't even want to get to know bald guys. It stands to reason that lesser-endowed men — the testosterone-deprived — would feel threatened by us large-tested types. But, biologically speaking, reason dictates that women would find us irresistible. Who is more likely to help them get on with the all-important work of perpetuating the species — Donald Trump, Merv Griffin, or me? Trump, Griffin, Leona Helmsley. People with good head-hair make buildings. They make money. They make traffic congestion, ulcers, pollution, Trouble with a capital T. Bald people make babies.

What the world needs to redress this non-adaptive snub of Darwininan biology is a new legal fiction, a concept commensurate with legal blindness. Legal blindness is a legal fiction because it describes a state of impairment short of total disability. With that in mind, I propose the establishment of "legal baldness." It would be different from legal blindness not only because the afflicted body part is different, but because it would shift the onus of affliction to where it belongs — from the bald person to people who laugh at him. Local human rights law would impose jail terms for persons violating natural law by excoriating or mocking anyone "going a little thin on top." The *Criminal Code* would deem the nickname "Cueball" an obscenity. Affirmative-action dating agencies would be established for those whose foreheads wouldn't quit but who nonetheless showed a hair-raising gift for raising fur on their shoulder blades, buttocks, knuckles, and toes.

The government would create the National Action Committee on the Status of Persons Who Have Lost Hair But Are Okay With It. Television and print advertising (possible poster-persons: Captain Picard from *Star Trek*, Uncle Fester from *The Addams Family*) would promote hair-status harmony. At election time, a whole hour would be set aside for candidates to debate hairless positions. Universities would set up entire departments to study merely fuzzy issues. Books would be written, papers published, songs sung, stories told. Problems would be faced, baldly and head-on.

Then again, apparently the bald occasionally do have friends in high places. Elisha the prophet, for example, the prophet Elijah's hand-picked successor, could be the patron saint of the follickly challenged. Elijah with a j was wise, but he knew nothing from *alopecia*: "He was an hairy man, and girt with a girdle of leather about his loins" (II Kings 1:8). On the other hand, Elisha, like your correspondent, had had it up, or perhaps down, to his hairline with skinhead jokes:

> *And he went up from thence onto Bethel; and as he was going up by the way, there came forth little children out of the city, and mocked him, and said unto him, Go up thou, bald head, Go up thou, bald head.*

And he turned back and looked on them, and cursed them in the name of the Lord. And there came forth two she-bears out of the wood, and tare forty and two children of them." (II Kings 2:23-24).

Friends, as I say, in high places.

According to John Woodforde's *The Strange Story of False Hair* (made possible by the publishers of *Understanding Your Nerves* and *Build Your Own Swimming Pool*), late in the last century Cosmo Lang, soon to be Archbishop of Canterbury, had chosen "Go up thou bald head" as his text to open the Oxford assizes. As a certain judge entered the church, his wig caught on the lintel "and remained for a moment suspended, revealing that he was as bald as an egg." It remains unclear, however, whether this was yet more proof of divinity among the hairless.

The barrister's wig came into fashion during the reign of Charles II (1660-1685). Because the early ones were cumbersomely full-bottomed, evolution began almost immediately toward the modern tye-type. Mind you, the current lord chancellor, Lord Irvine of Lairg, aka Lord Wallpaper (in recognition of his lordship's penchant for redecorating his official residence in renaissance Italian court-style on the taxpayer's slate), has rebelled. As a news story put it:

'Cool Britannia' less formal

London: The Lord Chancellor . . . is tired of wearing a seventeenth-century costume to work and has asked Parliament if he could, please, wear a suit for every day and save the knee breeches, silk stockings and buckled shoes for special occasions. . . .

In fact, his lordship also asked if it was really necessary that he disport himself in his full-bottomed wig and impressive floor-length, black damask, gold-trimmed gown quite so often. Apparently tradition demanded fancy dress at all phases of legislative process except the committee stage (when his lordship could wear a designer suit), and that he had to wear the wig and gown during Question Period.

Yet it seems that what was good for the goose did not apply to the *shlepper*. In his (London) *Times* "Diary," Jasper Gerard wrote:

> *That lucky man Hayden Phillips, who is to become the Lord Chancellor's chief bag-carrier, has had to buy a new wardrobe. He will have to don two Gilbert and Sullivan-style outfits when he begins working for Lord Irvine of Lairg next month. For the opening of Parliament, Phillips has to wear a black tailcoat with laced cuffs, black knee breeches with silver buckles, a jabot [jacket], pumps with silver buckles, silk stockings and sword.*
>
> *At the start of a new Parliament, his attire needs to be only slightly less grand; tailcoat without cuffs, black trousers, silk gown and wig.*

Of course, traditionalists blame Labour for the lord chancellor's desire to slum around the House in his bunny slippers. It all started a few months earlier, when Buckingham Palace informed Lord Irvine that on state occasions he would no longer have to risk his neck backing down stairways after paying obeisance to Her Majesty. The LC's office was quick to insist that his lordship did not have "doddering legs," but he had no problem with turning his back on the monarch, or installing hand-carved oak beds in his Lord's residence at a cost of about $80,000. Those who worry about slippery steps, er, slopes, began whinging: "What next, High Mass in blue jeans?"

Actually, they already do that in some places, with out-of-tune guitars. And Lord Irvine's requests themselves are not without precedent. Lord Eldon, Lord Chancellor for the first third of the 1800s, once petitioned the king for permission to eschew his full-bottom wig on those occasions when it was not perched over the woolsack (the LC's seat in the House of Lords). His wife evidently found the thing less than attractive. "So lately as the reigns of James I and Charles I," his lordship advised His Majesty, "judicial wigs were unknown." The king was "willing, if you like it, that you should do as they did; for though they certainly had no wigs, yet they wore long beards." History does not record whether Lord Eldon replied that, not long after the period in issue, the benchers of the Inner Temple ordered that no member "should wear his beard above three weeks' growth on pain of forfeiting 20s."

Today, beards are not much in barristerial favor. Probably this is because, given the choice between looking Establishment and looking intelligent, most men would ask themselves, "Which one gets the babes?" Lawyers generally, anyway, even bald ones, seem to be pogonophobic — morbidly afraid of beards, a word I learned from *It Grows on You: A Hair-Raising Survey of Human Plumage*, by Roy Blount, Jr., who does not have any hair on his face. This may account for why I cannot find *pogonophobia* in the dictionary, a problem I also encountered with Mr. Blount's definition of *baby* as "the small curl on the tail of a judge's wig." It's up to you whether you want to trust him on flour: "In the eighteenth century, the British rich used up so much flour powdering their wigs that the British poor had a bread shortage."

This has the ring of truth to it, as does Blount's remark that Samuel Sewall, a judge who presided over the Salem "witch" persecutions, decried wigs as "godless emblems of iniquity." It is certainly true that "people have left their wigs to people in their wills" — or at least they have done the equivalent, according to some commentators. Sir Joseph Jekyll, a master of the rolls, left his estate to pay off Britain's national debt. Not surprisingly, his relatives challenged the will "on the ground of imbecility." Lord Mansfield remarked that Sir Joseph "might as well have attempted to stop the middle arch of Blackfriars bridge with his full-bottomed wig."

Of course, even before Samson, hair was symbolic of virility and power. I suppose that this is why streaming coiffures are so popular with heavy metal rock bands, and why skinheads like to show us they're so tough they don't need any. Unless you are a skinhead, or Kojak, it is a sign of defeat to pull out your hair or rend your beard. Roy Blount says that bald emperors passed laws requiring everyone else to cut their hair short.

Religious law often mandates that men display beards but that women hide their locks. Then again, religious law often mandates that men humble themselves by shaving their heads, and, as Blount points out, Mary Magdalene dried the feet of Jesus with her tresses. He calls this "the sexiest Christian scene," although he seems even more impressed by the hairy pagan story of Osiris. When the Egyptian fertility god died without an heir, his widow Isis warmed him with her hair until his penis reactivated sufficiently to impregnate her.

The cult of Isis was a strong force against Christianity. Not to be outdone, in the 1976 case of *Re Willard L. Mikesell*, a Promethean Michigan judge declared that he would reduce bail from $10,000 to $500 if the accused would get his hair cut "in a fashion similar" to his honor's — one-quarter inch all the way around. Partly on account of this decision, the judge was removed from the bench.

56 Self-expression gets really heated

The law may forbid you to yell "Fire!" in a crowded theater, but what if your athletic supporter shorts out in a packed casino? While *Nevada v. Anderson* doesn't raise this exact question, it brings all sorts of unexpected issues to mind, and makes a surprisingly convincing case for the "original intendment" argument of constitutional interpretation.

Philip Anderson was a professional "card counter" — a man who successfully played blackjack for a living by keeping track of which cards have already been dealt and are therefore out of circulation. Many casino managers are so impressed with the feats of memory displayed by counters that they ban them. But unlike the memory artists, Anderson, a businessman, had gone hi-tech.

Anderson counted cards by using "computer shoes." He cut the toes out of his socks so that when he tapped his foot against switches in the shoe, he transmitted signals to a computer strapped to his calf, telling it which cards had been dealt. Through a wire running up his leg, the computer sent little electric shocks to Anderson through his jockstrap, telling him how to play his hand. The computer ran off a battery he carried in his back pocket. In order to avoid painful burns — and telltale squirming at the blackjack table — Anderson had placed slightly inflated balloons between his body and the hardware.

In 1986, the state of Nevada charged Anderson with burglary — "entering a building with the intent to use a cheating device" — and "possession of a cheating device." In answer, he argued that the law violated the First Amendment of the U.S. constitution by "impeding the transfer of information from his toes to his buttocks."

It is widely known that casinos are bad losers, "happy to have drunks sit at the table and lose," as Andrew Blumen, Anderson's lawyer, put it. (Computer shoes and all, even Anderson was down $1,600 when he was arrested.) But Blumen has not convinced any court that jolting your nether parts is a form of expression protected by the U.S. constitution.

On the face of it, if you can put it that way, such behavior seems like yelling "Fire!" in your own gene pool. On that basis alone, you might argue that it failed the benchmark test of free expression law in the United States. There was a "clear and present danger" to Anderson's progeny, distinct U.S. citizens even if only in the abstract.

For that matter, shorting shorts were bound to be a hazard to the *existing* public, especially in places where dozens were prone to hang simultaneously from metal slot machines. Then again, journalists, authors, and other polemicists regularly trot out the First Amendment to complain that lawsuits have a "chilling effect" on free expression. Anderson might well have said that forced removal of his computerized supporter would have worked a like effect on him, and who could argue with that, especially in February?

Jocularity is probably the response claims like Anderson's deserve. The prosecution in the case called the First Amendment claim "silly," and in its brief filed with the Nevada Supreme Court it remarked, "There was no debate or communication of ideas . . . between the defendant and his hidden computer that remotely has any connection to the First Amendment." In an *amicus curiae* brief, the state attorney general agreed: "The defendant was not attempting to continue the building of our politics and culture." After ruling that the Nevada statute barring card-counting devices from casinos was not unconstitutionally vague, the supreme court tersely held: "Respondent's other contentions have been considered. They are without merit. Reversed and remanded" — to the trial court, for prosecution against Anderson as charged.

According to Blumen the court observed that if Anderson had been using a pencil and paper or an abacus or some other low-technology device, it would have been "hard-pressed to enforce the statute's validity." I do not find this anywhere in the court's written reasons. While casinos might be perfectly happy to wager that a sucker is born every microsecond, they don't hold a gun to anybody's head. The really clear and present danger could simply have been that Anderson and his computer would have made plain to the other gamblers that they were saps. In this sense, the *Anderson* case reminds us of every political scandal and high-level fraud we read about in the daily newspapers. Beating the system at its own game may not be technically illegal, but it offends everyone who accepts the spirit of fair play that defines the status quo.

Using the law to beat the system would not be a profound affront if it concerned nothing but a gambling dispute. Constitutional rights and freedoms are another matter. If someone wants to electrify his undershorts, that's his own business. Ditto maybe even where Smith wants to dance naked on saloon tables while Jones watches. (In 1980, a prosecutor in Toronto urged that a stripper was free to express herself by exposing her 73-inch breasts in a nightclub, but it was legally indecent for her to invite awestruck patrons to touch the extraordinary glands: "It was a minor version of a live sex act. One hopes that this is not going to be the thin end of the wedge."*) Yet some lawyers argue that to ask for constitutional protection for jock-zapping and nude dancing is to make mock of our fundamental constitutional freedoms.

It might in fact be the kind of tactic that makes people lump lawyers in with the criminals they represent — winning at any cost, including the cheapening of civil rights. Reactionary though they might sometimes be, "original intenters" — lawyers who insist that constitutions must be interpreted only in reference to what their original framers intended — remind us that the First Amendment was designed to protect democracy itself, expression of belief and opinion, even "the thought we hate." And the Fourteenth Amendment guarantee of equal treatment under the law, upon which Anderson also relied (to get himself out of state and into constitutional

---

*In general, the law has been loathe to regard breasts as sexual organs. In Nova Scotia in 1980, this led to the surprising court decision that if a man grabbed a woman's breast, he was not committing a sexual assault. In 1984, a woman in Toronto was charged with performing an indecent act by masturbating a man with her breasts in the front seat of a truck. The prosecution was obliged to withdraw the charge when the judge ruled that this was impossible. See page 158.

jurisdiction), was the post-Civil War response to the *Dred Scott* case, itself a primer on how legal cynics use newspeak: before the Fourteenth, *Scott* denied recently freed slaves citizenship and all the rights that accompanied it.

While it is true that even frivolous cases can make important law (recent controversial litigation about the supposed free-expression right to burn the American flag is an example), it is more often a fact that *Anderson*-type arguments strain already thin and clotted judicial resources, violating civil rights in more urgent cases.

CHAPTER NINE

IF YOU CAN'T SAY SOMETHING NICE

Libel, Slander, Contempt, and Generally Minding One's Tongue

57 "I go mainly on the word *rotten*": A selected history of the law of contempt of court

"The Norman Conquest is a catastrophe which determines the whole future history of English law." Mostly, Pollock and Maitland explain (as their blood pressure returns to normal) in their *History of English Law*, 1898, the "catastrophe" is a matter of linguistics — the fact that the language of our law owes more to French than to Anglo-Saxon. "It would be hardly too much to say," the scholars observe, "that at the present day almost all our words that have a definite legal import are in a certain sense French words. *Contract, agreement, covenant, obligation, debt, condition, bill, note, master, servant, partner, guarantee, tort, trespass, . . .* " They multiply examples for the rest of the page. And, sure enough, from the 13th through the 16th centuries, the everyday language of English law continued to be French, largely because it was also the everyday language of the British royal court. But as Pollock and Maitland note in a pointed aside, "To dignify with the name 'Norman-French' the mere 'dog-French' that we find in law reports of the sixteenth century is ridiculous."

Probably the most notorious example of that "dog-French" — this mongrel Frenglish that signified the last gasp of direct Norman influence in Britain — is one of the earliest reports of contempt of court in our legal system. According to this case from 1631, upon being convicted of a felony a prisoner "ject un Brickbat a le dit justice que narrowly mist" — "threw a brickbat at the said justice, which narrowly missed him." The justice was Richardson, Chief Justice of the Common Bench, and the brickbat, according to some reports, was a large flintstone. Fortunately, Chief Justice Richardson was "leaning low of his elbow, in a lazie recklesse manner," so the stone carried away his hat without touching his head. After the narrow escape, Chief Justice Richardson is said to have remarked to some friends, "You see, now, if I had been an upright judge, I had been slain." But his lordship apparently did not find the attempted battery amusing at the time. As another report puts it:

> For this [the throwing of the flintstone] Noy* immediately drew up an indictment against the prisoner, whose right hand was cut off and fixed on the gibbet where he, himself, was immediately hanged in the presence of the court. (Et pur ceo immediately fuit Indictment drawn per Noy envers le prisoner, & son dexter manus ampute & fix al Gibbet sur que luy mesme immediatement hange in presence de Court.)

---

*William Noy (or Noye), 1577–1634, attorney-general under Charles I. He sometimes proved relentless in his advocacy for the Establishment, and was only recently appointed the king's chief law officer at the time of the brickbat assault.

In his *Second Miscellany-at-Law*, Sir Robert Megarry records another instance of a disgruntled litigant, one Cosgrave, expressing his displeasure by projectile. Cosgrave threw an egg at Vice-Chancellor Malins, which missile nearly hit the vice-chancellor's head but instead broke against the canopy where he sat. No one has been able to document it, but at evading egg on his judicial face, Vice-Chancellor Malins is reported to have remarked gravely, "That must have been intended for my brother Bacon" — also a vice-chancellor of the court.

Whether Vice-Chancellor Bacon's riposte was ready wit or apocryphal, the prisoner, though he was carrying a pistol that he thoughtfully did not use on his lordship, paid dearly. Cosgrave served more than five months in Holloway Prison before deportation to his native U.S.A.

Sticks and stones are not just child's play, it seems, nor are defamatory words. Thirty-eight years before the brickbat case, but less famously, a man named Constable had put it about that Sir Christopher Hilliard, Justice of the Peace, was "a blood-sucker, and sucketh blood; that if any man will give him a bribe, as sheep, or a couple of capons, he will take them." When Sir Christopher sued, the trial judges found that only the first bit, about blood-sucking, might be criminally libelous. Could it have been that justices of the peace were expected to take bribes?

Constable appealed and was acquitted on the Monty Pythonesque ground that he might just as well have been paying Sir Christopher a compliment: a good J.P., after all, made it his business to go for the jugular:

> For it is usual when a justice of the peace pursues offenders, and does his office, to call him "blood-sucker"; and it is not any slander unto him and may be taken in some good sense in executing his office.

Just two years on the other side of the brickbat case, an angry citizen who lives on anonymously in the law reports called an also-anonymous justice "a logger-headed and sloutch-headed bursen-bellied hound." The image seems to interbreed a kangaroo with a bloodhound and a Neanderthal man: *loggerhead* is a literal form of *blockhead*, and *bursen-bellied* seems to come from *burse*, meaning "purse" — as in *bursary* — perhaps the one that serves as an insignia for the lord chancellor (confirming the public's worst suspicions about lawyers). One may wonder how such a creature could earn his living trying cases, but the words were nonetheless held to be legally harmless.

Sore losers span the centuries, of course. In his *Law and Life*, lawyer and recorder Geoffrey Dorling Roberts tells how a prisoner screamed at him, "I shall appeal here and now, you big-nosed ——ing bastard —nt." The elisions are those of Roberts, who, "hoping for sympathy," told his wife of the incident. She found it unfair: "You haven't got a big nose."

Then there are the less expressive, sometimes oblivious contempts. In the 1877 Australian case of *Re Dakin*, the contemnor was cited for doing nothing other than his business — hammering together signboards. He had attempted to perform this work "as quietly as possible" but, as the courts of justice were hard by, Chief Justice Higginbotham expressed indignation, explaining that many cases involving personal liberty had been argued amidst the din, including two on capital charges.

More often than judges, it is process servers who bear the contempt of a litigant, and it remains good law that you commit contempt of court by attacking its officers. In 1773, a defendant "Johns" was ordered to show cause why he should not be held in contempt for "making the person who served him with a subpoena ... eat the same ... and otherwise ill-treating him." The added trouble was, once burnt, twice shy: "by reason of [Johns'] ferocious and terrible disposition," no one in the county employ would serve

Johns with the order that he was to appear to answer a contempt allegation. The court ruled that a process server could simply leave the order at his door.

A similar problem had been pre-emptively solved in 1711. An unnamed defendant had become subject to imprisonment when, on being served with notice of a criminal information against him, he remarked that "he did not care a fart for the rule of the court." A prosecutor proposed that the defendant be ordered to appear before the court to show cause why he should not be committed for contempt, but the justices simply issued an arrest warrant, reasoning that the scofflaw was unlikely to find this second court order any more attractive than the first.

Of course, lawyers have frequently been accused of contempt, and not always because they become emotionally caught up in their clients' affairs. In 1775, for example, a solicitors' group was cited after they had filed suit on behalf of a highwayman claiming "breach of partnership" against his colleague in iniquity. The latter bandit had refused to share the mutually ill-gotten gains.

Less common, probably, are instances such as that of a century earlier, when the court cited a sheriff acting in the line of duty. The sheriff had originally been ordered to specify by metes and bounds a wife's one-third dower share in her husband's house. Rather than assigning the woman a given number of rooms, on some whim the sheriff chalked out a third part of each room. Unamused, the Elizabethan justices found the sheriff's joke "idle and malicious."

The leading contempt case in the legal history of the British Commonwealth is at least as interesting as its vivid antecedents. *R. v. Gray* is a prosecution notable both for the abuse that occasioned it, and for the fact that of the two reported versions of the case, judges rarely cite the one that quotes exactly what Gray said that was scandalous.

The more candid version, in the *Law Times Reports*, tells how Gray, an Edinburgh newspaperman, took both personal and professional umbrage at remarks Justice Darling made at the beginning of an obscenity trial. Before hearing the case, Justice Darling warned the press that if they reported the details of the evidence, he would personally "make it his business" to prosecute them as well. Remarking that Justice Darling would have better spent his time trying the backload of court cases rather than running newspapers, Gray called his lordship, among other things, "little Tich ["shorty" or "squirt"] upholding his dignity on a point of honour in a public-house," and "an impudent little man in horsehair." He concluded his diatribe: "One of Mr. Justice Darling's biographers states that 'an eccentric relative left him much money.' That misguided testator spoiled a successful bus conductor."

More recently, in what has become another leading case, an itinerant law clerk had occasion to characterize the British judge who sent him to prison for six months for contempt as a "humourless automaton." The clerk had been working at yet another obscenity prosecution which he found tedious. Hoping to "enliven" the proceedings (to use Lord Justice Denning's felicitous description), the contemnor stole a canister of nitrous oxide from a hospital parking lot and planned to introduce the "laughing gas" through the court ventilation system into the trial. He was found out before he could put the plan into action, which was just as well, even if no one had a laugh: in overturning the conviction the entire court of appeal doubted that anyone could be convicted of attempted contempt, and they were certain that the physical act of contempt itself was not completed in this case. Indeed, even if the clerk had made it to the courthouse roof and managed to release the gas into the vents, when the nitrous oxide entered the courtroom air it would have been too dilute to produce any effect at all.

In Canada, the *Gray* case has its immediate counterpart in the factually striking *R. v. Kopyto (No. 2)*. *Kopyto* arose out of a Toronto lawyer's unremitting advocacy for a socialist activist who believed that the Royal Canadian Mounted Police had schemed in sundry ways to make him lose his position on the executive of the League for Socialist Action. For five dogged years, the lawyer, Harry Kopyto, had filed writ after motion after appeal, exhausting every legal alternative. As a last resort, he spent another three years moiling away in Small Claims Court, with its last-chance ceiling of $3,000 on damage awards. When that failed, as well, on the infuriating ground that after eight years of storming the battlements Kopyto had filed the claim too late, Kopyto headed full-steam for the court of public opinion.

"This decision is a mockery of justice," he told a writer for the *Globe and Mail*, who reported the words to all of Canada the next day.

> *It stinks to high hell. It says it is okay to break the law and you are immune so long as someone above you said to do it. Mr. Dowson and I have lost faith in the judicial system to render justice. We're wondering what is the point of appealing and continuing this charade of the courts in this country which are warped in favor of protecting the police. The courts and the RCMP are sticking so close together you'd think they were put together with Krazy Glue.*

Although the offense of scandalizing the court is a British import, there have been no successful prosecutions under British law for 70 years. Canada, on the other hand, may well hold the modern record for scandalizing prosecutions in the free world. Of the better-known recent cases, in 1970 the British Columbia Supreme Court acquitted journalist Allan Fotheringham of scandalizing a coroner's court, and in 1971, Manitoba Minister of Transport Joe Borowski (more lately famous for sponsoring anti-abortion litigation) was convicted after he remarked in a radio interview that a judge had shown political bias in a case that was "an insult to Canadian justice."

When Harry Kopyto was tried in the Supreme Court of Ontario during the fall of 1986, the legal profession rallied uncharacteristically to his defense. A platoon of some of the most prominent criminal defense lawyers in the country worked on his case free of charge, and the Criminal Lawyers' Association won intervenor status. Represented by former crown counsel David Doherty (who shortly after became a justice of appeal), the Association admitted that freedom of expression should be limited to the extent that it genuinely threatened the fair administration of justice. But they were also convinced that criminal defense lawyers such as Kopyto, those most closely in touch with the criminal justice system, must feel uninhibited to hold that system publicly accountable. In fact, the view among barristers in general was that in bringing the scandalizing charge against Kopyto, the attorney general was compromising counsels' ability to defend their clients as they saw fit, as well as threatening their professional principles, morale, and livelihood.

Still, Justice Montgomery found that Kopyto's comments were contemptuous: they embodied "a vitriolic, unmitigated attack" on the small-claims judge that went "far beyond criticism" to deliberate vilification. The Krazy Glue remark was "a blatant attack on all judges of all courts . . . likely to lower the authority of the court and its respect in the public eye." After hearing from the crown that a jail term would only make Kopyto a martyr, Justice Montgomery forbade Kopyto to practice in the courts until he purged his contempt by apologizing to all the judges of the province.

A year later, a five-judge panel of the Ontario Court of Appeal unanimously overturned the conviction. Kopyto told the press, "It's a victory for the legal profession, it's a victory for the public, it's a victory for freedom of speech." But the entire appeal court seems to have found at least some of his published remarks repugnant. Justice Peter de Carteret Cory characterized them as "a puerile manifestation of petulant pique" in "the poorest possible taste," and "no more than the whining of an unhappy loser. It was unreasonable, unprofessional, and unworthy of even the most marginal and most recent member of the profession. It was, in a word, disgraceful." But a majority of three judges held that, as prosecuted in this instance, "scandalizing the court" violated freedom of expression as guaranteed by Canada's *Charter of Rights and Freedoms*. And in that light, *Kopyto* is an interesting cultural artifact, a totem, really, of Canada in its jurisprudential adolescence, struggling to rationalize its Old World parentage in the brave New World of North America.

Of course counsel appear quite frequently in the law reports because of remarks they are wont to make about the court. Frequently, however, lawyers are not shy about directing their comments to the court's face. Sometimes counsel include their professional opponents in the opprobrium, as with the 1978 case where a barrister called the opposing Crown lawyer corrupt. When the judge asked him what he meant by "corrupt," he replied that he meant "rotten," "depraved," "not fully capable," "worthless," "wicked," and "dissolute," but, when all was said and done, "I go mainly on the word 'rotten.'"

58 Troublesome women, rabble-rousing men

Never mind Scrooge or the old curmudgeon down the street: it is impossible for a man to be a common scold. A man might be a common "barrator," a quarrelsome or litigious person, but in our common law scolding is sex specific. The 18th-century legal historian William Blackstone says that the form of charge was originally "*com-*

munix rixatrix, for our law Latin confines it to the feminine gender" (-ix being a feminine ending; a man would be a *rixator*.)

Illegal scolds are "troublesome and angry women who . . . break the public peace, increase discord, and become a public nuisance to the neighbourhood." A Pennsylvania court has held that if defense lawyers find such law sexist or ungallant, they should take it up with government:

> *As for the unreasonableness of holding women liable for a too free use of their tongue, it is enough to say that the common law, which is the expressed wisdom of the ages, adjudges that it is not unreasonable. . . . The argument drawn from the indelicacy and unreasonableness of such a prosecution of a female should be addressed, therefore, to the legislature rather than to the courts.*

The leading case seems to be *U.S. v. Royall*, the result of three charges laid against Ann Royall in 1829, in the District of Columbia. Royall was accused of "being an evil-disposed person, a common slanderer and disturber of the peace and happiness of her good and honest neighbors . . ."; of being a common scold; and of being "a common brawler and sower of discord."

Perhaps the neighbors were throwing everything they had at Ann, to see what would stick. Only the "common scold" count did, it turned out, as the single charge capable of such "general" description. In other words, while the charges were all vague (and a person has the right to know clearly the charges she must answer), the law did not require the indictment to specify the words of Royall's calumny.

At trial, Royall's lawyer had argued that the crime was anachronistic, if ever known to Maryland law, and inconsistent with the state's *Bill of Rights*. All the old authorities held that the punishment for scolding was ducking on a ducking or "cucking" stool, which was not only "cruel and unusual" but obsolete even in England (even in 1829) whence it came.* If the punishment was red-coated obsolete, the lawyer claimed, so must be the offense: it was plain old UnAmerican, with a capital U.

The earlier leading case on ducking scolds, *R. v. Foxby*, was very English, indeed. At trial in 1703, the justices convicted Foxby, explaining that "scolding alone is not the offence, but it is the frequent repetition of it to the disturbance of the neighbourhood which makes it a nuisance." Foxby's lawyer moved to appeal on the ground that the indictment had charged her with being a common *calumniatrix* instead of the technically correct *rixatrix*, at which point Chief Justice Holt wondered aloud if such an appeal would be wise as "it was better ducking in a Trinity term" — springtime — "than in a Michaelmas term," when Foxby's appeal would come up, in late autumn. The court anyway

> *enlarged the time until the next Term, to see how she would behave herself in the meantime: for Holt, Chief Justice, said, "that ducking would rather harden than cure her; and if she were once ducked, she would scold on all the days of her life."*

Foxby got off on a technicality, with a scolding from the court. But in the *Royall* case, Chief District Court Judge Cranch found that, as an indictable common law offense (a crime that existed independently of the district's statutes), scolding was punishable by means other than

---

*Ducking as practiced in Britain could be very unpleasant, all right, a form of temporary outlawry from the small communities where it was commonly employed: the offender was paraded through the streets, sometimes in a commode, then dunked in a cold pond, river, or, occasionally, sewage dump. But in some ways the alternative, a mouth trap, was worse. Inside the trap, which locked over the jaw, was a sharp flange. The flange abutted the wearer's tongue so that she would be injured if she talked. For more on the history and use of the ducking stool or "castigator," see my *Naked Promises*, p. 53 and notes.

ducking and was therefore not tied to an obsolete barbarity. Judge Cranch convicted Royall and assessed her a ten-dollar fine, costs, and security on a pledge to be of good behavior for a year.

Despite the severity of the punishments scolding might attract, it was a minor offense. Spreading false news has always been a far more serious matter, signalled perhaps by the fact that it is usually men who have been accused of it, and also by the fact that the offense has been prosecuted in North America in recent years, with great notoriety.

"Publishing or spreading false news" is a type of defamation. In the most serious cases, it also looks a lot like sedition or treason, the perceived danger being that the false news will cause serious harm to society at large. The offense originated in the *Statute of Westminster*, 1275, styled as *scandalum magnatum*:

> *Forasmuch as there have been oftentimes found in the Country Devisors of Tales whereby Discord, or Occasion of Discord, hath many times arisen between the King and his People, or great Men of the Realm; For the damage that hath and may thereof ensue, it is commanded, That from henceforth, none be so hardy to tell or publish any false News or Tales, whereby Discord or Occasion of Discord or Slander may grow between the King and his People, or the great Men of the Realm; and he that doth so, shall be taken and kept in Prison, until he hath brought him into the Court, which was the first Author of the Tale.*

In Elizabethan times, when the Queen was extremely, and not always unreasonably, sensitive to political machinations, *scandalum magnatum* was punished by amputation of the ears for a slander and amputation of a hand for a writing. In his 1877 *Digest of the Criminal Law* (a codification of British criminal law), Sir James Fitzjames Stephens included a contemporary equivalent of *scandalum magnatum*:

> *Every one commits a misdemeanor who cites or publishes any false news or tales whereby discord or occasion of discord or slander may grow between the Queen and her people or the great men of the realm (or which may produce other mischiefs).*

The offense was repealed in England in 1888, but, thanks to Stephens' model, it has survived elsewhere. As recently as 1987, a German immigrant to Toronto was convicted of spreading false news after he published booklets attacking generally accepted views on the persecution and murder of Jews by the Nazis. The historical revisionist appealed, arguing that the *Canadian Charter of Rights and Freedoms* guaranteed his right of free speech in such matters. A five-judge appeal panel unanimously concluded that the "spreading false news" law (section 177 of the *Criminal Code**) was a reasonable limitation on freedom of expression, and was sufficiently specific in its means and ends, in that instance, protecting "the public interest in racial and social tolerance."

The publications were the usual sort of anti-Semitic drivel — one was called "Did Six Million Really Die?" — but the appeal court (and evidently the jury) felt that they posed a real and present danger to public order. The court of course had the very heavy weight of history on its side.

---

*Section 177 reads: "Every one who wilfully publishes a statement, tale or news that he knows is false and that causes or is likely to cause injury or mischief to a public interest is guilty of an indictable offence and is liable to imprisonment for two years." The mental element "wilfully" is made explicit, and Stephens' mischief element is no longer incidental. In fact, in recent years the mischief element has come to play a more important legal role. While the common law in England was focusing more and more on the public mischief done, until 1953 the Canadian *Code* version of the law was categorized under "Seditious Offences." In 1953, the word *statement* was added, and the entire provision was moved to "Nuisances," under "Part IV: Sexual Offences, Public Morals and Disorderly Conduct."

The law, statutory and common, has never required that actual harm be done. In the Holocaust denial case, the Ontario Court of Appeal seems to suggest that publishing literature which attacks the conventional view of the number of Jews tortured and killed by Nazi Germany could be illegal, no matter that the tenor of the times makes it less likely that the publication will result in obvious physical harm.

Sad to say, not much has changed in at least 270 years, not even in light of the Holocaust. In 1732, one Osborn put a rumor about that recent Jewish immigrants to England from Portugal had set afire "a bastard child begotten by a Christian on the body of a Jewish woman." The immigrants were assailed by a mob. On a preliminary motion, a court expressed doubt that the false news prosecution would succeed insofar as no specific victim of the libel was named. But a more sensitive court later decided that the entire Jewish community was laid open to harm by such lies, and therefore the prosecution could proceed.

In 1778, Alexander Scott appeared in the Old Bailey charged with printing false news of an impending war with France. Similarly, but conversely, in 1814, a group of men put it about that peace would soon be made between George III and Napoleon, and even that Napoleon was dead, their aim being to raise the price of government securities. Their lawyer argued that spreading "false reports, rumours, arts and contrivances" was an offense unknown to English law, and that, if anything, higher prices on government securities would be to the public good. The presiding judges did not view it that way, although their judgments seem founded more in the law of conspiracy than in *scandalum magnatum*. Still, the chief justice, Lord Ellenborough, did say that "the purpose itself is mischievous" (the purpose of the conspiracy, that is), a notable remark today considering that mischief is the foundation of the offense as embodied in the law where it remains on the books.

Also of modern interest is the view in that case that the prosecution was not obliged to prove continuing hostilities between

England and France. A judge could simply take notice of what was already widely known. In the "Holocaust revisionism" prosecution, the Ontario Court of Appeal refused to decide whether the courts would take judicial notice of the Holocaust — whether, in other words, they could simply have accepted the Holocaust as a fact without hearing evidence on the subject. Obviously, this disappointed both sides in the case.

The earlier two Canadian cases on "spreading false news" are separated by 62 years. In 1907, an American shopkeeper living in Taber, Alberta, appeared before the Supreme Court of the Northwest Territories for what amounted to an outburst of bitterness. George Hoaglin had put posters up in the windows of his store, and had printed flyers, proclaiming that he was holding a "closing out sale" because he was leaving Canada. "Americans not wanted in Canada," he announced. "Investigate before buying lands and taking homesteads in this country."

In fact, Canada was hungry for American immigration, despite Hoaglin's unhappy experience of the country. He had become disgruntled, apparently, after the federal government prosecuted him for some "infraction under the Inland Revenue Law." The Supreme Court convicted him of spreading false news, but noted that the words he used were not necessarily offensive in themselves. The *context*, the court held, made them unlawful. If a newspaper "in discussing public policy" stated that immigration by Americans was contrary to Canadian interest, this could be fair comment, as could the simple caveat to new immigrants that they should buy land or take homesteads with a wary eye. Then again, the court added, if the posters were untrue but mere merchant's puffery — "Going Out of Business, Unbeatable Bargains" — there would be no offense under the *Criminal Code*. But the additional falsehood about the unpopularity of Americans could, when coupled with "Going out of business," have caused genuine public harm.

In 1969, a trial court fined the editor of a Montreal underground newspaper $100, and bound him over to keep the peace, after he published the false news that Jean Drapeau, then mayor of the city, "had been shot by a dope-crazed hippie." But the Quebec Court of Appeal overturned the conviction. The accused had published the story, claiming that the counter-cultural assailant had stabbed Mayor Drapeau with a hypodermic needle, as part of a parody of the *Montreal Gazette*. The parody was designed to be invisible until the newspaper was unfolded, but because in some cases the paper had been sold reverse-folded, several readers purchased it on the misapprehension that it was the genuine *Gazette*.

Even though 50 anxious readers had phoned the night editor of the *Gazette*, and two had called the Mayor's office, Justice Hyde found it "difficult to imagine that anyone could have been misled into believing that the story was genuine." Justice Hyde could not see where the public mischief lay. "While I consider the page was stupid, pointless, and in bad taste," he wrote, "I cannot agree that, *per se*, it was reasonably sure to cause trouble or insecurity."

59 You say *cocotte*, I say bleached blond bastard

Legal translation is a complex game. English law does not speak English, you might say, let alone French or Spanish. Nor, apparently, does Tanganyikan law speak Russian. Charles Berlitz tells of delegates at the United Nations discussing Tanganyikan legislation called *The Organic Act*. The Russian translator rendered it literally as *Organicheskiy Akt*, which was mechanically correct but also means "sexual intercourse." As the discussion went on the "fascinated Russian delegates first chortled, then laughed outright, even exchanging waves with the Ukrainian, Byelorussian, Bulgarian, Polish, Czech, and Yugoslavian delegates." At last, the translator "brought down the house" with her translation of a reply to the question "What do the natives think of the *Organic Act*?" "In general," the translator informed her delegates, "they maintain a passive attitude."

Occasionally the law has asked jurors to act as semi-professional translators in these *double-entendre* situations. Particularly memorable is a 1925 defamation action in New York, *Rogira v. Boget*. Elena Rogira was a stewardess on the *S.S. Orizaba*, which called at ports in Cuba and Spain. The second steward, Andrew Boget, was enamored of Rogira, a widow with four children, to the point that he became jealous when she performed shipboard work for the chief steward.

As the *Orizaba* steamed out of Havana one evening for Spain, some of the crew were seated at dinner. Rogira asked Boget to arrange for water to be brought to the table. According to her evidence, Boget replied, "Why don't you go to your friend's room and ask him for ice water?"

"I have no friends," Rogira responded. "I just am nice to everybody, and I have no friends."

"Go ahead," Boget said. "You are worse than a *cocotte*."

"With this, the plaintiff fainted," the New York Court of Appeal reports, "not, however, until she had slapped his face." The court found that the other crew members at the table understood French and that *cocotte* was "a French word meaning a woman who leads a fast life, one who gives herself up for money. The interpreter said it implies to some men the same ideas as the word *prostitute*. In other associations it may mean a poached egg."

The trial and lower appellate court dismissed Rogira's complaint, but the appeal court decided that, as Boget's use of *cocotte* might have "imputed unchastity" to Rogira, she could have had a valid slander action. The court ordered a new trial, but the law remains bereft of a settled definition of *cocotte*. Rogira dropped her lawsuit before it reached a second hearing. Perhaps someone would have pointed out there that *ma cocotte* can mean something like "sweetie-pie," and that the most common usage of the word is to describe an everyday casserole pot.

What amounts to an imputation of "unchastity" is of course a product of the times. One day in the early 1600s, for example, a man named Knight said to Joan Califord, "Thou art Mutcome's hackney," a hackney normally being a horse, of course, but it could also mean a woman who offered rides for a price. In case there was any doubt, Knight elaborated: "Thou art a thieving whore and a pocky whore, and I will prove thee a pocky whore."

Like fat men called Slim, Knight must have been ironically named, or perhaps he found it a strain to live up to his moniker's courteous pretense. He had some luck in court, however. When Joan Califord's husband sued him for slander, the justices proved themselves unrelentingly literal-minded. As thieving was not a felony, calling a woman a "thieving whore," they held, left no remarkable stain on her reputation. To call her "pocky whore" would have been actionable if it implied promiscuity, but "pocky" in itself did not signify the *French* pox "when it is not shewn by any other circumstance, as to say that she was laid of them, or the like." (*The Dictionary of the Vulgar Tongue*, 1811, gives *French disease* as "the venereal disease, said to have been imported from France.") Never mind that you just called the woman a whore; she could have got the pox otherwise, you know . . . somehow.

Forty-three years later, a different court saw the illogic of this when Bridget Marshal's father sued neighbor Chickall. Chickall had called Bridget "a whore, and a pocky-ars'd whore." It was not actionable, the court ruled, to say simply "thou art a whore," and "thou hast had the pox" (again, calling a woman a "whore" did not necessarily mean she was "unchaste"), but to link the calumnies — "Thou art a whore and hast had the pox" — was to invite penalty, the implication being that the pox was not chicken- or small-, but, indeed, French.

Even within a year of the Califord case, an English court seemed to rule that if you supplied some repulsively graphic details, being called a pocky whore could indeed attract money damages. The words there were, "Mrs. Miller is a whore and hath had the pox and hast holes one may turn his finger in them. Mr. Ring the apothecary gave her drink for it, and therefore take heed how you drink with her."

In fact, in the even earlier *Levet's Case*, a much tamer aspersion was held to be slanderous. The defendant had said, "Thy house is infected with the pox and thy wife was laid of the pox," which was offensive not because of the words "thy wife was laid of the pox," but because the "house" was an inn. The words were therefore "a discredit to the plaintiff, and the guests would not resort thither." The court awarded Levet £50 in damages.

Yes, at times our law has valued women at less than business assets. But by the early 1900s, our courts reflected society's greatly increased sensitivity to woman's good name. A young plaintiff successfully sued for libel when a New York reporter wrote that she was a "dancer at Coney Island." This, the court held, put the woman before "the public gaze not only as unchaste but as belonging to one of the lowest classes of the great army of fallen women."

More surprisingly, perhaps, the modern cases also say that, even in times when putative illegitimacy could dash one's hopes of property and inheritance, it wasn't very often that *bastard* was an actionable slander, no matter who you were, and no matter the associated "imputation of unchastity." In 1950 a New York couple called their landlady, Mrs. Notarmuzzi, a "bleached blond bastard." She sued in slander but, according to the state's supreme court, it didn't matter that the Shevacks also called her a "lousy tramp" (translation: *cocotte*), "rotten son of a bitch" (albeit bleached blond male tramps were presumably very rare at the time), "black marketeer," and "bootlegger." Circa 1950 in the U.S., alleged bleached-blondism, not to mention bastardy, did not seriously impugn Notarmuzzi's character.

Indeed, as with the case of *cocotte* in dictionaries, law reports that predate *Notarmuzzi* translate *bastard* as an endearment. The American journalist Walter Winchell was once prosecuted for criminal libel after using *bastard* in his column. The complainant evidently suspected that the insult would not be defamatory civilly, but his resort to criminal justice was no more productive. Acquitting Winchell, the court found that great men such as Erasmus and Alexander Hamilton were "illegitimate," and that men regularly called friends "you old bastard."

A similar finding was made in South Africa in 1943, arising out of a dispute between two railway foremen. The alleged defamation occurred after "threats of violence were exchanged, interposed with the usual pleasantries" — racial slurs, scatological commands, and a theory that the plaintiff was bred of "half bastard, half yellow-belly." But Justice van den Heever found that railroaders "habitually use strong language spiced with salacious terms subolent [sic] of the sewer" and in railway workshops "the word 'bastard' is frequently used as a term of endearment." The plaintiff therefore could not recover for that denigration, but was awarded £80 for the observation that "he should have been in an internment camp long ago."

The case law also demonstrates that even the most polite language — or at least language not prone to slang interpretations as *cocotte* might be — can be translated into imputations of dastardliness, if not bastardliness. At the Bodmin Assizes in the 1930s Justice Wright had just convicted a farm laborer of bestiality. "Prisoner at the bar," he began,

> *the jury have convicted you on the clearest evidence, of disgusting and degrading offences. Your conduct is viewed by all right-minded*

> *men with abhorrence. The sentence of the court is that you be kept in penal servitude for seven years.*

The prisoner had not taken in all of this little lecture, so Justice Wright asked the warder, standing near the prisoner, to repeat it. Apparently the warder found his lordship's rhetorical flight a bit high-minded and obscure. He told the prisoner, "His lordship says that you are a dirty old bastard, and he's put you away for seventeen years."

Still, the last word belonged to the Court. "Warder," Justice Wright said, "I have no objection to your paraphrasing my sentence, but you have no power to increase it."

60 Gazoomping the sarker takes real chutzpah, dahlink

Gazump became a lawyers' word by way of a real estate boom in Britain during the 1960s and '70s. When a buyer agreed to sell his house to Black for one price, then turned around and sold it to White for a higher price, real estate lawyers and brokers began saying that Black got gazumped. More generally, it means double-dealing for fatter profit. Until Parliament intervened, a lot of homebuyers got gazumped, which made the term seem just minted. But under *gazoomph*, the *Oxford English Dictionary* gives printed usages since 1928:

> Daily Express 19 Dec. 2/7 'Gazoomphing the sarker' is a method of parting a rich man from his money. An article is auctioned over and over again, and the money bid each time is added to it.

In 1971, the *Guardian* reported that gazumping came from "car trade slang for selling to one buyer and then, as values rise, to a second buyer." Folk etymology says the word's origin is Yiddish, but a little digging suggests that it is more likely oafish mimicry of Yiddish. Leo Rosten, author of *The Joys of Yiddish* and *Hooray for Yiddish* has told me, "My experts do not give any Yiddish cognate for *gazoomph*. There's a Yiddish *gozlen* (robber, bandit) which, as a verb, means to plunder. I suspect English cockneys coined *gazoomph*."

But some clearly genuine Yiddish has made it into the law reports, probably the most notorious example being a footnote in the majority opinion in the 1979 case, *California v. Arno*. The appellants had been convicted in Los Angeles Municipal Court of dealing in films with such dubiously inviting titles as "Hard Core Girls" and "Raped Rectum." The *Arno* appeal focused on evidence gathered by police officer Johnson while he was on a hilltop opposite Arno's offices in the Playboy Building on Sunset Boulevard.

Officer Johnson swore that, through ten-power binoculars and from a distance equal to two or three football fields, he had seen "Arno and others handle a distinctively marked flip-top box displaying a label with a picture of a nude woman." Associate Justice Thompson, for the majority, held that the binocular evidence was inadmissable as an invasion of privacy: the handling of the box was meant to be "protected from the uninvited eye." He allowed the appeal.

In a dissent about five football fields longer than the majority opinion (14 pages to three), Justice Hanson wrote that "pornography, narcotics, prostitution, pimping, bookmaking, and the like" are not victimless crimes. "There are no victimless crimes. Society is the victim. The majority opinion in my view unduly restricts law enforcement officers from protecting society's interests."

Justice Thompson replied, in his footnote number two,

We feel compelled by the nature of the attack in the dissenting

opinion to spell out a response:
> 1. *Some answer is required to dissent's charge.*
> 2. *Certainly we do not endorse "victimless crime."*
> 3. *How that question is involved escapes us.*
> 4. *Moreover, the constitutional issue is significant.*
> 5. *Ultimately it must be addressed in light of precedent.*
> 6. *Certainly the course of precedent is clear.*
> 7. *Knowing that, our result is compelled.*
>
> (See Funk & Wagnall's The New Cassell's German Dict., p. 408.)

The part of *Cassell's German Dictionary* Justice Thompson refers to seems to be the entry for *schmuck*, or at least that is what some readers have deduced from "spelling out" the first letters of each of the footnote's numbered sentences.

According to Gerald Uelmen, writing in the ABA *Journal* ("American Bar Association" when it is spelled out), Justice Hanson "protested that press accounts of the footnote used the Yiddish definition" found in *Webster's*, not the German one found in *Cassell's*. The *Cassell's* meaning is "ornament, decoration, jewels." How this became the *Webster's* Yiddish meaning of penis, "prick," may have something to do with our English expression "family jewels," and also with German or Jewish *hausfraus* adoring their young sons at bath.

In any event, the reply to Justice Hanson's complaint came:

> One certainly cannot fault the Los Angeles Times *for using an English dictionary since California published opinions for over 125 years have been written in English and our jurisdiction obviously does not extend 7,000 miles to the Rhine in Germany.*

As Uelmen suggests, by the time of *Arno*, the Yiddish *chutzpah* was already something of an accepted term of legal art. That same year, it was applied to a Maryland man convicted of attempting to bribe a judge. Playing along, the judge had accepted $2,500 to throw a case. After the briber was convicted, he appealed his sentence, adding a motion for the return of the $2,500. "The appellee," wrote Chief Judge Gilbert, "for whatever else he may lack, suffers not for want of *chutzpah*." For those not right up to date on their legal words and phrases, the chief judge defined the word in a footnote: "Chutzpah is of Yiddish origin. It means that a person has 'gall, moxie, nerve and audacity compounded with brazen assertiveness.'"

Seven years earlier, in *Williams v. Georgia*, Judge Clark of the Court of Appeals had applied *chutzpah* to a man accused of breaking into a sheriff's office in the county courthouse to steal eight pistols, five shotguns, and ammunition from three locked cabinets. In the end, his honor found that a "Scotch verdict" ("not proven guilty" instead of "not guilty") would have been the most appropriate, because the circumstantial evidence was strong, but not conclusive. In a closing note, he added:

> As this opinion began with a Hebrew word and ends on a reference to Scotland, it should be noted this is not inappropriate because many historians have traced the Seythians or Seuthae, who populated Scotland, to be descendants of the Ten Lost Tribes of Israel.

In an earlier note, his honor had explained that *chutzpah* meant:

> ... colossal *effrontery*" or "brazen gall" but as stated in The Joy of Yiddish *by Leo Rosten, "The classic definition of 'chutzpah' is that quality enshrined in a man who, having killed his mother and father, throws himself upon the mercy of the court because he is an orphan."*

The ensuing years saw the *chutzpah* quotient in North American court judgments explode. In an Internet article updated from their 1993 *Yale Law Review* essay, "Lawsuit, Shmawsuit," Justice Alex

Kozinski, a U.S. appeals judge, and Eugene Volokh, a law professor at the University of California at Los Angeles, allege that, largely by dint of *chutzpah*, "Yiddish is quickly supplanting Latin as the spice in American legal argot." They document 231 uses of *chutzpah* by U.S. judges, 220 of those occurring from 1980 on. "*Maven* has appeared in 14 cases," the authors advise, "*klutz* in three. . . . Also appearing in other cases . . . : *schlock* (1974 and again in 1993), *no-goodnik* (1991), *tzimmes* (1971) [a confusion], *rachmones* (1992) [pity], 'a writ of *rachmones* does not lie' (1998) . . ."

In the 1993 case *White v. Samsung Electronics America*, Justice Kozinski himself became the first to use *schtick* in a U.S. judgment, he says. At issue was whether Vanna White, the toothsome hostess on "Wheel of Fortune," could sue Samsung for a commercial parody of her work. The commercial, Justice Kozinski writes in dissent,

> starred a robot dressed in a wig, gown and jewelry reminiscent of Vanna White's hair and dress; the robot was posed next to a "Wheel-of-Fortune"-like game board. . . . The caption read "Longest-running game show. 2012 A.D." The gag here, I take it, was that Samsung would still be around when White had been replaced by a robot.

Disagreeing with the majority that White had a cause of action for appropriation of her publicity rights, Justice Kozinski asks, "Should White have the exclusive right to something as broad and amorphous as her 'identity?' Samsung's ad didn't simply copy White's *schtick* — like all parody, it created something new."

Searches of Canadian jurisprudence in the Quicklaw and Lexis-Nexis databases yielded only two jurisprudential *schticks* north of the border, both of them spelled *shtick*, and only one of them from a judge. (The other was supplied by a witness in a wrongful dismissal action at a rumbustious radio station.) In holding that certain tour guides were independent contractors and their employer was not liable to pay employment insurance premiums on their behalf, Tax Court Judge William MacLatchy writes of one guide, "She never saw herself as an employee; was not required to do as she was told. In effect, as the show business says, 'She did her own shtick.'"

But Canadian judges are not to be outdone in the chutzpah department. *Chutzpah* garnered 11 hits and, in 1995, there was one *hutzpah*. Some of the usages had a decidedly Canadian gentility. In a wrongful dismissal judgment dated February, 2001, Justice R. Bruce Harvey of the British Columbia Supreme Court considered whether an employer was correct that the plaintiff displayed *chutzpah* in requesting a letter of reference. "I understand *chutzpah* to mean something much more than the English word *nerve*," Justice Harvey found.

That may be so, although in a 1997 case, Justice Stephen Borins, then of the Ontario Court (General Division), found that *chutzpah* was perhaps inadequate to describe the failure of the provincial government to consult Toronto-area municipalities regarding their amalgamation into one megacity. When the municipalities brought a constitutional challenge to the forced amalgamation, Justice Borins held,

> *It may be that the government displayed megachutzpah in proceeding as it did, and in believing that the inhabitants of Metro Toronto would submit to the imposition of the megacity without being given an opportunity to have a real say in how they were to live and be governed. However, the question for the court is not the government's political posture, but rather its legal and constitutional authority to proceed as it did. In any event, the* Charter *[the* Canadian Charter of Rights and Freedoms, *which comprises the first part of the constitution] does not guarantee an individual the right to live his or her life free from government chutzpah or imperiousness.*

Justice Francis Muldoon of the Federal Court has shown a persistent fondness for *chutzpah*. In 1993, an infringement action bristling with complicated chemical terminology stimulated his lordship into truly multilingual flight:

> *It would take more* chutzpah *than is possessed by this judge to let it go as textual infringement, 'the end of the matter,' so the opposite quality residing in the old, familiar notion of ex abundanti cautela, exacts that the alternative of substantial or pith-and-marrow infringement must also, now, be explored.*

To attempt to explain this would take more megachutzpah than is possessed by this writer, but his lordship's drift is clear when, five years later, he recalls an immigration case "where an applicant from Rawalpindi went to the Cairo visa office and then had the *chutzpah* to ask for costs." And around the time that this book was in final revision, his lordship expanded the horizons of words and phrases legally defined by finding "mutual chutzpah" where opposing counsel sought costs of an injunction application after conducting "themselves toward each other in an impolite and unprofessional manner."

Judges often define *chutzpah* by reference to Leo Rosten's famous example of the murderous orphan. Kozinski (who "sits on the U.S. Court of Appeals for the Ninth Circuit") and Volokh ("who sits on his tuchis in his office" at U.C.L.A.) give another usage: A man asks a lawyer how much he charges. "A thousand dollars for three questions," the lawyer says.

"Isn't that kind of expensive?" the potential client wonders.

"Yes, it is," says the lawyer. "What's your third question?"

61 Bench and Bar and that old sporting life

There is a sporting side to practice at the bar, the notion of contest and "may the best player win" that attracts those who fancy themselves high rollers. Perhaps it is the same sort of appeal that, in less democratic times, made barristerism seem a gentleman's game, a genteel outlet for aggression and domination, championship combat without spilling much of your own blood.

As late as 1957, English barrister Geoffrey Lincoln was advising young advocates that the first phrase they should commit to memory was "Don't fence." It could be used, he said, any time "you run out of ideas while cross-examining," no matter how cooperative the witness was. (Then again, Lincoln also advises regular use of "What about the dog?" — even when the witness has been called to give expert evidence about handwriting on a cheque. When in the face of continued threats and dark suggestions the witness still protests ignorance, the barrister delivers the *coup de grâce*: "What dog? Why the dog Mr. Justice Cowpie said he wouldn't hang on your evidence last week!")

But the tables have turned. Sports have become a profession and law a trade. Ball players are philosophers ("If you can't imitate him, don't copy him," says baseballer Yogi Berra), while lawyers do the plumbing on their tax shelters. And a divot has become an idle, sodding piece of lawn whacked up by golfers, where, in the 16th century, it described generally larger slices of turf, used for roofing and building walls. Thicker, heavier slices were called *fails* or *feals*. So, in Scottish law, *feal and divot* described a legal right running with real property to remove turf for fences and thatching. Such, indeed, is the evolution of *divot* that today it is a synonym for *rug*, the sort of rug, that is, which sportscaster Howard Cosell used to wear on his bean (as in *beanball*).

Then, there is *hurdle*. Only relatively recently has it been something for horses and graphically sinewed humans to leap at and bark their shins on. When English was becoming English it was (as *hyrbil*) already a small fence or pen woven of bark or twigs. And from the 15th century, until the practice was abolished in 1870, traitors were dragged through the streets on a hurdle — a frame which resembled a section of a fence — to the site of their execution.

If you follow cricket, you will have heard of scoreless periods called "maiden overs," an over being that part of the game when balls are bowled from one end of the wicket (before switching *over* to the other end). A maiden, of course, is a young, inexperienced woman, and in older usage, one who has not married and produced offspring. Thus, a *maiden assize* or *circuit* or *session* was one which (perversely) produced no death penalties. In later and less sanguinary days, it described judicial sessions that simply failed to produce a trial. In his journal for April 17, 1826, Sir Walter Scott wrote, "The judge was presented with a pair of white gloves, in consideration of its being a maiden assize."

Still, even the most ardent cricket follower might have been ignorant of *aloo* until a fan repeatedly shouted the word through a megaphone at star batsman Inzamam-ul-Haq during a 1999 test match in Toronto. The appellation sparked an international incident, and nearly became a legal term of art, when Inzamam had finally had enough and, brandishing his bat, chased the critic through the large crowd of spectators during a drinks break. Inzamam was 25 pounds overweight at the time, and considered *aloo* to be defamatory insofar as it means "potato."

Like legal tribunals, sports have judges, referees, and umpires, the last being named by a word maybe six centuries old. At that, *umpire* is a later form of *noumpere*, a "non-peer" or indifferent party. Over time, the *n* got transferred to the indefinite article: "A noumpere" became "an umpire."

Finally, I once heard a bitterly fought trial characterized as "a real rhubarb" — a venerable baseball metaphor. A discussion on a baseball field becomes a rhubarb usually when an umpire's decision is hotly under attack, generally by more than one snarling and gesticulating member of the offended team. More often than not, the team manager will have stormed out of the dugout to give his opinion, and more often than not, someone, player or manager, will be ejected from the game.

There is a long history in English of figurative uses of "rhubarb" to connote bitterness, often in love suits if not lawsuits. In *Astrophel and Stella*, a cycle of love poems from 1586, Sir Philip Sidney already brings us close to the baseball and litigation usage: "Have I not paine enough, my friend . . . / But with your rubarbe words ye must contend to grieve me worse?" No doubt many an umpire, and the occasional litigant, has said the same thing — or something close to it, anyway.

As with many baseballisms, Red Barber, the Brooklyn Dodgers broadcaster of the 1930s and '40s, is credited with popularizing the sports adaptation of "rhubarb." He says that he got it from sports journalist Tom Meany via another sportswriter, Garry Schumacher. Meany, in his turn, supposedly got it from a bartender who had witnessed a shooting, the gore of which reminded him of the sanguinary and tart garden vegetable.

To complicate matters further, Schumacher has claimed invention of this usage himself, via his "subconscious memory" of rhubarb sandwiches that, in his childhood, were favored as missiles in food fights rather than as high-fiber nutrition with the laxative properties of castor oil.

The better view is that modern applications of *rhubarb* derive from an old movie and theater ruse: actors will mutter the word over and over when they want to simulate the hub-bub of an angry mob — the sort of rabble that lynches innocent bystanders, and throws rhubarb sandwiches, when it can find them.

62 Stop "wining," please, if you can't take a joke

Doing stand-up comedy one night at the Great American Music Hall in San Francisco, Robin Williams wandered onto the subject of wines. Home Box Office broadcast the performance, and it was also distributed on videocassettes, record albums and tapes, under the title "Throbbing Python of Love." "Whoa — white wine," Williams said during the wine bit, holding a bottle.

> This is a little wine here. If it's not wine, it's been through somebody already. Oh — there are white wines, there are red wines, but why are there no black wines, like Rege, a motherfucker? It goes with fish, meat, any damn thing it wants to. I like my wine like I like my women — ready to pass out.

Williams pronounced "Rege" "Reggie," and his remarks were not scripted. On the video versions, Williams speculates how useful it would be to have someone like footballer Mean Joe Green advertize this versatile black wine: "'You better buy this or I'll nail your ass to a tree.'"

When David Rege, a winemaker who also pronounces "Rege" "Reggie," became aware of the Robin Williams' wine jokes, he sued. He claimed "trade libel," personal defamation, intentional and negligent infliction of emotional distress, invasion of privacy, and intentional and negligent interference with prospective economic advantage — not to mention that linking Rege wines with black people associated the product with "a socio-economic group of persons commonly considered to be the antithesis of wine connoisseurs."

There was venerable legal precedent for the claim. In 1639, a brewer named Fenne sued Dixe for telling some of Fenne's customers, "I will give my mare a peck of malt, and give her water after it, and she shall piss as good beer as Thomas Fenne breweth." The judges threw the lawsuit out on the argument that Fenne did not prove that the criticism had caused him to lose any business. Justice Barckley in particular noted that "the words are only comparative" and jocular.

> *And he said that it had been adjudged that where one says of a lawyer, that he had as much law as a monkey, that the words were not actionable [i.e., the lawyer could not successfully sue for defamation]; because he hath as much law, and more also. But if he [the lawyer's critic] had said that he hath no more law than a monkey, those words are actionable.*

Legal careers are still made on such fine distinctions. Indeed, 350 years later, the California Court of Appeal came to a similar conclusion, at least respecting jocular comparisons and intoxicating liquors. It issued a rare writ of mandate forbidding Rege to sue Robin Williams over the wine joke. Writing for the court, Justice Kline refused to create a special First Amendment (free expression) exemption for certain forms of comedy, pointing to the morass such distinctions had made of obscenity law. Justice Kline added that judges are not professionally noted for a liberal sense of humor:

> *If judges assumed the responsibility to decide what is amusing and made the protections of the First Amendment turn upon their views, perhaps less putative humor would be safeguarded than our restrained approach permits.*

But his honor also found that the joke, by its context and effect, was obviously a joke. "To hold otherwise would run afoul of the First Amendment and chill the free speech rights of all comedy performers and humorists, to the genuine detriment of our society."

As for Rege's contention that blacks are not commonly held to be wine connoisseurs, Justice Kline found it "repugnant to values embedded in our Constitution and [it] must be resoundingly rejected."

For the law on what to do where a name and product used in jest resemble a plaintiff's name and product, Justice Kline recalled the famous Miss Wyoming case. The subject matter there was a story marked "Humor" in *Penthouse* magazine, about a Miss America Pageant contestant from Wyoming named Charlene. As Charlene prepares to perform her baton-twirling number in the talent section of the pageant, she, in the words of Chief Judge Seth of the U.S. Court of Appeals, Tenth Circuit, "thinks of Wyoming and an incident there when she was with a football player from her high school. It describes an act of fellatio when she causes him to levitate."

On stage, Charlene "performs a fellatio-like act on her baton which stops the orchestra." Offstage once more, she fantasizes how her orthodontal skills could promote peace when practiced (in those days when the Berlin Wall stood) on the entire Soviet Central Committee, Marshal Tito, and Fidel Castro, and then proudly "levitates" her coach, before all America and the world.

The real Miss Wyoming complained that the story suggested that she had:

> *committed fellatio on one Monty Applewhite and also upon her coach, Corky Corcoran, in the presence of a national television audience at the Miss America Pageant. The article also creates the impression that plaintiff committed fellatio-like acts upon her baton at the Miss America contest.*

The Court of Appeals found the *Penthouse* story "gross, unpleasant, crude, distorted," with "no redeeming features whatsoever." But under the First Amendment, the court said, the trial jury was entitled to protect the author. The story "described something physically impossible in an impossible setting," and it was therefore a reasonable inference that no real Miss Wyoming was portrayed.

Sydney Smith, the English man of letters, once wrote to Bishop Blomfeld that the bishop "must not think me necessarily foolish because I am facetious, nor will I consider you necessarily wise because you are grave." Plaintiff's lawyers should copy down those words. And when a client comes screaming libel, whether screaming in real heat or out of cold calculation, maybe the wisest course — not necessarily the most lucrative course, but the most reasonable and decent one — would be to share the thought.

63   Mad as hell and not eating beef any more

As one wag put it, "In many states it is now easier to defame a tomato than a human being." It was true, anyway, that in Texas you couldn't say "beef stinks," but you could sell a bumper sticker declaring, "The only mad cow in Texas is Oprah Winfrey."

It all started, apparently, with Alar. Back in the 1970s, we stopped eating apples because they were sprayed with the chemical, the agricultural version of Clearasil. When the television news magazine "60 Minutes" said that Alar caused cancer, apple-growers sued CBS. Although the cancer allegation turned out to be suspect, the lawsuit failed. Several state legislatures responded with what have become known as "banana bills" and "veggie libel laws," statutes that say "producers" of perishable food can sue for "false disparagement" of the food. At this writing, more than a dozen such statutes are on the books, and another nine or so are in the bill stage.

As for mad cows in Texas, on April 16, 1996, Oprah Winfrey devoted ten minutes of her hour-long show to whether bovine spongiform encephalopathy, "mad cow disease," could infect North American consumers. She interviewed Howard Lyman, whom the press doggedly describe as "a former rancher turned vegetarian." Lyman told Winfrey that U.S. beef producers feed their animals the ground remains of their brothers and sisters, by virtue of which the potential mad cow problem "could make AIDS look like a common cold." Later, it would become clear that this wasn't necessarily an exaggeration. At the time, Winfrey asked her studio audience, "Now, doesn't that concern you all a little bit?" And in one of those signal moments in the history of American law, not to mention American television, she added, "It has just stopped me cold from eating another burger."

Alan Greenspan couldn't have caused more kerfuffle. Beef futures on the Mercantile Exchange in Chicago, headquarters of Winfrey's production company and show, fell like the fatted calf. Calling it the "Oprah Crash," Texas cattle interests launched a $10-million class action against Winfrey, her company, her distributor, and Lyman, basing their claim on the state's *False Disparagement of Perishable Food Products Act*. During the trial, Winfrey broadcast her daily show from Amarillo, the trial site, where you could buy bumper stickers proclaiming love for the TV idol, as well as bumper stickers proclaiming the same woman a bovine lunatic.

Of the 11 in-force food disparagement laws that I subsequently found on the Internet (courtesy of the Rutgers Animal Rights Law Center), the Texas version was, in fact, one of the less draconian. There was what lawyers call a fairly high *scienter* or "knowledge" factor: to be liable under the law, the disseminator of the information had to state or imply falsely that the food was unsafe, and that person must have known the statement was false.

Where most of the statutes said that the information was presumptively false if not based on reasonable scientific inquiry, in Texas this was a matter which seemed to apply only to weighing up the conflicting evidence: "In determining if information is false, the trier of fact shall consider whether the information was based on reasonable and reliable scientific inquiry, facts, or data," the statute said. Of course, the court in Winfrey's case might have interpreted this as creating a presumption against off-the-cuff remarks like the television celebrity's: the Texas action was the first food libel to be prosecuted under any of these statutes.

By contrast, in Alabama "it is no defense . . . that the actor did not intend, or was unaware of," the disparagement. Presumably, a publisher in Osaka could be liable if some hack at the publisher's daily in Tuscaloosa slags off an Alabama huckleberry. In Oklahoma, one could actionably disparage a zucchini if she knew *or should have known* that the information about it was false. And "disparagement" extended to "dissemination of information to the public in any manner which *casts doubt* on the safety of any perishable agricultural food product to the consuming public." If you don't like the look of the potato salad today, you are best advised to keep it to yourself.

The South Dakota statute awarded treble damages against "any person who disparages a perishable agricultural food product with intent to harm the producer." Ohio allowed "up to" treble damages in the same circumstances. In Idaho, however, home to America's most famous potatoes and anti-government survivalists, the plaintiff always was limited to "actual pecuniary damages" (actual tangible losses). The Idaho law had a narrower definition of disparagement, casting an eye toward conventional libel law and perhaps constitutional guarantees of free expression. Absent publication "to a third party of a false factual statement" (*sic*) there could be no "disparagement" that you could sue over. Adopting the language of libel claims, the statute required that the statement be "of and concerning the plaintiff's specific perishable agricultural food product." It must also have "imputed" (*sic*) the safety of the product. The defendant must have intended to harm a pecuniary interest or have acted recklessly in that respect, *and* the defendant had to know that the statement was false or had to have acted recklessly as to its truth.

But during the Oprah trial the American press did not seem interested in distinctions in the laws state to state. As far as journalists were concerned, the laws were all presumptively unconstitutional. Mind you, Nancy Benanc of the Associate Press had a point when she said, "You can burn a flag, but you had better think twice before insulting an onion." Then again, there was the journalist who predicted: "Well, that Oprah may never eat beef again, but she sure as hell is gonna eat her words." As the world now knows, it was the journalist who had to dine on his prediction, and Creuzfeld-Jakob Disease — the always-terminal brain disease that humans can contract from mad cows — remains a serious problem in our factory-farm economy.

NOTES

(Note to the notes: The material for this book incorporates more than 18 years of peripatetic research. Some of my notes have gone missing or are spotty to the point that I would have had to start nearly from scratch to recover certain details. In such cases, I have tried to give at least some beginning point for those prepared to do the extra digging.)

<u>1</u>   R. v. Walcott (1694), 4 Mod. 395; affirmed (1696), Shaw P.C. 127.

Holt v. Astrigg (1607), Cro. Jac. 184; and see Megarry, *A Miscellany-at-Law*, (Sevens and Sons, 1981), 192.

<u>2</u>   Sidley's Case (1663), 1 Sid. 168, *sub nom Sir Charles Sydlyes' Case*, 1 Keb. 620, 84; E.R. 1146.

<u>3</u>   Jessin v. County of Shasta 79 Cal. Rptr. 359 (1969).

Blackstone on mayhem, *Commentaries*, IV, 205.

Disabling the testicles: *Sensobaugh v. State*, 244 S.W. 379 (C.C.A. Tex., 1922).

Involuntary tattooing: *People v. Page*, 163 Cal. Rptr. 839 (Cal. App. Dist. 1 04/15/1980).

Cockroft v. Smith (1705), 11 Mod. 43.

State v. Bass, 120 S.E.2d 580 (S.C.N.C., 1961).

1603 case from Coke: *Bass* case, 583.

Blackstone on duelling: *Commentaries*, IV, 199.

Bar fights can be legal: Compare *R. v. Dix* (1972), 10 C.C.C. (2d) 324 to *R. v. McTavish* (1972), 8 C.C.C. (2d) 206.

Uruguayan duel: Reuter News Service, February 26 and March 5, 1990.

<u>4</u>   1918 Rhode Island sex novelties case: *Manes Co. v. Glass*, 102 A. 964. Record supplied by the Supreme Court of Rhode Island.

<u>5</u>   *R. v. Laframboise*, Ont. Gen. Div. Action No. M310/92, Feb. 16, 1993.

R. v. Zurfluh, Ontario Lawyers Weekly, April 5, 1985, p.16.

Baxter v. The Queen, Ont. Gen. Div. Action No. 3869/92, April 21, 1993.

R. v. Reynolds, Alberta Prov. Ct. file 20640785P101101, Oct. 28, 1992.

<u>7</u>   "Get Stuffed Sunshine," Theodore Dalrymple, *The Independent*, October 11, 1998, p. 29.

Harris, Judith, *The Nurture Assumption* (The Free Press, 1998).

Slang Thesaurus (Elm Tree, 1986).

<u>8</u>   *R. v. Evans*, [1996] 1 S.C.R. 8.

Robson v. Hallett, [1967] 2 All E.R. 407 at 412.

<u>9</u>   I gathered the material for this essay from the standard biographies of Shakespeare and a 1986 essay by Anatole Broyard in the *New York Times Book Review*. I have been unable to locate any of my notes that would supply more detail.

<u>10</u>   Stealing eggs, etc.: *R. v. Cox* (1844), 1 Car. and K. 494, 495; *R. v. Halloway* (1823), 1 C. & P. 127.

R. v. Pace (1965), 48 D.L.R. (2d) 532.

R. v. Brown (1890), 24 Q.B. 357.

<u>11</u>   Lord Chancellor's foot: *Table Talk of John Selden*, Pollock, ed., 1927, p. 4.

Shoemaker not a cobbler: *Redman v. Pyne* (1669), 1 Mod. 19.

Musical stockings: *The Times* (London), October 18, 1994.

Marla Maples' shoes: My trail of the Jones prosecution started with a "Talk of the Town" article in the *New Yorker*, February 21, 1993. See also *Jones v. Maples*, No. 903N (N.Y. App. Div. 1st Dept. 05/27/1999).

<u>12</u>   Paul Armorgie *fait clameur de haro*: *Globe and Mail* (Toronto), May 26, 1993.

<u>13</u>   *In re Grosvenor*, [1944] Ch. 138; [1945] A.C. 304 (H.L.).

National Research Council scientists count angels: February 6, 1984, *Globe and Mail* (Toronto).

<u>14</u>   Jeanne Calment on bad deals: Reuter News Service, Dec. 28, 1995. Likewise, I collected much of the rest of the information on Calment and

Rattray from news services. Jeanne Calment died on August 4, 1997.

15 *Mason v. Westside Cemeteries*, (1996), 135 D.L.R. (4th) 361.

Haynes's Case (1614), 12 Co. 113.

16 143 bikinis: Canadian Press, June 14, 1984.

Thief gets stolen underwear back: Associated Press, September 13, 1986.

Bouwhuis Protective Undergarment: *Globe and Mail* (Toronto), July 16, 1984.

Vodka unzipped: Canadian Press, August 23, 1985.

17 *Queen v. Cognos*, [1993] 1 S.C.R. 87.

Hedley, Byrne & Co. v. Heller Partners, [1963] 2 All. E.R. 575.

19 1947 South African case: *R. v. M.* (1947), 4 S.A. 489 at 491.

North Carolina laxative case (in note): *State v. Monroe*, 28 S.E. 547 (1897, S.C. North Carolina).

R. v. Ladue (1965), 45 C.R. 287.

"There's no harm in asking": Magruder, "Mental and Emotional Disturbance in the Law of Torts," *Harvard Law Review*, May, 1936, 1033 at 1055.

Ishmael Reed kindly responded by letter to my questions about *Reckless Eyeballing*. I was unable to locate the issue of *Ebony* he mentions.

Against Our Will: Men, Women, and Rape (Simon and Schuster, 1975).

Ogling swimmer: In "Evidence of ogling is clear, board told," Robert MacLeod, *Globe and Mail* (Toronto), September 1, 1989, gives a short summary of the case.

20 "Glasgerion": The great ballad scholar Francis Child collects "Glasgerion" and its variants in volume II, page 136 of his *English and Scottish Popular Ballads*, 1886. The late, lamented English "folk baroque" group, The Pentangle, have recorded a moody, evocative interpretation on their "Cruel Sister" album, rechristening the hero Jack Orion. (Jack the valet becomes Tom.) Their musical setting follows "Glasgerion's" plot line in the best tradition of musical story-telling.

R. v. Collins, [1973] Q.B. 100.

The big, bad wolf in the family bed: See, e.g., *R. v. Young*, (1878), 14 Cox C.C. 114; *R. v. Clarke* (1854), 6 Cox C.C. 412; *R. v. Barrow* (1868), 11 Cox C.C. 199.

R. v. Williams, [1923] 1 K.B. 340.

"Doc": The Rape of the Town of Lovell, Jack Olsen, Atheneum, 1989.

Quack doctor rapes: See, e.g., *R. v. Case* (1850), 4 Cox C.C. 220; *R. v. Flattery*, [1877] 2 Q.B.D. 410.

1878 Irish case: *Hegarty v. Shine*, 14 Cox C.C. 124.

Herpes in Virginia, *Lawyers Weekly*, March 9, 1990, p. 13.

Commonwealth v. Appleby 402 N.E.2d 1051 (S.C. Mass., 1980).

1934 English caning case: *R. v. Donovan*, [1934] 2 K.B. 498.

21 *Donoguhe v. Stevenson*, [1932] A.C. 562.

Palsgraf v. Long Island Rwy., 162 N.E. 99 (1928, N.Y.).

23 *Shlensky v. Wrigley*, 237 N.E. 2d. 776 (1968, Ill.).

25 In 1998, the *Wine Spectator* published several stories on French wine scandals. See, for example, in the January 31, 1998 issue, "The Sweet With the Sour," by Per-Henrik Mansson.

Sommelier compares wine to plastic surgery: quoted by Kristy Lang of the *Sunday Times* (London).

26 *La Bonne Table* (New York: Godine, 1989).

27 The "Plaster Caster" case was widely reported in the daily press during the last two weeks of April, 1993.

Judge Stevens on the cast's bronze progeny, and Geoffrey Glass on damages: *National Law Journal*, May 17, 1993.

Etchingham versus Albritton: *The Times* (London), Dec. 11, 12, 13, 18, 1993; April 3, 4, 6, 1996.

30 *John W. Carson v. Here's Johnny Portable Toilets Inc.*, 698 F. 2d 831 (1983, U.S.C.A., Sixth Circ.).

Mutual of Omaha v. Novak, 648 F. Supp. 905 (U.S.D.C.); aff'd 775 F 2d 147 (1985, U.S.C.A.), 836 F.2d 397 (8th Cir., 1987).

Lardashe case: *Jordache Ent. v. Hogg Wyld*, 828 F.2d 1482 (10th Cir., 1987).

Dallas Cowboys Cheerleaders Inc. v. Pussycat Cinema, Ltd., 604 F. 2d 200, 205 (2d Circ., 1979).

Girl Scouts of the United States v. Personality Posters Manufacturing Co., 304 F.Supp. 1228 (S.D.N.Y. 1969).

Jordache Ent. v. Hogg Wyld, 828 F.2d 1482 (10th Cir., 1987).

31 *Morning Star Co-Operative Society Ltd. v. Express Newspapers Ltd.*, [1979] F.S.R. 113.

Bernard Levin's *Times* piece (Oct. 31, 1978) is reprinted as "The man who missed the Clapham Omnibus?" in (1979), 13 Law Society of Upper Canada Gazette 141.

The Bank of England v. Boggs: The Times (London), Nov. 2, 1986 and magazine for that date; Jan. 6, 14, 26; Apr. 9; May 5; Nov. 1, 24, 27, 29, all 1987. Lawrence Weschler published a profile of Boggs, including a description of the trial and events leading to it, in *The New Yorker*, Jan. 18 and 25, 1988.

Mr. Submarine Ltd. v. Emma Foods Ltd., [1976] O.J. No. 806 (Quicklaw).

Walt Disney Productions v. Triple Five Corporation (1992), 130 A.R. 321.

Miss Nude Universe: *Miss Universe, Inc. v. Bohna*, [1992] 3 F.C. 682 (Quicklaw).

32 Gay Olympic trademark action: *San Francisco Arts & Athletics Inc. v. U.S. Olympic Committee*, 55 L.W. 5061 (1987, U.S. Ct. App., 9th Cir.).

Maple leaf symbol owned by U.S. company: "Maple leaf can bloom on Expo souvenirs," Stephen Godfrey, *Globe and Mail* (Toronto), Oct. 14, 1985.

33 I collected much of the information in this essay from the website of Interprofession Gruyère, and the article "AOC gruyère: qu'est-ce qu'elle a ma meule?" also posted on the Internet and linked to the website of TV5, the international French-language television service.

34   *Chemical Corp. v. Anheuser-Busch, Inc.*, 306 F.2d 433 (5th Cir., 1962), cert. denied by U.S.S.C.

Dallas Cowboys Cheerleaders Inc. v. Pussycat Cinema, Ltd., 604 F. 2d 200, 205 (2d Circ., 1979).

35   "Miami J'yce: Love Walks Right Out of 'Ulysses' Symposium," Brenda Maddox, *New York Times Book Review*, Feb. 26, 1989, p. 7.

"'Corrected' edition sparks academic battle," Peter Cooney, Reuter News Service, June 21, 1989.

Robert Spoo generously provided his views via e-mail and copies of his articles "Copyright Protectionism and Its Discontents: The Case of James Joyce's *Ulysses* in America," Yale L.J., Vol. 108, No. 3 (December 1998), 633–67 and his expansion of that piece in the 1999 *Joyce Studies Annual*.

Aeolian piano case: I believe that Dunaj is referring to *White-Smith Music Publishing Co. v. Apollo Co.*, 209 U.S. 1 (1908) .

36   Judge Beezer on Napster: *A&M Records, Inc. v. Napster, Inc.* No. 00–16401 (9th Cir., Feb. 12, 2001).

Alleged Ewok infringement: *Preston v. 20th Century Fox Canada Ltd.* (1990), 38 F.T.R. 183.

Lenz Hardware Inc. v. Wilson, N.Y. App. Div. Dept.3 07/08/1999.

37   La Fave and Scott, *Substantive Criminal Law*, West Publishing, 1986, vol. II, at 259.

Blackstone on provocation: *Bl. Comm.* IV, at 191–192.

Maddy's Case, (1671) 2 Keb. 829, 1 Vent. 158; *sub nom. Manning*, T. Raym. 212. The branding indicated, of course, that Maddy had used up his share of the king's mercy.

The "honor defence": See, for example, "Comment, Recognition of the Honor Defense Under the Insanity Plea" (1934), 43 Yale Law Journal, 809.

Legislation in Utah, New Mexico, Texas: La Fave and Scott, at 268–270.

Rembar on *infangthief*: (New York: Simon and Schuster) 1980, at 100.

Sensobaugh v. State, 244 S.W. 379 (C.C.A. Tex., 1922). In his *Institutes*, Chapter 3, section 62, Lord Coke records a case from 1228 where a man and wife castrated "John the monk" after the man caught the wife and cleric *in flagrante delicto*.

Juries and the unwritten law: See, e.g. La Fave, at 270 and "Comment," 43 Yale L.J. (above), at 809.

Killing to prevent adultery is justifiable homicide: *Campbell v. State*, 49 S.E. 2d 867 (1948, Ga. S.C.).

Burger v. State, 231 S.E.2d 769 (1977) at 770.

Twinkie defence: "Is There Really A Twinkie Defence?" *Lawyers Weekly*, Jeffrey Miller, Jan. 16, 1987, pp. 10–11.

Murder of a wife for nagging: Shirley Frondorf, *Death of a "Jewish American Princess,"* (New York: Villard Books), 1988.

38 *Barnacle v. Barnacle*, [1948] Probate Cases 257.

Love on public pathway: *Mellin v. Taylor* (1836), 3 Bing. N.C. 109.

Love in a truck: *Yuill v. Yuill*, [1945] 1 All E.R. 183.

Manual satisfaction: *Sapsford v. Sapsford* [1954], 2 All E.R. 373.

What constitutes masturbation: *Ontario Lawyers Weekly*, May 3, 1984, p. 2.

Maclennan v. Maclennan, [1958] Sess. Cas. 105.

39 Toronto parade: *Globe and Mail* (Toronto), Nov. 28, 1988.

Beastly Law, David and Charles, 1986.

40 In his *Joys of Yiddish* (Pocket Books, 1970), p. 218, Leo Rosten says the rabbi's advice about in-laws (*makhetayneste*) comes from "one of the oldest Jewish stories."

41 "Sheriff of Nottingham banishes Robin at last," Andrew Pierce, *The Times* (London), March 26, 1996; "The Sheriff Strikes Back," *ibid*.

42 Catherine Drinker Bowen's biography, *Francis Bacon: The Temper of a Man* (Atlantic Monthly, 1963), supplied some of the background for this essay. In *The Law of the Land* (New York: Simon and Schuster) 1980, Charles Rembar discusses the Coke-Bacon common law-equity wars at pp. 283–285 and 291 and robbing hoods at p. 98.

43   Benefit of clergy: See, e.g., Blackstone, *Commentaries*, Vol. IV at pp. 42–3, and Graham Parker, *Introduction to Criminal Law*, (third ed., Methuen, 1987), 261.

R. v. Roose: see Megarry, *op. cit.*, p. 334, and the statute cited as 22 Hen. 8, c. 9.

Outlawry: see, e.g., Charles Rembar, *The Law of the Land, op.cit. passim*.

R.G. Hamilton on sanctuary: Professional Books of Britain publish Hamilton's books on legal history.

Peine forte et dure: Blackstone, *op. cit.*, p. 340, and Rembar, pp. 165–7.

The Queen v. Anonymous: Many of the details of this case were generously supplied by the prosecutor, Martin Rudland.

Footnote on standing mute: *R. v. Paling* (1978), 67 Cr. App. R. 299.

44   William Buckley: *Atlantic High* (Doubleday, 1982).

Eel pies and ice cream on the Lord's Day: *Bullen v. Ward* (1905), 74 K.B. 916; *Slater v. Evans*, [1916] 2 K.B. 124. Both are discussed in more detail in my *Naked Promises*.

45   *Fishery Products International Limited v. Midland Transport Limited* (1994), 113 D.L.R. (4th) 651.

Secretary of State for War v. Midland Great Western Railway, 2 I.R. 102.

46   *Constitutional Law of Canada*, Carswell, 1977.

47   Robbie and the Stone: See, for example, "Scots scramble to house nation's heart of stone," Gillian Bowditch, *The Times* (London), July 4, 1996.

49   Accidental whaling: *Cameron v. M.N.R.* (1971), 71 D.T.C. 440 (Tax App. Bd.).

Rumack v. M.N.R. (1992), 140 N.R. 267, 92 D.T.C. 6142 (F.C.A.).

A suit for Christmas: *Wilkins v. Rogerson*, [1961] Ch. 133.

Canada v. Cranswick (1982), 40 N.R. 296 C.T.C. 69, 82 D.T.C. 6073 (F.C.A.).

Car-racing case: *Huband v. M.N.R.* (1974), 74 D.T.C. 1039 (Tax Rev. Bd.).

Pirate's treasure case: *Tobias v. Canada*, [1978] F.C.J. No. 4 (F.C.T.D.).

50   Albert Haddock is no gentleman: *Rex v. Haddock, Uncommon Law* (1935,

Methuen) 18 (as reported by A.P. Herbert).

Nash v. Battersby (1703), 2 Ld. Raym. 986; *sub. nom. Battersby v. Marsh*, 6 Mod. 80.

Messor v. Molyneux, cited in *R. v. Brough* (1718), 1 Wils. K.B. 244.

53 *The Fatal Shore* (Alfred A. Knopf, 1986).

55 *Re Willard Mikesell*, 243 N.W.2d 86 (1976, Mich. S.C.).

56 *Nevada v. Anderson*: The district attorney's office in Clark County kindly supplied me the record of the case, including prosecution, defense, and *amicus* briefs. Mr. Blumen also sent me a note on his defense arguments. See, as well, a *Wall Street Journal* article by Ken Wells reprinted in the *Toronto Star*, Jan. 17, 1990, p. H3 ("Computer shoe gives gambler that winning feeling").

Touching breasts: *The Queen v. "Chesty" Morgan*, *Globe and Mail* (Toronto), Dec. 23, 1980.

57 The prisoner who "ject un brickbat": *R. v. Anonymous* (1631), 73 E.R. 416. And see R.E. Megarry, *Miscellany-at-Law*, (Stevens and Sons: 1958), at 295.

Second *Miscellany-at-Law* (Stevens and Sons: 1973).

Intended for brother Bacon: Whatever Vice-Chancellor Malins said, if anything, the rest of the details are reported (Sir Robert writes) at [1877] *The Times*, March 17 at 13.

Re Dakin (1887), 13 V.L.R. 522.

Process server forced to eat subpoena: *Williams v. Johns* (1773), Dick 477.

Not caring a fart for the court: *R. v. Anonymous* (1711), 1 Salk. 84.

Highwaymen as "partners": See (1893), 9 L.Q.R. 199 and Megarry, *Miscellany-At-Law* (Stevens and Sons: 1958) at 76–78.

Abingdon's Case: see Megarry, *Miscellany-At-Law* at 22.

R. v. Gray (1900), 82 L.T.R. 534; [1900] 2 Q.B. 36.

Laughing-gas case: *Balogh v. Crown Court at St. Albans*, [1974] 3 All E.R. 283 (C.A.).

R. v. Kopyto (No. 2) (1988), 62 O.R. (2d) 449 (C.A.).

R. v. Fotheringham, [1970] 4 C.C.C. (2d) 126 (B.C.S.C.).

Re Borowski, [1971] 3 C.C.C. (2d) 402 (Man. Q.B.).

Contempt of opposing counsel: *R. v. Paul* (1978), 44 C.C.C. (2d) 257 (Ont. C.A.).

<u>58</u>   Blackstone on scolds: *Commentaries*, IV, 169.

Sexist scolding in Pennsylvania: *Pennsylvania v. Mohn* (1887), 1 Am. Dec. 153.

U.S. v. Royall, 27 Fed. Cas., 907, 908 (1829).

R. v. Foxby (1703–04), 6 Mod. 11, 178, 213, 239.

Holocaust revisionism: *R. v. Zundel*, (1987), 31 C.C.C. (3d) 97.

Portuguese anti-semitism: *R. v. Osborn* (1732), 2 Barn. K.B. 138, 166.

False news of war with France: See the note to *R. v. Hoaglin* (1907), 12 C.C.C. 226 at 229. And see F.R. Scott, "Publishing False News," (1952) Can. Bar Rev. 37.

Rumors of Napoleon's death greatly exaggerated: *R. v. De Berenger* (1814), 3 M. & S. 67.

R. v. Hoaglin (1907), 12 C.C.C. 226 at 229.

Mayor Drapeau and the hyped hippie: *R. v. Kirby* (1970) 1 C.C.C. (2d) 286.

<u>59</u>   Berlitz: *Native Tongues* (Grosset and Dunlap: 1982), p. 155.

Rogira v. Boget, 148 N.E. 534 (N.Y.C.A.).

Califord v. Knight (1618), Cro. Jac. 514.

Mrs. Miller's pox: *Miller's Case* (1617), 1 Cro. Jac. 430, 15 Jac 1.

Levet's Case (1591), 1 Cro. Eliz. 289.

Marshal v. Chickall (l66l), 1 Sid. 50.

Coney Island dancer: *Gates v. New York Recorder Co.*, 155 N.Y. 228.

Notarmuzzi v. Shevack, 108 N.Y.S. (2d) 172, 1951).

Bastard as endearment: *Marruchi v. Harris*, 1943 O.P.D. 15.

Warder increases sentence: The story's origin is barrister and recorder Geoffrey Dorling Roberts.

60   *California v. Arno* (1979), 153 Cal. Rprtr. 624.

The Joys of Yiddish, op. cit.; *Hooray for Yiddish* (Simon and Schuster, 1982). See also: *Solicitor's Journal*, Feb. 11, 1972, 110 and *Damm v. Damm* (1974), 234 E.G. 365.

Uelmen on Yiddish: *ABA Journal*, June, 1985, pp. 78–80.

Chief Judge Gilbert on *chutzpah: Maryland v. Strickland*, 400 A. 2d, 452 (1979, Special Appeals).

Williams v. State, 190 S.E. 2d 785 (1972, Ga. C.A.).

White v. Samsung Electronics America, 989 F. 2d 1512 (9th Cir. 03/18/1993).

Megachutzpah in Toronto: *East York (Borough) v. Ontario (Attorney General)* (1997), 34 O.R. (3d) 789.

Immigration *chutzpah*: *Estevez v. Canada* (Minister of Citizenship and Immigration), [1998] F.C.J. No. 897 (Quicklaw).

Mutual *chutzpah*: *Sandy Bay Ojibway First Nation Band v. Beaulieu* (2001), 2001 FCT 318, Docket T_1041_99.

61   Cricket "potato" insult: Derek Pringle, "Cricket: Pakistan hope Inzamam can tip the balance," *The Independent*, December 7, 2000, p. 29.

62   David Rege v. Robin Williams: *Polygram v. Superior Court of California*, 216 Cal. Rprtr. 252 (Cal. App. 1 Dist., 1985).

Fenne the brewer: 1. Roll. Abr. 58; (1639) March N.R. 59; W. Jo. 444. March identifies the brewer as Dickes (that is, Dickes is the plaintiff, Fenne the defendant). Fenne becomes Fen in William Jowitt's report; in Roll's Fenne is called Fenn.

Miss Wyoming case: *Pring v. Penthouse International*, 695 F. 2d 438 (U.S.C.A. 10th Cir.).

INDEX

"60 Minutes" (television program), 270

Ackroyd, Dan, 137
Act more effectively to prevent cursing and swearing, 213
Acte for poysonyng (1530), 178
adultery,
    "definitions" of, 156-60
    provocation and, 149-55
    with syringe, 158-59
Aeolian Piano case, 142
"affinity," 164
Alar (agricultural spray), 270
Albritton, Cynthia, 105-07
Alfred, King of England, 181
All Jangle and Riot (Hamilton), 181
Allen, Woody, 104
Alverstone, Lord Justice, 189
Amadeus, 216
American Standard hardware, 223
ancient lights, 71-72
Anderson, Philip, 232-33
Andrias, Justice Richard (New York), 44
Angels and Us, The (Adler), 48
angels dancing on pinhead, 47
Anheuser-Busch brewery, 137-38
animals in law, 162
anonymous accused, 185-86
appellation contrôllé
    cheese, 133-36
    wine, 134
Armorgie, Paul, 45
Arundel, Lord, 175
Astrophel and Stella (Sidney), 266
attempts to commit crime,
    impossible attempts, 40-41
"attorney-at-law," 164-65

Babington Conspiracy, 4-5
Bacon, Sir Francis, 171-76
Bacon, Vice-Chancellor, 239
baldness, unfair discrimination and, 225-28
Barber, Red, 266
Barckley, Justice (England), 268
Bardet, Phillipe, 133-36
Barry, Dave, 223
"bastard" not defamatory, 255-56
battery, kiss, etc. as, 73-75, 85-86, 218
Beastly Law, (Bresler), 162
beaver trap, patent on, 117
beef, alleged libel of, 270-73
beer, slander of, 267-68
Beethoven, Ludwig van, 215, 217
Beezer, Judge Robert (U.S.), 145
beheading, propriety of, 3
Benanc, Nancy, 273
benefit of clergy, 177-80
benefit of peerage, 179
Bentley, John (sanctuary and), 181
Berlitz, Charles, 252
Berra, Yogi, 264
bestiality
    on bitch, 40-41
    on ducks, 40-41
Bishop of Rochester, 178
Bitove, John, 97
Black's Law Dictionary, 70, 193, 220
Blackstone, William, 9, 14, 16, 150-52, 174, 179, 182-83, 245

Blair, Prime Minister Tony, 168
Blair, Robert, 115
"bleached blond bastard" not
    slanderous, 255-56
Blomfeld, Bishop, 270
Blue Guide to New York, 92
Blumen, Andrew, 232-33
Boget, Andrew, 253
Boggs, J.S.G., 126-27
Bohème, La, 216
Bonaparte, Napoleon, 105
Bond, James, 4
Bonne Table, La (Bemelmans), 104
Boots pharmaceutical concern, 168
"Bordeaux milkshake," 101
Borins, Justice Stephen (Ontario), 262
Borowski, Joe, 243
Bouwhuis Protective Undergarment, 62
bovine spongiform encephalopathy, 271
Bowditch, Gillian, 200
Bracton, Henry de, 181
British North America Act, 196-97
Brownmiller, Susan, 76-77
Brunton, Jim, 200
Buckley, William F., 189
Budweiser beer, trademark protection,
    136-37
Burdon, Eric, 107
burglary, rape versus, 82, 86-87
Burgundy, wine scandal in, 100-02
Burr, Aaron, 15
"bursen-bellied hound," 240
Burshtein, Sheldon, 145
Bury St Edmunds Gaol, 219
Bush, George W., 222

buttocks, tortious surgery on, 88-90
"bylaw," 164-66

Calment, Jeanne, 54-56
Cameron, Bill, 204-06
Cameron, Justice Margaret
    (Newfoundland), 193
"Canada" as trademark, 133
Canada Customs and Revenue
    Agency, 207
*Canadian Charter of Rights and
    Freedoms*, 196-97, 245, 249, 262
Canadian constitution, 195-98
Canadian Encyclopedia, 15
Canadian Taxpayers' Federation, 212
canon law, 164
card counting, 231-33
Carlyle, Thomas, 201-02
Carmen, 216
Carson, Johnny, 112, 122-23
Casteja, Phillipe, 102
Center for Bead Research, 91
Channel Islands, clamor of haro and,
    45-47
"charivari," 160-63
Charles I (Britain), 2, 212, 230
Charles II (Britain), 228
cheese, Swiss, regulation of produc-
    tion, 133-36
Chemical Corporation of America,
    137-38
Chicago Cubs baseball team, 94-95
"Choirmaster Case," 82-83
Christ Church Meadow (sign outside),
    165

INDEX

chutzpah, 259-63
Clark, Judge (Maryland), 260
Claveria, Saul, 16-17
clergy, benefit of, 177-80
cocotte not slanderous, 252-54, 256
Cognos Inc., 67-68
Cohen, Herb, 107-08
Coke, Sir Edward, 8, 12, 172-74, 182
Coleridge, Lord Justice
    case of bestiality with duck, 40-41
Commentaries on the Law of England, see "Blackstone"
compurgation, trial by, see "Trial"
Congreve, William, 218
"consanguinity," 164
consent
    fighting and, 13
    mayhem and, 11-13
    to sexual activity, 73-86
contempt of court, 237-45
Copyright Act (U.S.), 140-41
corporate social responsibility, 93-96
Corvair (automobile), 23-24
Cory, Justice Peter (Ontario), 244
Coventry Act, 10
cow, acquitted of trespassing, 162
    copulation by as indecent, 6
Cowley, John, 165
Cranch, Judge (U.S.), 247-48
Cranswick, J.E., 207-08
Creuzfeld-Jakob Disease, 273
cricket as tortious, 72
Criminal Code (Canada), 14, 75, 152n, 227, 249, 251
Cromwell, Oliver, 29

cross-examination, 117
Cubitt, William, 219-20

Daily Star (newspaper), 125-26
Daley, Myong S., 147
Dallas Cowboys football club, 123-24, 138-39
Dalrymple, Theodore, 28-29
"dancer at Coney Island" libelous, 255
Danneman, Monika, 108-11
Darling, Justice, 242
Dawn of the Dead, 215
De Vries, Peter, 103
Dea, Justice J. B. (Canada), 128
dead body, interfering with, 75-76
Dean, Jay Hanna ("Dizzy"), 96
defamation, 146-47, 252-57, 267-68
Denning, Lord Justice, 242
Des Barres, Pamela, 106-07
Diana's temple, 180
Dictionary of National Biography, 7
Dictionary of the Vulgar Tongue, 254
Digest of the Criminal Law (Stephens), 248
Dionysius, 181
disembowelment of convicts, 1-6
Doc (Olsen), 84
Dodd, Alfred, 175
Doherty, David, 244
donkeys, 162
Donoghue, May, 87-88, 90
Drapeau, Mayor Jean, 252
drawing and quartering, 1-6
Dred Scott case, 235
driving offenses
    while impaired, 20-23

Drobot, Eve, 104-05
du Maupassant, Guy, 56-57
Dublin, Archbishop of, 220
ducking (punishment), 216-17
duelling, 13-17
Dunaj, William, 140, 142-44

Edmund Davies (Justice), 80-81
Edward I (England), 182, 198
Einstein, Albert, 105
Eldon, Lord Justice, 229-30
Elegy for Himself (Tichbourne), 4
Elgin Marbles, 201
Elijah (biblical personage), 227
Elisha (biblical personage), 227
Elizabeth I (Britain), 4-5, 171-72, 194
Elizabeth II (Britain), 192
    head of armed forces, 39-40
    Rideau Canal swans and, 66
Ellenborough, Lord Justice, 220, 250
Encyclopedia Britannica, 15, 91
English Gardening School, The
    (Alexander), 71
Environmental Policy and Conservation
    Act (U.S.), 222
Erasmus, 256
Estey, Justice Willard (Canada), 127-28
Etchingham, Kathy, 108-11
etiquette and tipping, 103-05
European Commission, wine
    regulations, 101
evidence, preponderance of, 69-70
experts, cross-examination of,
    drunken, 117-122
Expo '86 logo, 133

expression, constitutional protection,
    231-35, 245, 268-69

False Disparagement of Perishable Food
    Products Act (Texas), 271
Fantasyland, trademark action, 128
Fassano, Federico, 16-17
Fatal Shore, The (Hughes), 219-21
feal and divot, 264
feet in law, 42-44
Figaro, Le, 51, 54, 56
Fiji, 189-91
First Amendment (U.S. constitution),
    232-35, 268
flag-burning, free expression and, 235
Follies and Fallacies In Medicine
    (Skrabanek and McCormick), 69
foot, lord chancellor's, 42
Foppiano, Jeri and Ernie, 215
force majeure, 192
Forgery and Counterfeiting Act (U.K.), 127
Foster, Justice (Chancery, England),
    125-26, 129
Foster, Lord Chief Justice, 8
Fotheringham, Allan, 243
Foul Bills and Dagger Money
    (Hamilton), 187
Fourteenth Amendment (U.S.
    Constitution), 234
Francis, Peter, 91-92
Freewax, trademark action regarding,
    136-37
French disease or pox, 254-55
French fries as meat, 189
French, Justice (England), 111

INDEX

French language, 212-13, 237-38, 252-54
French law, 134, 188
Freud, Sigmund, 177
Friedman, Milton, 94
Frommer, Arthur, 191
Frost, A.J., 206
fruit of poisoned tree doctrine (evidence law), 70-71
Fry, Steven, 220
Future of Swearing and Improper Language (Graves), 29

Gabler, Hans, 139-40, 142-44
Gaginni, John, 218
Gainers meat packers, 114
Galchinksy, Judge Herb (Colorado), 164-65
Gale, Mary, 88-90
garden, law and, 70-72
Garr, Ira, 44
Gay Olympic Games, 130
gazump, use of in law, 257-58
General Motors, 25
gentleman, definition, 213-14
Gentleman Usher of the Black Rod, 212
Gerard, Jasper, 229
gifts, panties as, 60
Gilbert, Judge (Maryland), 260
Girl Scouts, trademark action, 124
Glasgerion (ballad), 80-82
Glass, Geoffrey, 108
Glass, Philip, 217
Golan (Israel), 180
Graves, Robert, 29

Gray, Charles, Q.C., 111
Greene, Joseph (vicar), 45
Greene, Lord Justice, 157
    angels on pinheads, 47, 49
Greensmith, Roy, 168, 170
gruyère cheese, production control of, 133
guilty with an explanation, plea of, 23-27
Guinness Book of World Records, 55

hair and law, 225-31
Hale, *History of Pleas of the Crown*, 182
Hamilton, Alexander, 15, 256
Hamilton, Ian, 199, 201
Hamilton, R.G., 181
Hanson, Justice (California), 258
haro, clameur de, 45-47
Hart, Clive, 140, 143
Hart, H.L.A., 203-04
Harvey, Justice R. Bruce (British Columbia), 262
Hebron, Israel, 180
Hendrix, Jimi, 105-11
Henry III (England), 182
Henry IV (England), 26
Henry VIII (England), 164, 178-79, 181, 187
Higginbotham, Chief Justice (Australia), 240
Hilliard, Sir William, 239
History of English Law (Pollock and Maitland), 237-38
History of Guernsey (Warburton), 47
History of New York (Lamb), 92

Hoaglin, George, 251
Hoffa, Jimmy, 25
Hogg, Peter W., 196-97
Holocaust denial, spreading false news as, 249-51
Holt, Chief Justice (Britain), 247
Homeowner magazine, 222
Hooray for Yiddish (Rosten), 258
Horridge, Justice Thomas, 189
Howell's State Trials, 4
Hugessen, Justice James, 205, 208
Hughes, Robert, 219-21
Human body, value of, 57-59
Humphrey, Keith, 217
hurdle, 264
Hyde, Justice, 252

ice cream as meat, 189
Immigration Act (Britain), 200
impaired driving, 20-23
    chewing underwear and, 21
    Halcion and, 20-21
impossible attempts, 40-41
Income Tax Act (Canada), 205, 209
indecency in legal history, 5-8
in-laws, defined, 163-66
Inner World of Jimi Hendrix, The (Danneman), 111
interfering with dead body, 75-76
International Date Line, 188
Interprofession Gruyère, L', 133
Irish Republican Army, 194
Ironside, Virginia, 72
Irvine of Lairg, Lord Chancellor, 228-29

Isabel of Bury (sanctuary and), 181-82, 186-87
Isis, 231
Islamic sentencing, 3
It Grows On You (Blount), 230-31

Jacob, biblical patriarch, 198
Jacobs, Elliott, 88-90
James I (England), 171, 173, 187, 230
James VI (Scotland), 200
Jekyll, Sir Joseph, 230
"Jewish American Princess defense," 155
"Jewish judgment," 3
John of Craumford, 187
Johnson, Samuel, 7
Jones, Charles, 43-44
Jones, Tom (singer), 61
Jordache (clothing designer), 124-25
Joyce, James, copyright problems, 139-44
Joys of Yiddish (Rosten), 258, 260
judicial combat, 14-15

Karminski, Justice (England), 158
Katherine of Aragon, 164
Kidd, John, 143
Kline, Justice (California), 268-69
Knollenberg, Joe, 223
Kohler hardware manufacturer, 223
Kopyto, Harry, 243-45
Kozinski, Alex, 260, 263

Lamb, Martha, 92-93
Lang, Cosmo, 228
Lardashe (clothing), 124-25

INDEX

Las Vegas casinos, 232
Law and Life (Roberts), 240
Law French, 238
Law of Property Act (England), 49
Law of the Land, The (Rembar), 152
"Lawsuit, Shmawsuit" (Kozinski and Volokh), 260-61
legal blindness, baldness, 226-27
Levin, Bernard, 125
lex talionis, 180
L'Heureux-Dubé, Justice Claire (Canada), 33
libel
 of wine, 267-68
 of food, 270-73
Lincoln, Geoffrey, 264
Lives of the Poets (Johnson), 7
Loch Ness monster, 200
Logan, Patrick, 221
Lohengrin (Wagner opera), 68
London Regional Passengers' Committee, 203
London Transport, 201-02
Lord's Day Act, 189-90
Lucas, George, 146
Lyell, Sir Nicholas, 110
Lyman, Howard, 271
Lynch-Staunton, John, 213
Lyric Opera of Chicago, 217-18

MacLatchy, Judge William, 262
"mad cow" disease, 270-73
Maddox, Brenda, 144
maiden (assize, etc.), 265
Major, John, 199

Major, Justice John (Canada), 30, 33
Malins, Vice-Chancellor, 239
Manhattan Island, purchase of, 91-93
Mansfield, Lord Justice, 230
maple leaf, as Canadian national symbol and logo, 133
Maples, Marla, 43-44
Mary Magdalene, 231
Mary, Queen of Scots, 4
mask
 pantyhose as, 62
 shorts as, 62
masturbation, definition of, 158
Matheke, Cynthia, 89
mayhem, 8-13
 amputations and, 11-12, 153
 tattoos and, 10
 vasectomies and, 11-13
McDonough, Alexa, 212
McLaren, Mary, 212-14
Meany, Tom, 266
Meat, French fries, eel pies as, 189
Megarry, Sir Robert, 178
Menendez case, 154
"Miami J'yce," 140, 143
Miller, Zell, 216-17
Minuit, Peter, 91-92
Miss Universe, trademark action, 128-29
Miss Wyoming, 269
Molloy, Justice Ann (Ontario), 58-59
Montgomery, Justice (Ontario), 244
Montreal Gazette, 252
Moore, Judge (North Carolina), 11, 13
Moreton Bay, Australia, 219-21
Morning Star (newspaper), 125-26

moron in a hurry (trademark law), 125–29
Morris, Judge (U.S), 122
Mozart, Wolfgang Amadeus, 214, 216
  Sonata for Two Pianos in D Major, 216–218
Mr. Submarine, trademark action, 127
Muldoon, Justice Frank (Canada), 263
music as deterrent, 214–18
"Mutcombe's hackney" not slanderous, 254
muteness, 182–85
Mutual of Omaha, trademark action, 123

Napster, 144–45, 147
Nash, Edward, 214
National Football League, 96
National Post newspaper, 217
National Research Council (Canada), 47, 50
Nature magazine, 216–18
negligent misstatement, 67–68
New York Post, 88–90
New York Review of Books, 140
New York Times Book Review, 105
New Yorker, The, 60
Newfoundland, 190–91
Newgate Prison, 181
Nixon, Richard Millhouse, 198
nolo contendere, plea of, 23–27
Noriega, Gen. Manuel, 180–82, 187
Norman law, 45, 181, 237
North American Free Trade Agreement, 223

Nottingham First, 167–68
Nottingham, Sheriff of, 167–71
Novak, Franklin, 123
novelties, obscenity and, 17–19
Noy, William, 238
Nurture Assumption (Harris), 28

offering indignity to a corpse, 75–76
Oink Incorporated, 124–25
"Olympic," property rights in, 130–33
Olympics, history of, 132–33
Ontario Association of Interval and Transition Houses, 160
Ontario Sewage and Liquid Waste Carriers Association, 115
opera, alleged battery at, 217–18
Orpheus, 80
Osiris, 231
"Otzi the Iceman," 114
outlaws, 166, 169, 181
Oxford English Dictionary, 45, 160–61, 257–58

Paley, Paul, 89
Palsgraf, Helen, 88, 90
Parker Jr., Robert, 102
Patel, Judge Marilyn (U.S.), 145
Paul (biblical figure), 181
Paul Revere and the Raiders, 107
peerage, benefit of, 179
peine forte et dure, 182–83
Pepino, Jane, 62
Pepys, Samuel, 7–8
Perman, Stacy, 223
Piers Plowman, 169

INDEX

Pig Latin, 144-47
Plaster Casters, 106-07
plastic surgery, exotic dancer and, 88-90
"pocky whore," whether slanderous, 254-55
Popper, Karl, 69
Porcheret, André, 100-01
Powell, Judge (Tennessee), 6
"pox" in defamation law, 254-55
prepositions, use of in law, 164-66
Preston, Dean, 146
privy, negligence re, 113
process servers, attacks on, 240-41
Progressive Conservative Party of Canada, 213
property, 35-63
  in human body, 57-59
  in panties, 60-62
provocation, defense of, 149-55
Psalm 51, 177, 180
public nuisance, breeding of horses as, 6
public or Queen's enemies, 191-94

queuing, 201-04

rape, 82-85
  attempted, of corpse, 75-76
Rattray, André-François, 55-56
Rauscher, Fran, 216, 218
Rawls, John, 204
"reckless eyeballing," 76-79
Reckless Eyeballing (Reed), 76
Red Cross, 130
Redding, Noel, 106-07

Reed, Ishmael, 76, 77-79
Rege, David, 267-68
Rembar, Charles, 15, 169, 173, 176, 182
Rent (play), 216
Republica, La, 16
Return of the Jedi (film), 146
rhubarb, 266
Richardson, Chief Justice (and brickbat), 238
Robbie the Pict, 198-201
Robert dictionary, 46, 213
Roberts, W. Lewis, 153
Robin Hood, "banishment" of 166-71
Robinson, Walter, 212
Rogerson, S.A., 206-07
Rogira, Elena, 253
Roose, Richard, 178
Rose, Alison, 60-61
Rosten, Leo, 258, 263
Royall, Ann, 246-48
Rumack, Marion, 205-06
Rumpole, Horace (fictional character), 175, 213
running (competitive), 209-11
Russell, Prof. Peter, 195-96
Rutgers Animal Rights Law Center, 271

sado-masochism, 85-86
Sale, Jonathan, 202
Samson (biblical personage), 231
sanctuary, 180-82, 187-88
"Saturday Night Live," 137
Saxon law, 181
Sayle, Alexei (British comedian), 51

scandalum magnatum, 248-50
Scheindlin, "Judge Judy," 98, 219, 221
schmuck, in court decision, 259
schtick in court decisions, 261-62
Schumacher, Garry, 266
scolds, common, 245-48
Scott, Alexander, 250
Scott, Sir Walter, 265
Scottish nationalism, 198-201
searches, police; smells and, 30-33
Sears Roebuck, 125
Second Miscellany-at-Law (Megarry), 239
Selden, John, 42
sentencing
    death sentence, 1-5
    disembowelment, 1-5
Seth, Chief Judge (U.S.), 269
Seven-Eleven convenience stores, 215
Seventh Day Adventists, 191
Sewall, Judge Samuel (U.S.), 230
Shakespeare, Anne, 36-38
Shakespeare, William
    Francis Bacon and, 172-73, 175-76
    gravestone of, 38
    oppressed Guatemalans and, 60
    Tempest, The, 36-37
    Twelfth Night, 36
    will (second-best bed), 35-38
Shasta County (California), vasectomies in, 11, 13
Shea, Justice (Alberta), 128
Shechem, 180
Shenker, Israel, 103
sheriff, contempt by, 241

Shlensky, William, 93-96
shotgun clause (shareholder agreements), 97-99
Siberia, 190
Sidley, Charles, 6-8
Simonds, Lord Justice
    angels on pins, 50
Slaight, Alan, 97
slander, 252-57
    and killing gardener, 3n
Slang Thesaurus (Green), 29
"Sleeping Beauty," 73-75
Smith, Sydney, 221, 270
Smokey Bear, 130
"Snow White," 73-75
Solomon, dispute resolution, 97-99
Sopinka, Justice John (Canada), 32
Spoo, Robert, 140-42
sport terminology in law, 264
spreading false news (offense), 248-52
Stafford, Lord, 3
Standing Committee on Finance (Canada), 208
Star Wars (film), 146
Statute of Westminster, 248
Steele, Kenneth, 217
Steinway piano maker, 125
Stephens, Sir James Fitzjames, 12, 248
Stevens, Judge Lillian (U.S.), 108
stockings
    barrister's musical, 43
    theft of, 39
Stone of Scone, 198-201
Strange Story of False Hair, The (Woodforde), 228

INDEX

Strayer, Justice (Canada), 129
Streisand, Barbra, 133
"strike," 191-94
Sunday Observance Act, 189
"sunshine" (person as), 27-30
swans, care and feeding of, 65-69
swearing, legal sanction for, 29-30
Sweeny, Robert, 15

tax deductions, 209-11
technicality, getting off on, 38-40
terroir (winemaking), 101, 135
theft
    of bikini bathing suits, 61
    of dog, 39
    of eggs, 38
    of furnace and turkies, 39
    of Marla Maples' clothing, 43-44
    of orange loaf, 39-40
    of shoes, 43-44
    of stockings, 39
    of vodka in pants, 62-63
    of winding sheets, 59
Theodosius, Emperor, 132
Theseus, tomb of, 180
Thompson, Justice (California), 258-59
Tichbourne, Chidiock, 4-5
Till, Emmet, 76-77
Time magazine, 223
tipping (gratuities), 103-05
Tishe B'Ab, property rights in, 130-33
toilets,
    as legal category, 112
    definition of, 114-15
    low-flow, 222-24

Tonga, 191
Toronto Raptors basketball club, 97, 99
Toronto Transit Commission, 214-15
tort law,
    everything Mom warned you about, 65n
    females as heroes of, 87-88, 90
    neighbor principle, 88
Torvill and Dean (ice dancers), 168
trade libel, wine and, 267
Traficant, James, 222
translation by jurors, 253
transportation of convicts, 66, 220
treadmill, 219-21
Treatise of the Pleas of the Crown, A (Hawkins), 13-14, 26, 149-50, 182-83
Trial
    by battle, 14-15
    by ordeal and compurgation, 14
Trudeau, Pierre Elliot, 223
Trump, Donald, 43-44, 226
Trump, Ivana, 44
"Turkish judgment," 3
Turner, John, 62
"Twinkie defense," 155
Twisden, Justice
    and shoemaker defamation, 42

Uelmen, Gerald, 259
Ulysses (Joyce), copyright in, 139-44
umpire, 265
"unchastity," imputations of, 254-56
Uncommon Law (Herbert), 213
underwear, law and, 60-63

United States, constitution of, 195–97

van den Heever, Justice (South Africa), 256
Van Graafeiland, Judge (U.S.), 138
vasectomies (are not mayhem), 11–16
venereal disease, consent to sex and, 85
Vespasian, Emperor, 133
viager (rente viager), law of, 51–57
Vincent, Justice Walter (Rhode Island), 18–19
Volokh, Eugene, 261, 263
Voyages and Travels of an Indian Interpreter (Long), 161

Wagner, John D., 222–23
Wagner, Richard, 68, 217
Walcott, Thomas and John, 1–6
Wall Street Journal, 133
Wallington, Justice (England), 156
Walt Disney Productions, 128
wampum (*wampumpeag*), 92
Warde, Major Henry, 15
Weaver, Alexander, 217–18
Wedderburn, Sir John, 175
Weeds Act (England), 71

Westminster Abbey, 199
whales (taxation of capture), 204–06
White, Vanna, 261
"whore" in defamation law, 254–55
wife-abuse, 160–63
wigs, lawyers' and judges', 228–30
Wilde (film), 220
Wilde, Oscar, 217–18
Williams, Robin (actor), 223, 267–69
Winchell, Walter, 256
windfall (taxation), 204–11
wine scandals in France, 100–02
Winfrey, Oprah, 270–73
Worthington, David, 203
Wright, Justice (England), 256–57
Wrigley, Philip K., 94–95

Yale Law Journal, 142
Yanovsky, Zal, 107
Yiddish, use of in law, 257–63

Zappa, Frank, 107–08
Zelinski, Justice Robert, 20–21